Planetwalker

Text and Illustrations

by

John Francis, Ph.D.

Best wishes
John Francis II

NATIONAL GEOGRAPHIC
WASHINGTON, D.C.

Originally published in 2005 by Elephant Mountain Press.
Published in 2008 by National Geographic Books by arrangement with
the author. First paperback printing 2009.

ISBN: 978-1-4262-0405-0

Founded in 1888, the National Geographic Society is one of the largest
nonprofit scientific and educational organizations in the world. It reaches
more than 285 million people worldwide each month through its official
journal, NATIONAL GEOGRAPHIC, and its four other magazines; the
National Geographic Channel; television documentaries; radio programs;
films; books; videos and DVDs; maps; and interactive media. National
Geographic has funded more than 8,000 scientific research projects and
supports an education program combating geographic illiteracy.

For more information, please call
1-800-NGS LINE (647-5463)
or write to the following address:

National Geographic Society
1145 17th Street N.W.
Washington, D.C. 20036-4688 U.S.A.

Visit us online at www.nationalgeographic.com

For information about special discounts
for bulk purchases, please contact
National Geographic Books Special Sales:
ngspecsales@ngs.org

For rights or permissions inquiries,
please contact National Geographic Books
Subsidiary Rights: ngbookrights@ngs.org

Excerpts are used in this book from *New Seeds of Contemplation* by
Thomas Merton, copyright © 1961 by The Abbey of Gethsemani, Inc.
Reprinted by permission of New Directions Publishing Corp.

Interior design: Susan Pinkerton

Printed in U.S.A.

For John and La Java

Acknowledgments

First, I would like to thank my wife, Martha, and sons, Samuel and Luke, for their support, interest, and encouragement during this project; my mother, La Java, for her quiet faith and watchful eye; my father, John, for sharing my journey; my brother, Dwayne, for keeping the lights burning; my cousins Shep for the music and Ed and Dorothy for their support and a place to call home; Lyn and Marty for their faith and for welcoming me into their family. I want to thank the communities of Point Reyes, California; Ashland, Oregon; Port Townsend, Washington; Missoula, Montana; Watertown, South Dakota; Madison, Wisconsin; Philadelphia, Pennsylvania; Cape May, New Jersey; and Washington, D.C., and all the other communities across the country that welcomed me into their midst as a pilgrim and one of their own sons. I want to thank Loti, for traveling so far to visit her papi, and Ray Gatchalian for his life of inspiration.

My gratitude also goes to my teachers, both formal and informal, at the University of Wisconsin-Madison, the Gaylord Nelson Institute for Environmental Studies, the University of Montana-Missoula, and Southern Oregon State University, especially John Steinhart, Gretchen Schoff, Ron Erickson, Mary Birch, Roger Dunsmore, Paul Lauren, Dexter Roberts, Tom Birch, Frank Lang, Lawson Inada, Ben Kimmelman, Akbar Ally, Ray Lincoln, Peace Pilgrim, Roderick Nash, Lynton Caldwell, and Seyyed Nasr. I especially would like to thank my editors, Alan Berolzheimer and Ann Bartz, and book designer, Susan Pinkerton, for their tireless efforts, as well as Cat Cowles and Sandy Duveen for typing and proofing my manuscript.

In any journey, whether it passes through a city or a desert, one encounters a number of people whose meetings also help create the human landscape. Some I know by name, others only by their spirit. I am grateful to all people whose spirits are a part of my journey. Thank you.

Finally, this book could not have been produced without the support of the following friends, companies, and organizations:

Benedikt Wobmann, Rishi Schweig, Rikki and Dulany Hill, Gary Ray, Paul Korhummel, Charlotte Zieve, Tracy Gary, Dede Sampson, Murray and Roberta Suid, Peter Barnes, Hathaway Barry, Stephen Straus, Deborah Hicks, Chris Boyes, Point Reyes Books, Building Supply, Horizon Cable, West Marin Fitness, the Bovine Bakery, Indian Peach Foods, The Station House, Service Argos Inc., and the Timberland Shoe Company. And finally, a special thanks goes to Ruth Chamblee for her friendship and hard work over the years in championing Planetwalker at NG.

Introduction

*The geographical pilgrimage is the symbolic acting out of an
inner journey. The inner journey is the interpolation of the
meaning and signs of the outer pilgrimage, one can have one
without the other. It's best to have both.*
— Thomas Merton, 1964

On January 17, 1971, I witnessed a crude oil spill of nearly
a half-million gallons in the waters near the Golden Gate
Bridge. The oil spill was my first experience with a major
environmental insult. As I drove my car over the Golden Gate I felt
some responsibility for the mess washing up onto the shore. It was
nearly a year afterwards, still feeling this responsibility, that I gave
up the use of motorized vehicles and started walking.

My community took note. Then to end the almost constant
bickering and arguments with my friends as to the question of
whether one person walking could make a difference, I stopped
speaking and spent a day in silence. My life altered. As that day of
silence stretched out before me, I realized I had begun a pilgrimage,
an outer and inner journey, walking and sailing around-the-world,
as part of my education dedicated to raise environmental
consciousness, and promote earth stewardship and world peace.

During the first century A.D., a Greek teacher and
philosopher, Apollonius of Tyana, embarked on a silent journey,
which reportedly lasted for five years. While some consider him the
first person to use silence as a discipline, given the breadth of
human history, that distinction may be difficult to believe.
Nevertheless, he at least gained some notoriety as he wandered

about the empire. People said he communicated very well without words through his eyes, nods of the head and his whole being. In the writings of Philostratus, Apollonius is credited for quelling riots with only a glance, bringing peace where words and reason failed.

More recently, in 1925, Meher Baba, a *sadu* (holy man) from India began his own silent journey, stating as he started that he would not speak in order "to save mankind from the monumental forces of ignorance." He would only end his silence "when the suffering on earth was at its height." In January 1969, Meher Baba died without having uttered a word.

Leaving my Northern California home in 1983, I walked in silence across the United States. During my silent walk I studied the environment formally in institutions of higher learning and informally on the trails, roads, and highways that stretched throughout the villages, towns, and cities across America.

When I started learning about the environment, it was the pollution of an oil spill that prompted me to action. Later I learned there were other issues besides pollution that demanded attention, like over population, and the loss of species and habitat. People talked and organizations worked on issues of conservation, restoration, preserving wilderness and now climate change. Yet, as important as those issues are, listening from my silence, environment for me became more. In this scenario people are part of the environment, not just caretakers, and we are at the core of our environmental troubles. Environment then, is also about human and civil rights, economic equity, gender equality, and from the standpoint of a pilgrim on the road, environment is about how we treat each other when we meet each other.

As with the practice of silence, the concept of pilgrimage is not new. It is as old as the urge to wander, and has its roots in all the major historical religions as well as a number of the smaller tribal cultures, including those of Egypt and Meso-America. The quantity of literature written on pilgramage and related themes is staggering. In recent times, Belgian ethnographer Arnold van Gennep (*The Rites of Passage,* 1908) and American anthropologist Victor Turner (*Dramas, Fields, and Metaphors: The Symbolic Action in Human Society,* 1974) have made substantial contributions to the empirical understanding of pilgrimage as a social process. Van Gennep defined three distinct phases through which every pilgrim must pass. The first is that of separation or detachment from the familiar; the second he referred to as liminal, a sort of ambiguous state during which the pilgrim is part of no fixed social structure; and the third is the reaggregation, which occurs when the pilgrimage is completed and the pilgrim returns to society.

The story of my pilgrimage begins with the separation from the familiar. As it progresses you may identify journeys within journeys as patterns of the three phases contract and expand.

While reading the Autobiography of Malcolm X, I was impressed with his shift from promoting a vehemently anti-white ideology to embracing one of global goodwill following his pilgrimage (hajj) to Mecca. He was the first American Black Muslim to journey to Mecca. Like Malcolm X, I experienced similar feelings of goodwill as those around me became aware of my journey. However, this book is not about those feelings as much as it is about pilgrimage, its history, and its present as understood by a pilgrim.

In the following pages, I investigate the ethical justification of my choices and actions through a method of "experiential reflection" on the life experience that awakened and delivered me onto this path of a pilgrim. Pilgrimage, as we will see, is a process. Throughout are woven the circumstances of tragedy, death, and realization in which we explore the finitude of life as well as its geography.

Geography is the study of environment and people and the ways they affect one another. The geography of this story attempts to justify the inner and outer journey of human experience on the land and explores how this experience influences the natural environment, and conversely the influence of the physical world on the metaphysical. All serve the experience of life and make it whole. In that wholeness we may find what philosopher Henry Bugbee calls "the moment of obligation in experience." Experiential reflection, with its retrospective orientation, is the method of choice because the ultimate justification in acting is primarily delivered out of the experience of acting.

How I came to be on this journey, as well as the meaning of pilgrimage for me, and society, is the subject of this book. Of course, we are all pilgrims of one kind or another and I hope that my story will help you begin, complete, or enhance your own pilgrimage. I use the pages from my daily journals to look back. This is how it begins.

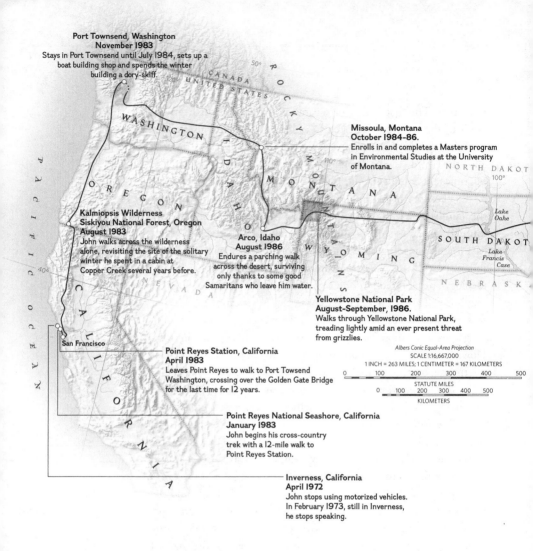

Port Townsend, Washington
November 1983
Stays in Port Townsend until July 1984, sets up a
boat building shop and spends the winter
building a dory-skiff.

Missoula, Montana
October 1984-86.
Enrolls in and completes a Masters program
in Environmental Studies at the University
of Montana.

Kalmiopsis Wilderness
Siskiyou National Forest, Oregon
August 1983
John walks across the wilderness
alone, revisiting the site of the solitary
winter he spent in a cabin at
Copper Creek several years before.

Arco, Idaho
August 1986
Endures a parching walk
across the desert, surviving
only thanks to some good
Samaritans who leave him water.

Yellowstone National Park
August-September, 1986.
Walks through Yellowstone National Park,
treading lightly amid an ever present threat
from grizzlies.

Point Reyes Station, California
April 1983
Leaves Point Reyes to walk to Port Towsend
Washington, crossing over the Golden Gate Bridge
for the last time for 12 years.

Albers Conic Equal-Area Projection
SCALE 1:16,667,000
1 INCH = 263 MILES; 1 CENTIMETER = 167 KILOMETERS

0   100   200   300   400   500
STATUTE MILES
0   100   200   300   400   500
KILOMETERS

Point Reyes National Seashore, California
January 1983
John begins his cross-country
trek with a 12-mile walk to
Point Reyes Station.

Inverness, California
April 1972
John stops using motorized vehicles.
In February 1973, still in Inverness,
he stops speaking.

Planetwalker

Map Key

○   Featured stop on the Route

──   Walk Route

- - - -   Bike Route

·········   Boat Route

— — ·   Plane Route

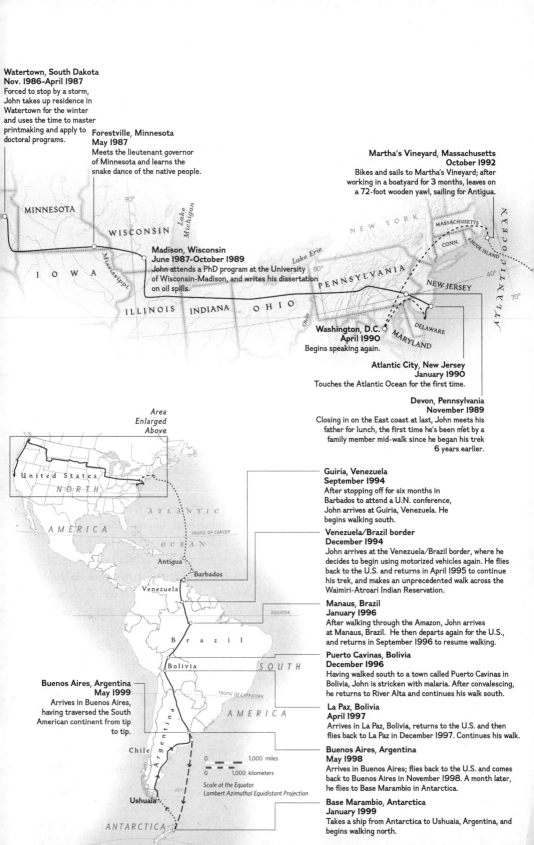

Watertown, South Dakota
Nov. 1986-April 1987
Forced to stop by a storm, John takes up residence in Watertown for the winter and uses the time to master printmaking and apply to doctoral programs.

Forestville, Minnesota
May 1987
Meets the lieutenant governor of Minnesota and learns the snake dance of the native people.

Martha's Vineyard, Massachusetts
October 1992
Bikes and sails to Martha's Vineyard; after working in a boatyard for 3 months, leaves on a 72-foot wooden yawl, sailing for Antigua.

MINNESOTA

90°

WISCONSIN

Lake Michigan

Mississippi

I O W A

Madison, Wisconsin
June 1987-October 1989
John attends a PhD program at the University of Wisconsin-Madison, and writes his dissertation on oil spills.

NEW YORK

MASSACHUSETTS

CONN. RHODE ISLAND

Lake Erie

80°

PENNSYLVANIA

NEW JERSEY

40°

70°

A T L A N T I C   O C E A N

ILLINOIS   INDIANA   OHIO

Ohio

DELAWARE

Washington, D.C.
April 1990
Begins speaking again.

MARYLAND

Atlantic City, New Jersey
January 1990
Touches the Atlantic Ocean for the first time.

Devon, Pennsylvania
November 1989
Closing in on the East coast at last, John meets his father for lunch, the first time he's been met by a family member mid-walk since he began his trek 6 years earlier.

Area
Enlarged
Above

United States

N O R T H

A T L A N T I C

O C E A N

A M E R I C A

TROPIC OF CANCER

Antigua

Barbados

Venezuela

EQUATOR

B r a z i l

Bolivia

S O U T H

TROPIC OF CAPRICORN

Buenos Aires, Argentina
May 1999
Arrives in Buenos Aires, having traversed the South American continent from tip to tip.

A M E R I C A

Chile

Argentina

0   1,000 miles

0   1,000 kilometers

Scale at the Equator
Lambert Azimuthal Equidistant Projection

Ushuaia

ANTARCTICA

Guiria, Venezuela
September 1994
After stopping off for six months in Barbados to attend a U.N. conference, John arrives at Guiria, Venezuela. He begins walking south.

Venezuela/Brazil border
December 1994
John arrives at the Venezuela/Brazil border, where he decides to begin using motorized vehicles again. He flies back to the U.S. and returns in April 1995 to continue his trek, and makes an unprecedented walk across the Waimiri-Atroari Indian Reservation.

Manaus, Brazil
January 1996
After walking through the Amazon, John arrives at Manaus, Brazil. He then departs again for the U.S., and returns in September 1996 to resume walking.

Puerto Cavinas, Bolivia
December 1996
Having walked south to a town called Puerto Cavinas in Bolivia, John is stricken with malaria. After convalescing, he returns to River Alta and continues his walk south.

La Paz, Bolivia
April 1997
Arrives in La Paz, Bolivia, returns to the U.S. and then flies back to La Paz in December 1997. Continues his walk.

Buenos Aires, Argentina
May 1998
Arrives in Buenos Aires; flies back to the U.S. and comes back to Buenos Aires in November 1998. A month later, he flies to Base Marambio in Antarctica.

Base Marambio, Antarctica
January 1999
Takes a ship from Antarctica to Ushuaia, Argentina, and begins walking north.

CHAPTER 1

Oil and Water: When Worlds Collide

The environmental crisis is an outward manifestation of a crisis of mind and spirit. There could be no greater misconception of its meaning than to believe it to be concerned only with endangered wildlife, human-made ugliness, and pollution. These are part of it, but, more importantly, the crisis is concerned with the kind of creatures we are and what we must become in order to survive.
— Lynton K. Caldwell

As a child growing up in Philadelphia, I never thought of myself as an environmentalist. In fact, I can't even remember hearing the word "environment" until I was grown and living in California. It sounded like something unimportant, having to do with smog in Los Angeles and recycling cans and paper in San Francisco. But things change, just like little-boy dreams and the weather along the northern California coast.

Clouds are not unusual for mid-January. The mild winters are expected to be cloudy and wet, and this year is no exception. Rain has been falling off and on between snatches of sun and blue sky. By evening a high-pressure ridge stretched from the western plateau across the state, ending the rain but leaving a cold cotton fog in place.

Then, in the early morning hours of January 18, 1971, shrouded by fog and night's darkness, two oil tankers collide beneath the Golden Gate Bridge. Eight hundred forty thousand gallons of crude spill out of the ships, the *Arizona Standard* and the *Oregon Standard,* into the choppy waters of San Francisco Bay.

The incoming tidal flow is nearly over when the collision occurs. As a result the oil reaches only 4 1/2 miles into the bay, then slowly drifts 7 miles out to sea before it floods back onto the coast. The fog that gathers close for a few hours hides the dying birds, fish, and seals whose bodies clutter the sandy beaches and rocky shores, mouths and lungs filled with black iridescent tar.

Oil and chemical spills are nothing new in San Francisco Bay. Only ten days earlier a Norwegian ship had dumped 12,000 gallons of fuel oil into an East Bay slough. In the years that followed the 1969 oil well blowout off the Santa Barbara coast, thousands of spills had been reported. Petroleum and petrochemicals were big business around San Francisco Bay, accounting for 20 percent of the cargo that floated across the bay's waters. Like the quakes that have shaken the city since the Big One in 1906 toppled buildings and ignited a fire that burned a city's soul, big spills have been disasters waiting to happen.

The sickly sweet smell of oil hidden in the morning fog drifts up from the water. My head swims and my stomach churns the way it did when I was a kid squeezed between two fat Philadelphia relatives in the backseat of a hot summer car—air conditioner failing, windows barely open. My stomach sagged and body bounced at each dip and pothole.

Within hours, and without being asked, thousands of volunteers swarm along the beaches to rescue stranded waterfowl and help with the cleanup. Schools dismiss classes and offices shut down early or never open. In marinas around the bay, boat owners feverishly haul their vessels out of the water to protect the finish of their hulls from the oil.

In Bolinas, north of San Francisco along Highway 1, knots of residents work frantically to prevent the contamination of one section of beach, and when that fails, they seek to protect another. They gather dead seabirds in a pile, carrying others still clinging to life to an animal rescue center to do what they can for them.

Painful snapshots capture the seemingly fruitless effort. At the edge of the Bolinas Lagoon, a young woman with waist-length hair wades neck deep in the dark water to capture distressed birds.

Attempting to escape her grasp they flap their sodden wings and slip farther beneath the surface.

On the shore, armed with shovels and pitchforks, workers collect straw dropped onto the oil by helicopters and small craft. Kneeling in the sand, a grown man cries as a blackened grebe dies in his hands.

On the shore, armed with shovels and pitchforks, workers collect straw dropped onto the oil by helicopters and small craft. Kneeling in the sand, a grown man cries as a blackened grebe dies in his hands.

I was six when I saw my first death—a robin crushed beneath an automobile's wheel on a Philadelphia city street in front of my home. Too young to fly, it had slipped out of its parents' nest in the tall elm with new electric green leaves. They hovered anxiously above the concrete curb. I begged my mother to let me take it in, to care for the baby bird until it could fly. It seemed as if everyone on the block was out on their porches that Saturday morning, sweeping sidewalks and washing granite steps, watching the drama unfold. The odors of bleach and pine oil cleansers wafted through the clean spring air. Finally my mother gave in. At that age it seemed as though I could always sweet-talk my mama.

"Yes," she said, but it was too late.

In excruciating slow motion the car wheel turned and crushed the life from the feathered body, leaving only the dream of flight. Standing on my parents' porch, I cried loud enough for all the neighbors to hear. They all sighed in concert. Voices rose making comments, expressing sympathy, like the inside of our Southern Baptist church.

The driver of the car had stopped, his blue eyes wide and mouth twisted open as he climbed out of his car. He had heard me and the neighbors cry.

"Oh, lady, I thought I had hit somebody," he said to my mother, "or ran over someone's dog."

His voice trembled as he told me he was sorry, and for a while we cried together on the steps. I didn't take the money he offered before he left. Alone, I wept and swept the robin's flattened body, still warm, filled with bloodied worms, into a pile of trash and last summer's leaves beside the curb.

My parents tried to soothe the hurt with love and wise words about life and death, but in the darkness of my room my mind replayed the robin's death. Clutching a pillow, I cried each night for weeks.

A year later my mother's family began to die. Tuberculosis. The disease racked the community and within the year three of my mother's siblings were taken away. It took Audrey, my youngest aunt, first. At 18 she was beautiful, with golden brown skin and soft thick lips. She sang opera, and they said she was going to be a star. I was flat out in love with her.

I didn't really understand the dying kind of death. I mean, I understood lying there with all the red life running out of you, the blood and guts of a squashed baby bird on a warm spring street, the irreversibleness of shattered glass. I could kind of understand that, though there seemed no fairness to it.

What was still a mystery to me was the lay-yourself-down, getting-sick-and-dying-in-the-back-bedroom kind of death. Audrey did it that way. Grandmom, with her silver hair and almost toothless smile, said she knew the moment when Audrey died because Audrey started singing, then stopped. I guess Audrey knew dying was close, too. She wasn't supposed to sing, not even talk, just lie up there in the back room of my grandmother's house and get her rest.

I wasn't allowed in the room because they said she was contagious. Sometimes, though, I would sneak in to visit her and she would smile when I came into the room, and in the quiet when we were alone she would whisper to me about how she missed me, and how she was getting better all the time. She would promise to take me to the zoo, the park, and the circus. I'd like that. I guess it was fair to say that Audrey flat out loved me as well.

So when they told me Audrey had died, I sort of laughed because I did not understand, and it did not make any kind of sense to me. A short time later, though, I somehow found myself dressed in my blue Sunday shorts on the way to Second Baptist Church to say goodbye to Audrey.

The church was built of large gray granite stones, irregular and dark with age. "It's called a viewing," my mother said, as we walked through the big red wooden doors that my father held open for us. Inside it was warmer than the summer day, and seemed filled with nearly everyone from our neighborhood and more. Ushers, stern faced, dressed in black suits with white flowers and white gloves, pointed us to the front pew where Grandmom sat with an assortment of uncles, aunts, and cousins. The organ was playing some sad then upbeat tune, and Reverend Washington, dressed in his flowing black robe, every now and again instructed everyone to turn to a certain page and sing along with the choir.

A slow procession started up past where Audrey was lying surrounded by more flowers than I had ever seen in one place. She seemed to smile at me, as if she were going to sit right up, laugh, and take me in her arms. I knew she would, too. Standing right next to the casket, I stared at her lightly powdered face, with hints of rouge. I waited for the embrace, the kiss with soft thick lips, the words "I love you, Johnny cakes." I would squirm and giggle. Instead, she didn't move, and after a few minutes the reality of what dying was about, and all this sorrow, the tears, and the sadness, began to sink in.

Before, on my parents' steps, I had cried at the sight of the dead baby bird. Here I could not find a single tear. All that came was a kind of weak laugh, and then again, a little stronger, until I could not control my hysteria. They carried me from the church. Afterward I felt ashamed.

In old Antigua, where my father's parents were from, people observed a lot of rituals when someone in the household died. For instance, if a child lived in the house he was sometimes tossed over the corpse three times during the wake by two relatives to keep the jumbie, or spirit, from hurting the child. After a few more friends and family members died of TB my parents took a more drastic approach. Although I had not contracted the illness, I was taken out of school and sent to a children's sanitarium in the Pennsylvania mountains, to be kept out of harm's way.

My parents did not tell me how long I would be away. We traveled hours in the night, and they promised to visit every weekend. I let them leave with only a few tears. Mrs. Christian, a short soul dressed in a starched white nurse's uniform, led me away to a dark quiet room. After she left, the room came alive with the sounds of whispering children.

"Hey, are you the new kid?"

"What's your name?"

Then I heard the sound of a dozen pairs of feet scampering across the cold linoleum floor. We made friends as children do and began our play, illnesses forgotten.

It was a warm but disconnected year. As time went on I grew tired of the walls of the dormitory and the hospital that housed the 50 or so boys and girls who had been isolated from their families. I grew tired as well of saying goodbye to the kids who were allowed to return home.

Only after the outbreak seemed to subside, a year later, was I brought home and allowed to return to school.

Until the fifth grade I remained a year behind in school. Once I had learned the fundamentals of reading and writing, school did not hold my interest. What seemed more important was how the world worked and how I fit into it. My parents pointed me toward medicine. Doctors and nurses were already in the family. To be a doctor meant that you could help people, they told me. I had been helped by doctors enough to know that. Becoming a doctor also meant success. That was a more subtle lesson, but a lesson nonetheless.

Born in Philadelphia, Pennsylvania, on February 23, 1946, I was named after my father, John Francis, Jr., a lineman for the electric company. He had been born in Panama, where his Antiguan parents had gone to find work building the canal. He immigrated to the United States with his folks, two sisters, and brother while he was still a little boy.

My mother, La Java Kirby, was from a Philadelphia family of 11 children. She could trace her roots back to Native Americans and North Carolina slaves.

We lived in the North Philadelphia neighborhood of Nicetown. Our street was lined with tall elms, broad-leafed maples, and sycamore trees. In the summer they made wonderful shade. In front of my house an old elm tree with massive roots buckled the concrete sidewalk. Somewhere among the branches fat gray squirrels lived. My parents let me put peanuts on the roof of our porch and I would watch from the bedroom window until the squirrels came and packed the nuts into their cheeks.

To me the city was a paradise. Just a few blocks away was Hunting Park, where the squirrels would take the peanuts right out of your hand. There was a merry-go-round, too, and a large swimming lake made of concrete and stone. The streetlights were jets of mantled gas that illuminated the sidewalks with a warm green-yellow glow.

The two-story brick row houses had been built in the 1920s. Each had a small front lawn, most decorated with beds of roses, tulips, and other flowers. Watering the lawn in the cool of a summer evening was a welcomed social event. On Saturday mornings my mother and the other mothers would scrub their front steps and the marble tiled vestibules, at least until their kids were old enough to earn a 50-cent-a-week allowance. Each house had a wooden porch, with outdoor furniture, metal gliders, and green-striped canvas awnings with fringed edges.

At night I would fall asleep listening to the sounds of traffic grumbling over the cobblestone streets and the Number 23 trolley with steel wheels that glided on ribbons of steel track.

I was surrounded warm and soft by the love of parents, grandparents, aunts, uncles, cousins, and family friends. Most lived within a few blocks of one another. So ensconced was I in daily life and the care given by relatives, I was nearly grown and out of my parents' home before I realized that for a time my mother worked during the days as a domestic and nights on an electronics assembly line for RCA.

When I was still very young but old enough to leave her and our city nest, La Java would take me on the train to spend the summers with her aunt Sadie and uncle Luke in the little hamlet of Harmony Village, Virginia.

My aunt and uncle lived on the shores of the Rappahannock River where it emptied into Chesapeake Bay, in a small wooden house at the end of a sandy dirt road. Fields on three sides and woods in the back surrounded it.

There was no electricity, and the water came from a hand-dug well in the yard. The well wall, made of stone, was taller than me. I had to stand on a little bench to look down to the water, and then only when Sadie or Luke was around to watch me. I would shout and listen to the echo. Above the well was a little peaked roof from which hung the cast-iron pulley, the wooden bucket, and rope. I was not strong enough to pull up the bucket once it had filled with water.

There were always stories of kids falling into a well. It had happened just up the road at the Jacksons' place. Their well had no walls. It was just a large hole in the ground covered by a few wooden boards. Over it was a tripod contraption with a long pole that worked like a seesaw. At each end of the pole was a rope and at the end of the rope closest to the well was a bucket. It took several children operating the contraption at both ends to get a bucket of water.

Our food came from the fields of sandy soil, the garden, and the river that stretched out into oyster beds and upside-down reflections of spiky pine forests in cerulean blue skies. Melons, tomatoes, squash, and all kinds of beans and greens, damp with beads of dew, could make me smile. I did not like the idea of eating oysters, much to the displeasure of Aunt Sadie. Oyster loaf was her specialty, but to me there was something otherworldly about their scrappy shells and slimy soft bodies.

On some Sundays the congregation of the Baptist church we attended gathered down by the river. The preacher dipped its new members with their white robes into the brackish water to wash their sins away. Then everyone would sing, "Wade in de wata, chillun." The men sang in deep resonant voices that made me listen in awe, while everyone swayed to the gospel beat. The little girls would giggle and talk about how the crabs nibbled at their toes.

In the afternoon Uncle Luke would catch a few chickens, tie their legs together, and cut off their heads with a small hatchet. Blood spurted and the headless chickens flapped about, to my horror and to the delight of my year-older cousin Eddie, who laughed and teased me. Aunt Sadie, a round squat woman with graying black hair, would toss the carcasses in boiling water for a few minutes, and then with whomever was on hand, pluck the birds clean.

I grew to love Aunt Sadie's fried chicken. Everybody did, and they came from miles around for Sadie's fried chicken dinner. Most everyone in Harmony Village walked, but some of the teenagers rode mules. The preacher showed up driving a dusty black car.

Our food came from the fields of sandy soil, the garden, and the river that stretched out into oyster beds and upside-down reflections of spiky pine forests in cerulean blue skies.

Inside a tan Toyota Land Cruiser on the road above the Bolinas beach, Jean Lohman sits idly wrapping and unwrapping twisted strands of hair from around her finger. Her eyes strain behind her wire-rimmed glasses as we watch the frantic activity and listen to radio newscasters describe the extent of the devastation. Then the voice challenges the whole audience of listeners: "And if you don't like the news, go out and make some of your own." It makes me uncomfortable.

Jean is a small, wiry woman with medium-length chestnut brown hair. It hangs straight down from her shoulders. A retired grade-school teacher and divorced housewife, she had returned to college and there discovered the 1960s Cultural Revolution. She is still awash in the euphoria of the People's Park takeover in Berkeley. At 45 she has the look and energy of a 20-year-old. Much to the consternation of her prominent "Gold Rush" family she talks incessantly about her origins, and how she can trace her roots back to California Indians and some freed slaves from Alabama. Nevertheless, her uncle Bev had left her a small fortune from his oil earnings, which made her a Standard Oil heiress according to her and the local papers. Even though they have squabbled in court and she is looking for a large financial settlement, she is still proud of her family. Today, though, she is almost apologetic about the mess that is washing up onto the shore. She wonders aloud how her brother is making out in San Francisco. He is still an oil executive with the company.

In San Francisco, emotions are running high over the spill and Standard Oil is under attack. In protest, half a dozen young people dump crankcase oil around the entrance to the company's headquarters. Standard Oil destroys and ecology grows out of the barrel of a gun are painted in red and green on the walls and sidewalk. Dead fish are dumped in the pond outside. On the other side of town, protesters throw sand mixed with oil onto a house believed to be that of Standard Oil's board chairman. As Jean talks about the spill, her brother, and the politics of oil I can hear the revolution—an old anger creeping into her voice.

"Come the revolution I'll get my money." It has been a recurring theme ever since we met. She had been wronged and nothing would be right until she had her money. She is on the case. Television and radio people are standing by to report the big day. Maybe tomorrow. All we have to do is wait. The oil spill, we both agree, is a mess, but when I turn to her and ask what she thinks we might do about it, I feel overwhelmed. It is difficult to see how her receiving a large financial settlement would affect the oil coating the coastline.

It is even more difficult to see how we personally can change to make a difference in the world. Volunteers are involved in the cleanup and attempting to save the wildlife, and I also want to do something. I want to get my hands dirty with oil and fur and feathers. I think this might take away the sudden sadness that now wells up in my stomach and nudges against the soft spot in my heart. Anything we talk about or consider that might help, though, is always at our convenience. She doesn't answer my question—instead, she lights a joint.

"We could live a simpler lifestyle and not need so many cars." I hear myself say the words, and think that I am repeating something I had read or that had been part of some past conversation. "We could stop driving cars. Stop riding in them," I add. This idea surprises us both.

"Yeah! That's a great idea." Then after a moment of thought, "But we can't afford to do it right now. We'll get some money, then we can do it."

"That sounds fair enough," I say. Jean and I like to hear ourselves talk. We have many times before constructed in our minds the utopian society built on how everyone ought to be. Living more simply and not driving automobiles sounds like a good idea, but even as I say the words, the complexity of my daily life, my 60-mile-an-hour habit, tells me it is not something we would give up easily. Besides, as Jean said, we can't afford to do it just yet. We need money first. I tell myself that the money will buy the time to slow my life down to a walk.

"When the money comes, I am going to start walking . . . that's a promise." But the words I speak are only words, and they drift lazily out the window with the curls of blue-gray marijuana smoke that clouds our minds. Jean restarts the engine and we follow slowly behind the procession of dim taillights, a circuitous route that leads back toward Inverness. As we leave behind the stench of the birds, oil-soaked and dead, the windshield wipers keep time to some unheard song.

Forty miles north of San Francisco, I live with Jean and her ten-year-old daughter, Ceci, in a small comfortable redwood cottage in Inverness, a bucolic summer village with a winter population of about 500 on the western shore of Tomales Bay. The village is situated on the Point Reyes Peninsula bordering the National Seashore and Tomales Bay State Park. Our home is in First Valley, near the end of a one-lane gravel road that skirts a small spring-fed brook. Just across from our yard the trail begins that can take hikers up into the trees, across the ridge, and out to the ocean and the beach. On clear days it seems you can see all the way to everywhere.

Downtown Inverness consists of half a dozen clapboard buildings of various shapes and dimensions along a pitted asphalt road. On the bay side are the grocery, library, and Chevron gas station. The library is a narrow one-room shack, barely wide enough to fit the librarian's desk. A little table occupies the center of the room, usually piled high with the books that could not fit on the shelves. Next to the library, the Inverness Store spreads itself wide, plain, and square with the only bit of sidewalk in town. Painted in big red letters on each of the picture windows looking out onto the street are the words, vegetables and meat.

Just off to the side, and to the rear of the parking lot, a little dock reaches out over shallow Tomales Bay. It is a place to sit and look out over the water, but at low tide it stands above the mud. Across the street the post office, a little bigger than the library, is squeezed between a real estate office and an art gallery.

Other houses and cottages are scattered about, tucked away here and there among the trees and on the mesa; most lie empty over the winter. Farther down the road, a motel and a few cottages cling to the shore. Beyond that are a dairy ranch or two, the Point Reyes lighthouse, and Great Beach, a ten-mile stretch of Pacific Ocean, sand, and solitude. The Beach is where we go when the walls of our cottage seem to be too close.

It is open country, the Point Reyes Peninsula. Shrouded in fog, wild and tame all at once, an "island in time" on the western side of the San Andreas Fault, it slips a few centimeters north each year. Strong, clean, and bracing, it is a long, long way from where I began. But now the stench of oil and images of dying birds gather close, hanging in the air like shreds of fog and Spanish moss in the tall, gnarled bishop pines that crest the ridge. It surprises me to fight back tears but not the need to cry.

Several months have passed since we visited the oil-infested beaches along the coast. Far from abandoning driving, Jean and I have driven our Land Cruiser to Mexico, where it is wrecked. We return home by bus. Now a VW bug is our only set of wheels.

A vagary of the wind brings in the sweet spring fragrance of wisteria hanging at the window. It rustles the curtains and rouses me from a sound, late-morning sleep. Smelling the wisteria from this direction is unusual. It means that a south wind is blowing, and that does not normally happen until the afternoon. When it does it means dangerous conditions on Tomales Bay.

I roll over and speak to Jean.

"That wind means something." I turn again, this time clutching the bedcovers. "I don't know what it means, but I know something is going to happen."

Later that day there is a knock on the door. It is Bob Gillespie, from next door. He tells us that Jerry Tanner, the son of a neighbor, has been lost on Tomales Bay. In a sudden storm that had come in from the south, the boat he and his family were in capsized when the engine failed. Miraculously, his wife and son were saved.

Jerry Tanner was about 25 and a deputy sheriff for the county. We made for unusual friends. I mistrusted the establishment and he took every opportunity to show his mistrust of me.

When I first moved into town in 1969, I had just dropped out of school for the third time and had come to Inverness only to visit some Philadelphia friends. I liked it so much I decided to stay.

In the first year Jerry and I managed little more than civility, but as time passed occasions arose when our distance and coolness felt silly and out of place. Once late at night we sat alone beside the road and talked—asking each other questions about who we were, our families, and how well we liked the community we shared.

Once an elementary teacher, Jean talked to Jerry in her schoolteacher voice that sounded as if she were about to box his ears and send him to the principal, even when he came to confiscate the marijuana she had planted in the garden.

Now Jerry has died and there are no words to express our feelings. We pick some peas and take them to his mother a few houses up the valley. But that is not enough. We want to do something more, something to celebrate life.

"We should go dancing in town," I suggest. Jean loves to dance, so she agrees.

It is still early afternoon and the music will not begin until later that night. It is a 40-minute drive and there is nothing to do before we need to leave. We think of taking a walk on the ridge. We know we want to walk; it is something we both like to do a lot.

After a good walk through the woods and over the hills to the beach we always feel renewed.

The next idea strikes us at the same time. It is only 20 miles to San Anselmo, where the Lion's Share nightclub is located. We could walk. The walk would be a life celebration in itself. We make arrangements to leave Ceci with neighbors. Then we gather our daypacks and leave.

It is dusk by the time we make our way over the first of the two hills that separate rural West Marin from the main body of the county. Walking on the shoulder of the asphalt road that we usually drive, cars buzzing by, is different from strolling on the peaceful grass of the deer trails and cow paths we take to the beach. We have little time for reflection. We wonder if taking this walk is a mistake. Our feet hurt something horrible.

The road winds through the redwoods of Samuel P. Taylor State Park. We stop to rest beside one of the giants. Night has fallen and the lights of the passing cars annoy us. There is a chill in the air, and we only have light jackets.

Several cars stop and the people inside ask us if we need a ride. Mostly we are met with words of encouragement; sometimes people shake their heads in disbelief as they drive away. A couple in a Jaguar sedan glides to a quiet stop beside us and an electric-powered window lowers at the touch of the elegantly dressed middle-aged woman. Beside her, her companion busies himself shifting luggage to make room in the backseat.

"We're going all the way to San Francisco," she says.

"No thanks, we're just walking," answers Jean.

"Well, we can just take you as far as the city."

Jean repeats herself.

"What! You don't want a ride? Really, it's all right, we have room."

On your first long walk, comfortable athletic shoes will do. Carry a light pack. As you add to the miles you walk in a day, and the weight you carry, invest in hiking boots that cushion and support your feet. Dress in layers and bring water, an energy snack, a small flashlight, and a few Band-Aids to help prevent and treat the inevitable blister. Enjoy the journey.

They drive off into the night, leaving us to enjoy our solitude and painful feet, the sounds of our footsteps and the sweet green smell of dew-wet grass in the night air. We are hungry.

It is nearly midnight when we drag ourselves into a Jack in the Box at the edge of town. Coming in off the road and out of the dark, the neon lights make us squint. As tired as we are, we bring in with us a certain exuberance of the night air, an adrenaline rush.

From behind the counter the cook, a pimply-faced kid still in his teens, looks up at us with a bewildered expression, as we did not arrive by car.

"What'll you have?" We order, but when he learns that we have walked from Inverness to go dancing, he refuses to let us pay. He says he has never met anyone who has done something like that.

When we reach the Lion's Share our friends are happy to see us, but it is past one in the morning and the band is already playing the last encore—"Get Together." We are too tired to dance anyway. We decline the offers of a ride home and struggle to the top of a little hill behind the club and drift off to sleep. We huddle together next to a cedar tree like two gray squirrels. The following morning we walk five more miles and register at the Holiday Inn.

After hot showers we spend the day sitting by the pool. The pain of the walk into town is a distant memory. We are looking forward to the walk back home.

We walk the return trip largely in silence, arriving home a little before dark. There is just enough light to see the toilet paper ribbons stretched across our front gate and balloons and a sign that reads Welcome home John and Jean painted on the bottom of an old cardboard box. Inside, Lance and Debbie, two friends, are waiting to congratulate us.

Lance and I had met two years earlier when we lived in the same communal house in Lagunitas, on the other side of the hill heading to town. That was when I was known as Pisces John. Then the only revolution we were waiting for was the advent of the Aquarian Age. Now Lance was married and expecting his first child.

We sit together on the queen-size bed, which takes up most of the living room, to catch up.

"So how was it?" Lance asks finally.

I do not have much enthusiasm for a conversation. I am tired and the fatigue has begun to strip away the adrenaline glow and the cool freshness of the outside that came in with us. I am nodding off into some deep thought when—POP!—the cork slips explosively from the champagne bottle, shoots up to the ceiling, and careens off the wall. Everyone is laughing.

"It was all right," I answer, feeling more and more like a party. "For a little while, though, I hoped we didn't have to come back."

Lance and Debbie peer over the tops of their glasses and look at me as if I had hurt them.

"What do you mean, John," Lance asks in a quiet voice, "don't you like it here?"

"No, that's not what I mean," I answer. "I like it here fine. Maybe that's part of it. I just didn't want to come back and fall into the same old way of living a life that I know has got to change. Maybe it was a taste of freedom."

"I like it here fine. Maybe that's part of it. I just didn't want to come back and fall into the same old way of living a life that I know has got to change. Maybe it was a taste of freedom."

As soon as I say the words, I know it is more than that. I knew as I walked back from over the hill and could not help thinking about Jerry. He seemed to have everything. He had youth, a beautiful wife, children, a good job, and the house with a picket fence. Then one morning it's all gone. His life is over. There are no promises in life that my sun will rise, that Jean's revolution will happen, that the money will come. The only sure thing is now, and in the experience of now I know what I need to do, to be.

Lance looks at me, bewildered.

"What do you have to change?" he asks.

Jean moves off the bed into the wicker chair and starts nervously twisting her hair around her finger.

"Don't look at me," she says. "I'm in the middle of a revolution and I have to drive. Besides, I like getting around too much to give it up."

Lance smiles at her from behind his reddish-blond beard.

"It's just that I've been telling myself that one day when I have the time and the money I was going to stop driving and—"

I don't get to finish the sentence before Debbie interrupts.

"Well, we are getting ready to have a baby so it's nothing we could do."

We change the subject and talk about refinishing the *Blue Jay*, a little wooden sailboat that sits in the front yard. Jean and I are tired. Lance and Debbie sense that we could use some time alone and leave.

The walk, the welcome home, and the conversation with Lance and Debbie stay with me through the night. I have taken the first step on a journey that will shape my life. I cannot stop now.

I have had similar feelings before. When I had been on a particularly fine camping or hiking trip, I dreaded getting back to the car for the drive home. I wanted to explore beyond the boundaries of a trip. I wanted the specialness of the experience to fill my life. And life, I had learned again with Jerry's death, is finite, something lived in the present and reflected on in the past. If I am ever going to have the time to explore a lifestyle on foot, it has to start now.

As I lie in bed I let the last few tired miles slip away into a waking dream. I think of taking a walk and not coming back. The sweet fragrance of wisteria drifts through the window and into the room.

In the morning I go to see Lance. I find him working in the garden with Debbie. Debbie offers me some lemonade. Lance and I have come to know one another pretty well over the last two years. Together we have tried to be vegetarians. He has seen me change from Pisces John, fasting for thirty days to purify my body, into a young man who smokes and drinks too much. And I have seen him transformed into a reputable construction worker, husband, and expectant father, and a respected member of our small community.

He can tell that I have something on my mind.

"I've decided not to drive anymore. Do you think that's crazy?"

He leans back against the outside wall and looks across the yard. A hummingbird buzzes up to the red-tipped feeder hanging from the eaves. We watch it until it buzzes away, disappearing into the trees.

"Hell no, that ain't crazy," he declares. "If you don't want to drive cars then you shouldn't. You know, lotsa times I get fed up with some tool or somethin' I'm using, so I just put 'er away until me or it has a change in attitude."

He lets out a roar of laughter that shatters the morning stillness. Debbie looks up from the garden and smiles. I laugh, too, and smile as I walk all the way home.

CHAPTER 2

Living on the Road:
Up in Smoke

The transition to life on foot, though voluntary, is not easy, and not everyone is happy with my decision. Already I have lost my job as the manager of a struggling avant-garde music group, Spectrum of Sight and Sound. My job is to book and promote concerts throughout the Bay Area, and chase the elusive recording contract. Relegating myself to foot and phone, I find that I am not effective. I am not surprised when I am let go.

Still, I try to do those things I was doing before I stopped riding in cars. When I am invited to play in an impromptu volleyball game in Point Reyes Station, I make the four-mile, one-hour trek while everyone else makes the five-minute drive. The game is nearly over by the time I get there. Going to the movie theater or meeting friends in San Rafael, 25 miles away, is even more problematic. I have to leave the day before.

I have been walking for only two months when the first big test of my new lifestyle arises. I can see it coming as I walk down First Valley and over one of the little wood bridges that cross the creek. When I arrive at the firehouse the large doors are open and I can see the shiny red La France fire truck that is the heart and soul of the Inverness Volunteer Fire Department. I have been a member of the fire department for nearly six months. Dick Graveson, the fire chief, is polishing a chrome fixture on the side of the big truck. He sees my reflection in the chrome, looks up, and motions me over.

His stooped shoulders, leathery neck, and bald head give him the appearance of a human turtle, old and wise. His moves are slow and deliberate. His voice is gravelly.

"Hi, John. Thanks for coming down."

"It's not a problem, Dick. What's on your mind?" I ask, but I already know the answer. It is the same thing that has been on my mind since I started walking everywhere. How do I fit into a sixty-mile-per-hour world when I am traveling at three?

"Well, people are saying that they've been seeing you doing a lot of walking between here and Point Reyes Station and that you're not riding in cars anymore." He smiles and chuckles to himself as he looks over the rim of his wire tortoiseshell glasses, then moves to another chrome fixture that is the pressure gauge for the water pump.

I think back to the road. It is not unusual to see someone walking along the road between Inverness and Point Reyes Station, nor is it unusual to be offered a ride from a passing motorist. Most of the people traveling this stretch of road during the weekdays are local residents. Beyond Inverness the road ends at the beaches and the Point Reyes lighthouse, a favorite spot for tourists.

I walk at almost any time, no matter the weather. Frequently I'm offered rides. I always refuse them. Most of the time this is the end of any discussion, and I continue on my way.

But sometimes the occupants of the cars want more—some explanation other than my simple desire to walk. Then I talk about the oil spills and air pollution that I do not want to be a part of. It is the only explanation I can give, besides being able to enjoy where I live for the first time. It is, despite their blank expressions, what they seem to want to hear. Some nod their heads slightly while others voice their agreement, telling me how they wish they had the time to walk. Many of these very same people had helped with the bird rescue and cleanup during the San Francisco spill. There is often an uncomfortable silence before they drive off, leaving me to my thoughts.

In his autobiography, Malcolm X, when commenting on his conversion from atheism to Islam, wrote that the hardest and greatest thing for any human being to do is to accept that which is already within and around him.

There is no question in my mind that walking is in me to do. Besides, more than two-thirds of the world's people still get around under their own power. Birds are born with wings, I was born with

feet. Again I remember spending summers walking on Uncle Luke and Aunt Sadie's farm along the Chesapeake Bay. There was no electricity or running water. Water was drawn from the well. There were no cars. Once we stepped off the train, we walked the sandy roads and trails, and we tended the oyster beds by sail.

I remember the horse-drawn wagons of the Amish in the countryside of my native Pennsylvania. We passed them slowly on our Sunday drives. I would wave excitedly, but they usually did not look and never waved back. My father told me that they didn't believe in driving cars. In my youth I wondered why. For me, two decades later, walking is a personal solution to my own and to some of society's ills—reaching back in search of something lost and striking out in the hope of finding something new. Whether I can survive on foot, physically or emotionally, in an automotive culture as the Amish do is another matter, and after word of why I am walking gets around a few people stop me on the road to argue the point.

Again I remember spending summers walking on Uncle Luke and Aunt Sadie's farm along the Chesapeake Bay. There was no electricity or running water.

I am surprised at the arguments that my giving up driving and riding in cars has caused in the community. Even though many people talk about wanting not to ride in cars because of the oil spill, everyone still does. The response to my decision is harsh and immediate. Once I am nearly assaulted for refusing a ride with someone: "What am I, not good enough for you to ride with me?"

In some instances I am told, "The reason you're doing this is just to make the rest of us feel bad." Granted, there is some truth to this. I naively expect at least part of the community to park their cars and pickups and, like the Pied Piper's children, walk off with me into an environmental utopia. This does not happen. However, the chief criticism the community has is put in the words of a close friend. "John," she says. "You are just crazy. One person walking is not going to make any difference in reducing air pollution or oil spills. In fact, it's just going to mean more gasoline for everyone else."

The comment gives me pause. Maybe I am crazy. How can one person make a difference?

One day just outside town a man stops me. He is a familiar, mustached face I have yet to attach to a name. The gravel crunches beneath the tires of his car as he pulls onto the shoulder of the road. Rolling down the window, he smiles and asks if I want a ride. I thank him but say I want to walk.

"Why don't you want a ride?" he asks. His eyes narrow. The

smile disappears from his face and I can tell he wants more than just the usual.

"I like to walk." But he doesn't wait for my answer.

"I heard about you." He snickers. His eyes narrow. "You don't want to ride because you think you're better than me. Isn't that right?"

I shake my head and try to explain about the oil spills and automotive pollution, but that makes little difference.

"Oh yeah, well, I like birds too. Are you trying to make me feel bad?" he shouts.

I find myself standing beside the road yelling at this man who is yelling at me while trying to make a point. I can soon see that nothing I say short of accepting his offer of a ride to town will make any difference. He tells me he looks at my decision not to ride in cars as a personal attack. While this is a very revealing point of view, I do not like the direction this yelling match is going and I'm more than relieved when Lance walks up and defuses the situation by making some enthusiastic remarks of his own about living in a free country.

I leave them there still talking and continue on to Point Reyes Station. My head is full, replaying real and imagined conversations, attempting to prove to myself that I am right. I do not like the anger I feel; it eats into my gut. I realize now that I have taken a stand that challenges a way of life, a way of seeing things. It is no wonder that people challenge me. I am challenging myself. I feel frustrated because though it is clear to me, I am unable to articulate beyond a simple phrase about why I walk. Even more difficult for me to understand is the burgeoning feeling of something spiritual and sacred in the ordinary act of walking. I start to feel that each step taken is part of an invisible journey for which there is no map and few road signs. I am not sure I am prepared, and the discomfort both frightens and excites me.

A few evenings later I stop at a phone booth and dial my parents' home in Philadelphia. My mother answers and we speak for a while about relatives and things. I casually mention that I have stopped riding in cars and how happy it makes me to walk. She laughs a wry laugh and asks me how I am going to get home to visit. The question has occurred to me. I do not have an answer.

"Well, that's very nice, Johnny," she says. "But when a person is really happy they don't have to tell people about it. It just shows."

I ask her what she thinks about my not driving. She says she thinks it is fine and then adds, more for herself than for me, "Don't worry, you'll be riding in cars again. This is only a phase you're going through."

The next day I find myself crying beside the road. Each time a car passes I feel as if the world is passing me by, and I am getting left behind. It occurs to me, as it often does, that only my stubbornness is keeping me on foot and I should start riding in cars again. It has been about two months since I began walking and I am getting tired of it. Sometimes I feel as if I am dying. Parts of me are.

Dick is still talking. Still polishing little bits of chrome.

"So if you aren't riding in automobiles, does that include fire trucks?" He stops polishing and looks me full in the face. The expectant expression tells me that he is hoping that I have written some caveat into my new lifestyle. "It's not like you're using a car for your own pleasure. When you're in the fire truck you'll be looking to help someone. Really, you'll be helping the whole community."

"No, Dick, it's all motorized vehicles—that includes the fire truck."

"That's too bad."

"I do know all the trails. I bet I can get to the fire before the La France."

"That may be true in some cases, but the idea of you running alongside the fire truck to get to a fire up on the Mesa might disturb some people."

"Yeah, you might be right about that."

"I know," he says. There is a twinkle in his watery blue eyes. "You can be the dispatcher. We need someone here at the fire station to operate the radio. That can be you. It's the perfect solution. Now, just don't stop talking." We both laugh.

One morning Jean and I are finishing our breakfast. When we get to the last cup of coffee she stops twisting the ends of some strands of hair and reaches across the table. She gently runs her fingers down the side of my neck. I grit my teeth to keep from wincing.

"How long have they been there?"

I know she is talking about the swollen lymph glands on my neck, but I ask the question just the same. "What?"

She points. "Those lumps growing out of your neck, that's what."

"Oh, that. I don't know, maybe about a month. They don't hurt, though." The fact is they do hurt, and I am worried about them. When they first started out as a cluster of raisin-sized growths on my neck where it meets the shoulder I tried to ignore them. Now they are grape-sized and impossible to disregard.

"You have to promise to walk over to Point Reyes Station and see the doctor. I'll walk over there with you."

I do not feel ill but I make the appointment. The next day I make the four-mile walk to Point Reyes Station to see my doctor. The doctor expresses even more alarm, and speaks guardedly about cancer, Hodgkin's disease. He suggests that the glands be removed as soon as possible. I am just as concerned but settle for a biopsy. It is a simple operation done with a local anesthetic, but it will have to be done in Petaluma, 25 miles away.

That evening on the phone I tell my mother about what the doctor said and she dismisses it by saying, "I wouldn't worry about it, cancer is not in our family history."

I decide to continue walking even if I am sick. If death is inevitable, I reason, then I might as well die living what I believe, no matter how naive. Anything else, I think, is giving myself up to sickness.

The Point Reyes–Petaluma road makes its way through some of the most rural landscape in the county. There are only two large hills to climb, and if I leave in the early morning I can reach Petaluma in a day, register at a motel close to the surgeon's office, spend the night, and make my appointment in the morning.

It is hot as I make my way up the last hill. All day turkey buzzards have been circling overhead, making me think of the dead and dying hidden among the summer-gold hills. I hurry past a fallen deer—roadkill. The putrid smell of its rotting flesh rises from sweet grass and makes me nauseous. I am growing tired, and my feet are starting to hurt. At the top of the hill I can see an old black oak offering shade at the side of the road. I tell myself, "That is where I will stop and rest. I will have a cigarette and sip on the water in my daypack."

Once beneath the tree I remove my shoes and lean back against the rough trunk and light up. The vultures still circle in the summer thermals—dark thoughts in a blue sky. Their lazy circles remind me why I am climbing the hill and why Petaluma is stretching out before me in the distance, and I think, "What if I do have cancer?" For the first time fear of dying seizes me.

I look away from the silhouettes in the sky and extract the pack of cigarettes from my pocket. Clouds of smoke are already wafting in the air when the absurdity of my actions strikes me. I wonder how I can in all honesty care about pollution caused by cars, or be so concerned about the health of the environment, when I do this to myself?

Then I realize that walking is not enough. Perhaps it is a beginning, but now I see that I am going to have to change not just on the outside but on the inside too, in more ways than I can now imagine. I think that maybe I have already begun this inner change. It seems that all change begins unseen or at least unnoticed in the journey that we call life. I shake my head as I read the familiar warning on the package label, cough a laugh, and give up smoking then and there.

I walk the rest of the way into Petaluma and arrive in time for my surgery. The following week I am back in Point Reyes Station and I find out the lymph nodes are not malignant. But on that hill outside of Petaluma, I vowed to live my life as if they were—to learn to balance on the edge between awe and taking life for granted.

My vow gives me a new understanding of Kurosawa's 1952 film *Ikiru*. It is about a bureaucrat who, upon finding out he has cancer and only a year to live, realizes that he has not really been living. He leaves his job and spurns his family to search for what he has been missing, which he mistakenly believes he finds in the affections of a young girl. Only when he is rebuffed and at the bottom of his depression does he discover that life for him is helping the residents of a poor district overcome the monumental obstacles they encounter when they attempt to build a park for their children. In one scene a writer who befriends Mr. Watanabe, our hero, shortly after he finds out about his illness, says, "How interesting it is that men seldom find the true value of life until they are faced with death."

The film makes an interesting comment about how undergoing a personal crisis can instigate an unusual and often altruistic action. In other instances researchers in social work have noted that successful survivors often engage in some secret service to others that gives them a sense that something constructive is coming out of the horrible circumstance. These people are said to look with great commitment for every opportunity to do something helpful, no matter how small. The people who really do well when undergoing a personal disaster are those who look at the problem as an opportunity for change and not as a threat.

I receive a letter from a friend who, with his family, has given up the use of automobiles for walking as the death of his father has become imminent. I write back and ask him what bearing the death of his father had on his decision. In his reply he says:

"Since a teenager I've felt the call to walk around the world. A couple of years ago I decided to start walking. When I returned from the New Mexico fire tower work this past summer—to St. Louis and my dying father—I knew it was time . . . and what better time to begin than on the arrival of Hiroshima Day—with its around-the-world connotations . . . and also better to begin with my father still alive . . . as a continuity with him and by way of including his life force in this work of mine."

The context of my walking expands into the realm of service.

At first glance I think the death of my neighbor, Jerry, has had this effect on me, and the realization of my own mortality is reinforcement. The context of my walking expands into the realm of service.

Not long after Jerry's death there was some talk in the community about establishing a bay watch. Tomales Bay is only about a mile across at its widest point, and on a clear day people on either side can see any boat that might be in trouble. Still, it had taken almost an hour before anyone responded to the capsizing of the Tanners' boat. I joined a group of Inverness residents and took a course in seamanship from the U.S. Coast Guard Auxiliary.

We had hoped to establish a coordinated search-and-rescue unit on Tomales Bay. However, the residents of the bay are an independent lot. There is resistance to conforming with the uniforms and regulations associated with a Coast Guard Auxiliary unit, so we work with another ad hoc association known as the West Marin Advisory Group, whose goal is to come up with a West Marin disaster plan. A fire that destroyed the town's historic hotel earlier in the year had brought the group in Marshall together.

The first objective of both groups is to make a house-to-house canvass in each area to locate buildings, water supplies, liquid propane gas tanks, and main electric circuit breakers. The ability to do these things will be relevant during any disaster. Under the heading of "search and rescue" the plan is to have people who live on the water report any emergency. An emergency number will be furnished and the community makes arrangements with Synanon, a drug rehabilitation facility, to dispatch a rescue boat tied up at their marina. I become the "walking coordinator and liaison" between the Inverness and Marshall sides of the bay. It is a good way for me to meet most of the people who live on the bay. It is a good way to introduce people to other aspects of my walking.

It's a 14-mile walk around the bay from Inverness to Marshall: 4 miles to Point Reyes Station and then 10 miles north on Highway 1. I had made the drive often to spend Saturday night drinking and dancing at the Marshall Tavern adjoining the hotel. After a few drinks the 14-mile trip back home can be deadly. It has claimed the lives of several friends. I have been lucky.

I still make the trip, but now on foot. It is a pleasant walk along the two-lane highway lined with cypress and pungent eucalyptus trees. The road rises, dips, twists, and turns along the eastern shore as it passes the occasional house, amid small herds of dairy and beef cattle behind barbed wire fences. Bright orange poppies crowd the shoulders of the road as it skirts a cluster of rustic fishing cottages and vacation homes. On weekends, especially in the summer, traffic is heavy and tiresome. When the tide is low I take the old railroad right-of-way close to the water. The tracks have long since been removed. Only the roadbed and the skeletons of the trestles that once crossed streams and mudflats remain. Sometimes, just a few yards from the highway, I feel as if I'm in another world. Like sailing on the bay, it is accessible solitude—a wilderness beside the road.

One stormy day I find myself rowing on a choppy Tomales Bay; having shunned motorized transportation I often spend many hours on the bay rowing a small dory or sailing our little *Blue Jay*.

As you walk look around, assess where you are, reflect on where you have been, and dream of where you are going. Every moment of the present contains the seeds of opportunity for change. Your life is an adventure. Live it fully.

The tide has changed and a south wind forces me to land this particular day on the shore near the Tomales Bay Oyster Company, which sits across the water from Inverness. I make my way over a barbed-wire fence and along the beach to a house set back beneath some cypress and knock.

Gordon Sanford opens the door. He is a rotund man, perhaps a bit overweight, who smiles from behind steamy glasses.

"We're closed," he says, removing his frames and wiping them across the front of his shirt.

"I know you're closed," I answer. "I just rowed up on your beach and I'm wondering if I can use your phone to call home. They might be worried with this storm coming up the way it has."

He looks surprised, peering past me into the gloom, then invites me in and shows me to the telephone.

"You been out rowing in this weather?" he asks.

I nod yes, and make my call. On the other end of the phone I have hardly been missed.

Gordon introduces me to his wife, Ruth, and insists that I stay for tea and something to eat. The conversation turns to oyster farming and I talk about spending my early summers in Virginia with my aunt, uncle, and cousin without electricity by the Chesapeake Bay, with hand-drawn water from a well and harvesting oysters from a small inlet. For a moment I am a kid again, feeling the mud of the Chesapeake between my toes and chasing fiddler crabs down into their holes.

It turns out that they once lived on the Chesapeake too. I am offered employment on the spot, and for the next several months I work there, harvesting and culling oysters. I learn about acquiring the seed, planting, rack construction, predation control, health standards for public consumption, and the importance of water quality, which after the oil spill in San Francisco Bay has special meaning for me. But even Gordon thinks it is odd when I refuse to use the motor launch to inspect the oyster beds. I row or pole instead. Then one day, straining against a flooding tide, I have to acquiesce. Gordon comes smiling and tows me in.

We sit on the worn gray wooden bench in the sun in front of a concrete work shack and talk. I learn that Gordon is a retired physicist.

"Heart problems forced me to look for a less stressful occupation," he says as he lights a cigarette, inhales deeply, and coughs.

Immediately I see his chain-smoking in a different light.

"Oyster farming seemed a natural."

We talk a little about that for a while and then he brings up my walking.

"You know, I really admire you for standing up for what you believe," he says. "But do you really think it's going to change anything?"

I shrug my shoulders and say, barely audibly, "Probably not."

A flock of seagulls rises on the wind from a mound of sun-bleached shells and hovers in the sky, screaming.

"Take oil, for instance," he says. "When we run out of that we'll just find something else."

Anticipating what the something else is, I tell him that I do not think nuclear energy is a good idea. It isn't safe. But so far no nuclear accidents have occurred and Gordon is ready with all the figures that make my simple statement sound ignorant and uninformed.

"Besides," he continues, "you're talking fission. The new technology will be fusion. Pure and clean unlimited energy."

For the next few minutes he tries to explain. I try to understand, and for a while I live in his world, where technology will save us. "It's just around the corner," he assures me. I have never met a physicist before, and I like Gordon a lot. When he talks about the Chesapeake he reminds me of home. Perhaps what he says is true. I don't know, and in a way it doesn't matter. I like the way I move over the land and water. I know I will continue just the same. For in the walking I discover a thread that runs through time, beyond the need of personal protest, connecting me to that life with Aunt Sadie and Uncle Luke on Chesapeake Bay. I never use the motor launch again.

CHAPTER 3

Bamboo and Silence: Learning to Listen

Having placed myself outside the mainstream of motorized transportation, I find that I have a lot of time on my hands. For Christmas Jean's 12-year-old daughter, Ceci, gives me a black hardbound book with blank pages and a set of children's watercolors. We are sitting in the living room with a tree we had cut a few days earlier from Lucy Shoemaker's land. The tree is sparsely decorated, but the twinkling lights are cheery.

"It isn't much, but I thought you might like to paint pictures of what you see when you go walking."

"No, this is really great! You know, I had been thinking about Picasso and how he inspires me. I heard he did some sort of art every day, even if it was to just make a mark on a piece of paper. I think that is impressive. I wish I could be so disciplined." I thumb through the blank pages and feel the promise of their emptiness. "I'll make a painting each day—a New Year's resolution."

I begin before dawn on New Year's Day. It is cold in the morning as I make my way down First Valley to Sir Francis Drake Boulevard. My breath makes ghostly vapors and the moisture condenses on my mustache hairs. Behind the Inverness Store I sit on the skinny wood pier that stretches out about fifteen feet over the bay and wait for the sun. A few minutes later I am painting the yellow-orange ball that is the sunrise, and I feel my life change.

The paintings add another dimension to my walking and sense of place. They begin as little more than blotches of muddy color on white paper, but I tell myself to continue to make one painting every day for as long as I am able. Some are unsatisfying except for the fact that at least I did a painting. But each page represents a day, and I believe in the promise that the next day will be better. In the end I turn the page. I spend each day looking, knowing that at some point I will find a subject to paint.

For the first month I usually choose some landscape or flower study. At first I am determined that my art contain only what I think of as natural subjects. I purposely leave out automobiles, houses, and telephone lines. They seem to be in the way of what I want to experience—yet I do not know what that is. But when February comes around I make an unusual discovery. I discover bamboo. It grows everywhere.

When I think of bamboo, I think of Japan. There bamboo is ubiquitous, and products from the plant are found in every aspect of Japanese life, from eating utensils to heavy construction, from smoking pipes to ceremonial fans. As a popular art motif it often symbolizes long life, and in one of Japan's earliest works of literature, *The Bamboo Cutter's Romance*, a stand of bamboo gives up its treasure, the daughter of the moon who had been exiled to Earth.

I had never really noticed it before except when I was a kid at the YMCA day camp in Philadelphia's Wissahickon Park. It was a bright green stalk that grew beside the streams. We pulled it up to make the spears and swords that were so much a part of our little boys' games. Bamboo never grew much taller than us. But back at the Y in the city, the lifeguards carried nine-foot bamboo poles to pull us from the pool. Bamboo kept me from drowning. I reached for slender knotted poles when I stood afraid, nine feet from the surface, the water closed over my head. Sometimes bamboo took the shape of furniture, dried and lacquered by the pool, or the surf-fishing rod my father used on the beach. In California, it was first pointed out to me during a weeding job in my neighbor's yard, low, dark green, and leafy. I didn't know how many varieties there were in the United States but I was told that if I looked, I could find it all over the country. A transplant from the Far East, it grows wild but is often found in local gardens because it requires little care. It endures.

The paintings add another dimension to my walking and sense of place. They begin as little more than blotches of muddy color on white paper, but I tell myself to continue to make one painting every day for as long as I am able.

I do not know what treasure bamboo has in store for me, but the next day I am out looking for it. Each day bamboo is all I paint. It grows in busy places along the roads and highways. It borders city streets in wooden pots and in quiet places—gardens with little Buddhist shrines, by ponds and streams. It is everywhere. Some days I draw it on the spot, and some days I sit and try to memorize it. Wherever it is does not matter, on a noisy street or by a quiet stream, I sit and stare—taking it all in, the moment, the quietness. At the end of the day I try to paint what is in me of the woody stems—the rustle of the leaves, the way the bamboo bends—the quiet that I find inside. The beauty of the simple grass. I do not know why my eyes turn to tears, except that often there is pain in beauty.

As dusk falls I sit down with a sprig of this newly rediscovered plant and paint until darkness falls. It is a thin soft green hint of stalk with flashes of elongated leaves. When I finish I feel as though I have touched something beyond putting paint to paper.

This is the first time I realize the meaning implied in the spaces, the places where paint is not. That night when I show Jean and Ceci, they nod approvingly while I smile and talk about how bamboo grows all over. Until this painting the primitive nature of my work has been more amusing than anything else.

"Yeah, I know, it grows all over," says Jean, as she sets the dinner table. "That's what is growing in the front yard by the fence."

"Really? I'm going to have to take a look." It is already dark, so I get a flashlight and walk out into the garden to see if it is growing by the fence as Jean says. It is.

I am embarrassed at not having noticed the bamboo that is growing in our own yard. It is not that I hadn't noticed it growing there, it is just that I hadn't noticed it enough to give it meaning. I remember it fuzzily, low and green without any detail. It makes me wonder how much of life goes by me that way.

In the morning the sky threatens rain. I spend the day walking over the green hills that come down from the ridge. They turn to golden dunes and flatten into a wide beach at the edge of the sea. White deer grazing on tender grass move in and out of drizzly fog. A local rancher has imported the deer from India as part of his stock development. Now they are wild, and have become almost sacred in the local mythology. Seeing them is akin to seeing a white buffalo or an albino rhino or elephant. They possess a kind of magic.

In the landscape there is magic too. I can find it in the quiet places. Today I find it in the saddle, a low meadow between Mount Vision and Inverness Ridge. From here I look back to see Tomales Bay and forward to the Pacific. Here I draw the bamboo that is in my mind, green and mud brown.

It is a bamboo meditation that began in the morning, growing in someone's garden by a still pond, with a bamboo fence keeping the noise and the hustle of the road away. I think about the next day. I will be 27. The numbers run through my head: three nines. Three nines make 27. I think three and nine have some mystical powers. Or maybe it is just the line in a Beatles song, "number nine, number nine, number nine" that allows me to fixate on what must be in part the math of the universe. No matter. For some reason I feel this birthday is special and that some great change will occur. I wonder how I will commemorate the day. Maybe I will spend it as I did New Year's Eve, in reflection.

I have already changed my life as dramatically and as drastically as I can imagine, but somehow it does not seem like enough. Something in the way I talk, argue, and defend walking is troubling. I think about past conversations and arguments that drive me to near distraction. I remember the phone call to my mother and how I told her I was happy. I wasn't, and she called me on it. If anything I am at least as confused about my walking as I imagine my parents are, but exaggeration and outright lying are not strangers to me. I don't like it, but that is the truth of it.

I sleep out on the Inverness mesa a little way up from the house. Stars are still shining in a partly cloudy sky. Later the predawn quiet is interrupted by the sound of rain. I feel the first few drops on my face and in the dark I reach automatically for the protection of the plastic tarp beside me and return to the edge of bamboo dreams, the rustle of bamboo leaves. I am not surprised: my dreams are filled with it and the two realities sometimes overlap.

In the morning the rain stops and large resplendent drops hang from slick green pine needles. The air is alive with moist smells. Beside me I hear the bamboo rustle. It is my 27th birthday, and to commemorate it I am struck by the idea of remaining silent for the day. It would be a birthday gift to my friends who have had to put up with my arguments and chatter. This idea of giving gifts to others on one's birthday comes to me from reading J. R. R. Tolkien's *The Hobbit*, and in the silence I smile to myself as a vision of a furry-footed hobbit scurries across a dreamscape of bamboo and disappears into soft thick leaves. There *is* magic on the mesa.

The idea of silence is interesting for me, as I was very talkative as a child and even more so in later years. While attending a Catholic high school I was attracted by the idea of spiritual devotion and I thought of pursuing a vocation as a Trappist monk, but the prospect of observing the order's strict vow of silence dissuaded me.

But the specialness of this day and my introspective state of mind bring about the decision for a bit of silence. It is nothing that I have ever done before. I wonder how it might change my life.

I put my sleeping bag and plastic tarp in a large red rucksack that holds my paints and journal along with some food and clothes, and head down one of the paths into First Valley. I cross a wooden bridge and walk the three doors past the tennis court before I turn into the yard. I stop a long minute and look at the low bamboo growing by the fence, then walk inside.

Jean is sitting in the bedroom still wrapped in her robe, with the radio tuned to the only San Francisco radio station we can get in the valley. Twisting her hair between her thumb and index finger, she looks up and smiles.

"Hey, happy birthday, honey. Did you have a nice sleepout? How about that rain, it's nice, huh?"

I nod yes and give her a big kiss and smile.

"Well, you must have had a great time, you're in such a good mood. Maybe you should do more walking and camping out." Her lips form a wry smile.

Silence. Usually I would be chattering back at her a mile a minute about where I have been, what I have seen, and where I am going. Now I only stare back at her. Instead of speaking I take off my pack, reach inside, and retrieve my black bound journal. I show her the pages of the last several days. All the paintings are of bamboo. Today's page is still blank.

"Yes . . . uh-huh . . . I see," she says, as she turns each page. "And you're not saying anything, so I guess you're going to be silent for your birthday. That is a great idea. You should walk out to Limantour Beach and spend a few days of quiet out there alone."

Between Jean and me there appears to be some form of telepathy. We understand each other with few words and few gestures. So, carrying some fresh clothes, fruit, and trail mix, I head off into the dreamscape in search of solitude.

Before I start the climb over Inverness Ridge, I find myself walking quietly down the rain-soaked path to the pitted asphalt road that leads into town. At the post office, Helen Giambastiani, the postal clerk, is just finishing sorting the first-class mail when I enter. From behind the counter she hands me a few letters retrieved from the general delivery slot.

"Good morning, John," she says, smiling as she turns back to the mail slots.

Inside I strain, wanting to reply in the usual manner, saying something like, "Good morning, Helen. How are you? Did you like that rain we had this morning? Thanks for my mail," but not a word escapes my lips. Instead, I am gripped by the reality of voluntarily not speaking. I ask myself, how am I to communicate if not with the words that are now swirling around in my head as thoughts begging to be said?

A grin stretches across my face and I make a feeble attempt at a salutation with my hand, but she is not looking at me, and I feel embarrassed. For a moment I am washed with a tide of relief, as I think that she will not notice I am not speaking and I will be able to get my mail and slip out before I have to explain something I now believe is odd—deciding not to speak for the day.

Then she turns from the mail slots and looks me square in the face. "What's the matter, cat got your tongue?"

Smiling again, half out of embarrassment, I place an index finger across sealed lips. I point to myself, and then light and blow out the imaginary flames of an invisible birthday cake that I create in front of me with a few circular gestures.

"It's . . . uh . . . your birthday?" she asks in a halting voice.

I nod yes, and place my index finger across my lips again as if I were going to let out a long "Shhhh . . . "

"And you're not going to talk?"

I nod.

"Oh, that's interesting, John," she chuckles. "And how long is this going to last?"

I smile and hold up one finger.

She hands me another envelope and cautions me to be careful. I am not sure why.

It takes almost five hours to reach the beach. I am in no hurry as I follow the trails over the ridge and along the small creeks that make up the watershed. Up high the twisted bishop pines drip with strands of Spanish moss to haunt my imagination with forest ghosts. I reach the beach as darkness falls, in time to find a protected place among the dune grass. I see the white deer, a half dozen or more down close to the water. The coastal fog closes around me.

From my pack I take out my paints and journal. I turn to the blank page that is today, and I paint a circle. Inside the circle I paint a dot. Afterward I peer into the dark, wet, diaphanous veil, lie down on the sand, and fall asleep to the shushing sound of the sea rolling onto a shallow beach.

In the morning when the dark of night turns to silver gray I wake up alone to the crashing sounds of the waves. I am still silent. There is no reason for me to speak, and at the edge of this sea each passing moment takes me farther and farther away from the chattering shore I left only the day before. I have never been here before. The experience of this newness begs me to stay and explore. The current drags me into water profoundly deep. In this new place, I decide to spend another day.

Several weeks later, I am still silent. I ask myself when I am going to speak again. And the answer is I do not know. The reaction of some of the townspeople and many of my friends to my silence is sometimes amusing, and often not. Some in the community think that my walking and now silence is a sign that the end of the world is close at hand, while some think it is the mark of my sainthood, and others simply write off my actions as those of a certified nut and pay little attention except for their own amusement. Still others are righteously angry.

I listen to all the compliments and criticism with no argument. Not speaking precludes argument. And the silence instructs me to listen.

The days continue to pass without my uttering a sound. I spend the next few months walking alone, usually up on the ridge and out to the beach at Limantour. I sleep there and listen to the pounding surf. Sometimes I visit a family in one of the several houses that were built before the land was purchased for the National Seashore. Other times I construct a driftwood shelter and build a campfire in the sand. I stay for several days, watching the birds and exploring the ever-changing beach.

On the ocean side of the ridge the tall bishop pines leave off and the old ranch trail makes its way along a green canyon wall that blooms in season with crimson paintbrush, purple lupine, and lilac shooting stars. It is a watershed and alders grow around the little brook that starts out as a spring higher up. The trees become denser and hide the panorama of the low green hills and the blue sea as the trail continues into the valley. This is where I come to be alone. Farther on is the pond where I fish. From here the rutted dirt road leads back up to the ridge. It is only a mile or so and can be driven in a four-wheel-drive vehicle. I have driven it many times, but walking makes it even more real, more remote.

The months pass slowly. The din of inner chatter fades into quiet echoes and I begin to keep a written journal. Now the daily watercolors in my black bound book take on new meaning. I look forward to the time each day as a meditation and use the paintings to communicate with friends and people I meet: stories in watercolored images without words.

From this new place lessons come, or perhaps realizations. The first is that most of my adult life I have not been listening fully. I only listened long enough to determine whether the speaker's ideas matched my own. If they did not, I would stop listening and my mind would race ahead to compose an argument against what I believed the speaker's idea or position to be, which I would interject at the first opportunity. Giving myself permission not to speak, not to attack some idea or position, also gives me permission to listen fully. Giving myself this permission gives the speaker permission to speak fully their idea or position without fear of rebuttal in a way that I could not have imagined.

Another realization is that it takes at least two people to argue just as it takes at least two people to communicate, and each person shares in the responsibility for both communication and argument.

On the ocean side of the ridge the tall bishop pines leave off and the old ranch trail makes its way along a green canyon wall that blooms in season with crimson paintbrush, purple lupine, and lilac shooting stars.

In a corner of our living room is a five-string Conqueror banjo. I pick it up and pluck at the strings.

Thwang . . . It is not in tune and the sound produces a frown that moves across my face like summer fog moving shadows across Tomales Bay.

It has been a year since I tried to learn how to play it. "Camptown Races" is as far as I got before I realized the futility and relegated it to a corner, unseen behind a stuffed chair. I've always wanted to learn to play music beyond the obligatory piano lessons I had as a child. The simple, crisp sound of a banjo long ago touched my heart.

The walking and silence, I decide, is going to be my opportunity to learn. I pluck the strings again. The sound produces the same effect as before, but this time the painful cloud slips across Jean's face as well.

"Are you finally going to learn how to play that thing?"

I shrug my shoulders and wipe the dust and cobwebs away with a rag.

"You ought to take lessons from someone."

I decide that I will carry the banjo wherever I go so I can learn from anyone I meet who knows how to play it. I sit in the chair and turn the tuning pegs. Then I stroke the strings again. *Thung* . . . It sounds worse, if that is possible. Jean winces again.

"You ought to find somebody who can teach you soon," she says, "the sooner the better."

I know she is right. I leave with my daypack, journal, and paints. The banjo is slung silently over my shoulder.

One day Inez Storer, a friend who teaches at a state college, tells me that my not talking makes her "mad as hell." I have nothing to say. Later in the month her feelings change and she surprises me when she presents me with a book she feels explains, at least for her, what my silence is about: *The Creative Process: Reflections on Invention in the Arts and Sciences,* edited by Brewster Ghiselin (1985). It consists of essays by various people in the creative arts attempting to discover what is common in the experience of creating. Each artist has a unique approach that seems to work for him or her. I am even more touched when she gives me a sable watercolor brush to replace the bristly brush I have been using.

"This will make a big difference," she says, smiling. I wonder at her transformation, but I am grateful to be helped along the road.

Still, as my days go by in silence, a cacophony of thoughts, conversations, and arguments persists inside my mind, begging to become words. Arguments rage in me about not speaking. I begin to question my sanity. Along with the "What are you doing?" and "When are you going to stop?" questions, a host of "dangling conversations" remain from before I stopped talking. It seems I cannot turn off the voices and internal chatter.

One day, after much thought about the merits of not talking, and to end my almost constant inner struggle, I decide to continue my silence, as an experiment, until my next birthday. The experiment is my attempt to make this a rational decision. Still, my mind races with a thousand and one ongoing conversations and unanswered questions. Any fantasies I might have had about some mystical inner peace or happiness that would automatically come with the closing of my mouth soon vanish in the dissonance of my own thoughts.

My friend Inez's feelings continue to change. One day she tells me she is so impressed with the evolution of my art that she wants to invite me to be a silent guest lecturer in one of her classes at Sonoma State College. She feels that her students need exposure to new ways of seeing the world. It takes two days to walk the 30 or so miles to the campus. When I arrive, she meets me in her office and takes me to an auditorium where the class is waiting. About half of the 20 students have chosen to be silent for the day, after hearing about my visit.

I load the projector with transparent slides of my watercolors and enlist the aid of a grinning mute student to change the image at my nod. Inez makes a brief introduction, and I launch into a little banjo riff while the house lights dim. The screen lights up with the title, "The Road, Friends, and Places," then dissolves into a watercolor montage of landscapes and people accompanied by my music.

I am surprised how much I enjoy myself in front of the class. I free myself of any inhibitions and stage fright until I feel as though I am flying. Afterward, when students ask questions, I feel the connection with the audience even more powerfully. I know that as artists and human beings searching for truth, we are speaking the same language.

Though I surprised my friends and neighbors when I gave up the use of motorized vehicles and began to walk, the shock waves that rolled across the country caused only mild tremors that hardly rattled my parents' china in their North Philadelphia home. But when I write to my parents about my decision not to speak, the ground opens Mississippi River–wide, breaking old china ideas covered with city dust and touching deep into my parents' souls. My father is on the next flight to California.

It is summer when my father arrives in San Francisco. Jean picks him up at the airport and drives him to Inverness in her old blue VW van. They find me walking alone along the road that skirts Tomales Bay and the San Andreas Fault. The van stops and he looks at me through the open window. We are both surprised. Fragrant laurel trees bend their heads in an arch and whisper in the wind above us.

"Hi, son." His greeting is warm but tentative, as if he is afraid to hear my answer.

I smile my biggest smile and reach to touch his hand.

"Do you want a ride to the hotel?"

I walk my fingers through the air and in the silence of my answer I can hear his breaking heart. I share the confusion of his pain.

"Damn! What is this?"

For a moment even he is speechless, as clouds move across the dry dark landscape of his face. I am not sure what keeps his tears from falling or me from opening the door and riding with him the mile to the hotel, but for the first time since I was a child, I feel the depth of his love and the gulf that pretends to separate us.

Later at the hotel we explore our relationship and our family in new ways. First he tries to understand my miming and acting out of the meanings I want to convey. That has become my way of communicating. By now I have realized the imposition put on people by my decision not to speak, and the patience and willingness required to explore it. But for my father it is just too much. I decide to write notes on small scraps of paper. But no matter what I write, it is not enough for him.

"It's not the walking so much," he finally says in exasperation, "it's the silence that's hard for me to understand."

I am not sure what keeps his tears from falling or me from opening the door and riding with him the mile to the hotel, but for the first time since I was a child, I feel the depth of his love and the gulf that pretends to separate us.

I search the pile of scribbled notes until I find a clean scrap of paper and write, "It keeps me from telling lies."

In not speaking, I have come to realize that lying is a practice I acquired as a kid growing up that stuck with me in my youth. When I finally came to terms with it, I could find no reason for lying other than that I had developed a bad habit. But as I explored the issue in my silence I came to see that I had not been satisfied with who I was. I felt more comfortable pretending to be someone else with knowledge, skills, and abilities that were not mine.

Growing up a Negro in America I had never heard of anything such as low self-esteem, but I did live it. Not so much in my family, though we were all trapped in it. It is pervasive in the media of popular culture, the newspapers, the radio, and TV. I remember at a young age not liking being who I was. I did not like being colored. I felt as though I was cursed, trapped, and I was embarrassed. Not really embarrassed by myself, but rather embarrassed by how the culture looked at and portrayed me. My defense was deception. I lied in order to pretend.

I deceived myself into believing that I was someone else, not black, not white, but a pretender, more chameleon than anything. It seems simple enough. If you don't like who you are, you just invent someone else. It was not that I never liked myself. I started out with parents and family who let me know pretty quickly that I was a unique and lovable individual with all the potential in the world. But back then I felt it was the world that did not live up to *my* expectations.

It has taken me years to understand that my propensity for deception is actually a reflection of my society, because society attempted to deceive me. In the short term the deception seemed to allow acceptance of self, but the ultimate outcome is the loss of self. By pretending not to be myself, I have lost track of who in fact I am.

The walking and silence save me. They not only give me the opportunity to slow down to listen and to watch others; they afford me the same opportunity with myself. Silence, I discover, is not something negative. It is not simply the absence of speech that happens when I stop talking. Silence is a whole and independent phenomenon, subsisting in and of itself. In the silence, I rediscover who I am.

From the phone booth outside the motel, my father calls my mother back in Philadelphia.

"Yes, I've seen him. He's standing right here." He pauses, and I watch him listen. "No, he seems healthy enough. He doesn't smoke and he doesn't drink. And the people here seem to like him." At the door of the phone booth I begin to play a nameless tune I have composed on the banjo. It is still raw and unsure. The notes topple from my fingers and my father speaks loudly over them. "Yeah, he paints and plays the banjo." The music annoys him. He shoos me away and closes the door. Now I can barely hear him, but I do, just enough to hear him say, "I think we should just leave him here and hope that he doesn't show up in Philadelphia. Yeah . . . Yeah . . . Okay. I'll see you when I get back."

Since I am at least physically healthy, my parents decide to leave me to my own devices in this part of California set precariously on the San Andreas Fault. My mother in her quiet way prays for me, intending to monitor any seismic activity through sporadic visits and weekly letters.

As my father stretches to understand my journey I realize that maybe you can't change the world by your actions alone, but you can change yourself. And when you do, the world around you may change by attempting to understand you, as we all try to understand each other.

Several days later my father returns to Philadelphia. Back at our home in First Valley, Jean is talking to me in the kitchen over breakfast.

"So last night you were speaking," she says nonchalantly as she puts butter to toast.

My ears prick up. I wonder if I have been talking in my sleep. It has been only a few months since I stopped talking and during that time I can count the instances on one hand when words slipped from my lips accidentally: once when I excused myself after bumping into someone at the grocery store, and the time I was in a motel watching *The Ten Commandments* on the television. When Charlton Heston, playing Moses, raised his hands and the Red Sea parted I gasped, "Oh my God!" On each of those occasions, lacking any evidence except my own awareness, I wondered if I had actually said anything. Now Jean is telling me that I am talking in my sleep. This is too much. Crestfallen, I look at her waiting for the rest, the details.

"That's not all," she continues, "you were riding in a car, too."

I know that Jean would not lie to me about something like that, and I am relieved to find out that she is talking about her dreams. I draw a big question mark in the space in front of her face. She looks at me with a blank stare. I draw the question mark again and flap my hand in front of my mouth as if I am talking and shrug my shoulders.

"Oh. What did you say?"

I nod yes.

"I don't know, I can't remember. All I know is that you were in the backseat of a car, talking, it was night, and we were driving somewhere with some other people. I remember I didn't think it strange at all for a little while. Then it dawned on me, hey, John is in the car and he's talking." She looks at me and asks, "What do you think it means?"

I shrug my shoulders again. I do not know. A few days later Ken Fox, a neighbor, tells me about his dream. He and I were sitting on the roof of a nearby house and we were talking.

"I don't know exactly what you were saying, but I got the feeling everything would be all right."

I soon learn that many of my friends and neighbors are having dreams about me talking to them. They are generally happy that I am talking. But no one can remember what I say.

The banjo accompanies me wherever I go, slung over my shoulder. On long solitary walks along the beaches, in the hills, or along the winding road between towns, music is with me, and the spirit of bamboo takes quiet root within.

CHAPTER 4

Stealing Spirits: Meeting Mr. Death

At the Sir Francis Drake garage in downtown Inverness I sit in the shade on a narrow wooden bench shoved against the light blue aluminum siding. I watch the cars and pickup trucks pull in and fill up. Most of them I recognize. I smile and nod in their direction, fulfilling my duty as the colorful local resident.

My clothes are variegated with a splash of worn-out this and a patch of faded that, dusty boots, and my ever-present banjo, topped off with a crocheted rainbow hat from Pearl, the wife of my cousin. Ted the mechanic is sitting beside me in greasy striped overalls. A shock of mussed blond hair sets off his square face that always seems bemused. We must look like a postcard scene sitting here, I with my legs crossed, quietly plucking rusty steel strings, just enjoying the day.

Then a stranger at the pump slyly pulls out a camera from his black sedan and starts to take our picture. Had this been several months earlier when I rode in cars and talked I do not imagine I would have thought twice about someone taking my picture, but since I have been walking and taken a vow of silence, I have become sensitive to the idea of having my photograph taken. I believe that cameras can capture your spirit.

Now, exactly where this belief comes from I do not know, perhaps from some long-ago television show or a story in *National Geographic* magazine, but there it is. I stop playing instantly and with every fiber in my being directed toward the would-be photographer I project, NO!

Thinking better of it, the man begins to put the camera away. Just then Ted comes to life and shouts out.

"Hey, go ahead and take our picture. We don't mind."

What, I think, doesn't he know that a camera can steal your soul? I turn and look at Ted, who is still bemused; he puts his arm around my shoulders, quickly draws me to him, and smiles a big smile. I look back toward the pump. The camera shutter clicks, the man ducks into his car, and without a word he drives away.

I sit there for a moment feeling wounded, a hole straight through my middle, but nothing leaks onto the ground.

"Aw, come on, John." Ted is standing now, wiping his hands on an oily rag. He sounds as if he has a mouthful of marbles. "It weren't all that bad, and it didn't hurt none, now, did it?"

I do not answer any of his questions. I am too busy writing down the license number, noting that it was an official State of California car. My mind races with fantasies of dark activities. The picture is for a secret database, a file kept somewhere for some evil purpose. Or maybe it is going to be published in a "Come to California" ad. No matter. The next day I walk the four miles to Point Reyes Station to see John Maderious, a local attorney.

What, I think, doesn't he know that a camera can steal your soul?

His office is above the old Western Saloon and looks out onto Highway 1 as it passes through town. Cecil Sanchez's horse is tied to the hitching post outside. I am ushered into John's office by his secretary. He comes out from behind his desk to meet me with an extended hand.

I explain everything that happened in Inverness through a performance of mime that would have made Marcel Marceau proud.

"There is really nothing you can do. You know you're a public figure, and unless people are going to use your image to make a profit, there is nothing you can do about them taking your picture."

He continues to explain the intricacies of privacy infringement as I pantomime ripping my soul from inside my chest and throwing it on the floor. He watches me with amused and sympathetic eyes as I express my fear that this picture will be used to hurt me. If I could find out what agency took my picture and what they intend to do with it, I could tell them how harmful this is for me. I see an idea come to him and he stops me in the middle of a silent sentence.

"I do know someone at the comptroller's office," he says as he thumbs through the Rolodex on his desk. "I'm not sure what they'll be able to do for you but they have public hearings at least once a month and I can schedule you to, uh . . . 'speak.'" He thinks for a moment. "I'm sure you will manage."

That is enough for me. I smile and walk my fingers across the back of my other hand, up my arm toward my elbow, through the air, and onto his desk to Sacramento.

The irony of my crusade does not escape me, as I have begun painting my third book of watercolors and in place of the usual landscapes I am painting the faces of people. It is a practice I have devised to keep connected to the community. Each day I have to ask a different person if I can paint their portrait. That way I share my silence with others. But is painting a portrait another way of stealing someone's soul, even if I have their permission? I feel a subtle warmth from the pages when I look at them and a connectedness when I share them. I decide the paintings are more a reflection of each person's spirit passing through my soul, a mingling of our spirits to leave us both with something more.

It will take five days to walk the hundred miles into the Central Valley to Sacramento, the state capital, at the confluence of the Sacramento and American rivers. My first long walk passes through an unfamiliar landscape of faces and geography. The valley is a great trough about 400 miles long and 50 miles wide, between the Sierra Nevada and the Coast ranges. The Sacramento and San Joaquin rivers drain most of the valley before converging in a huge delta and flowing into San Francisco Bay.

After four days I arrive in Davis, about ten miles southwest of Sacramento, whose residents affectionately call it the bicycle capital of the world. In town, bicycle racks line both sides of the streets with a multicolored assortment of mountain, hybrid, and racing bikes lined up side by side. Signs proclaim that bicycles and pedestrians have the right-of-way. I find a place to camp just outside town and walk in to meet Debbie Nelson at Denny's restaurant. Debbie is a friend who lives on Tomales Bay. She has offered to help interpret my sign language to the Comptroller Board. My language now consists of pantomime and some sign language gleaned from a book by Iron Eyes Cody (Espera De Corti, 1904-1999) on Indian Sign Language.

The son of a Cherokee Indian named Thomas Long Plume, Iron Eyes learned Indian Sign Language from Two Gun White Calf, a Blackfoot Buffalo Man, a Cheyenne and the Arapaho Chief White Horse. He traveled throughout the United States and Canada as an expert in Indian Sign Language. He was also a prize-winning dancer who once danced for the king and queen of England. However, he is best known in the United States for the public service announcement of the "Crying Indian" that aired on the first Earth Day in 1971. In the spot Iron Eyes paddles a canoe up a polluted stream past a smokestack belching black clouds into the air. Then he walks along the edge of a busy highway piled with trash. When the camera moves in for a close-up, a single tear rolls down his cheek, and the narrator says, "People start pollution. People can stop it."

A few weeks after I stopped speaking, I found Iron Eyes' book in the library. I was so touched by his television spot and so inspired by Native American concern for the environment that I did something I had never done before: I wrote a fan letter. A short time later I received a letter from his wife and an autographed book and photo of Iron Eyes in an eagle headdress. She wrote to say how much Iron Eyes appreciated my letter and that he encouraged me to continue to work for a clean environment. I carried the letter and the book with me a long time, until the cover wore away.

In the early morning darkness I walk the last several miles to the capital city and the hearing where I am to present my grievances. Inside the chambers state officials gather around the state comptroller as he calls the meeting to order to conduct the business of the state. All eyes turn to me as I enter, dressed in brightly patched denim jeans, a frayed denim shirt, a Day-Glo orange safety vest, and my skullcap. My banjo is slung over my left shoulder on a knitted strap in the same rainbow colors as my cap. There is silence.

The comptroller whispers something to a woman beside him and she nods and he clears his throat.

"We have with us this morning a visitor from Inverness." He looks down and shuffles through some papers. "Uh . . . a Mr. . . . uh . . . John Francis." He looks up and smiles. "He walked all the way here from Point Reyes to address this committee." The committee is wide-eyed, and mouths are beginning to open.

Debbie edges past me into the center of the room.

"Because John Francis has taken a vow of silence, I will translate his sign language," she says.

I move to Debbie's side but keep my eyes focused on the 15 or so people that ring the small room. Moving my gaze from one to another I grab at the empty space outside my chest and throw it violently to the ground.

"My heart feels bad," translates Debbie.

Eyes widen.

I touch my chest with the palm of my hand, and make a *V* shape with two fingers and twirl them in the air in an ever-expanding circle like a tornado. With the same hand I snatch away the invisible storm.

"My spirit has been taken."

A sigh escapes into the room.

I go on to pantomime cameras, cars, and tears rolling down my unhappy face, and the walking that had taken five days, showing the rising and setting sun with a circle coming up and disappearing behind my hand. Both hands continue and tremble, showing fear, supplication, my plea for help, until there is no more to tell except to thank the people who sit there in total silence. Then the comptroller speaks.

"Well, that was quite a story," he says, talking to Debbie. "All of us here appreciate how Mr. Francis feels." He clears his throat again. "What would Mr. Francis like us to do?" He looks at me and I hold out my left hand palm up and touch it with the forefinger of the right.

"He wants the photograph back."

"Well, we don't have the photograph," he says, "but we can assure him that if we did, we would give it back. The best we can do is make some inquiries and if we find out who took his picture we will get it and give it back to him."

He nods again to the woman on his right, who scribbles something in a notebook and shows it to him. He takes a moment to read the page, then looks at me.

"Your friend Mr. Maderious in Point Reyes Station mailed us the license number of the car, the time and date, so I think that's all the information we need."

I seem to become deaf or invisible again as he looks at Debbie and says, "Please thank Mr. Francis for coming all this way to speak to us today. You can tell him that he can go back to Inverness and not to worry. We will take care of everything."

Moments later we are back out on the street. Debbie asks me how I feel. I shrug my shoulders. I am not sure if I ever thought that I would actually get my photograph back, or what I would do with it if I did. I am no expert in putting back a spirit that has been stolen. I don't think I ever heard that part of the stolen spirit myth. Maybe I would burn the picture and smudge myself with the smoke, and scatter the ashes to the four winds or keep them in a little medicine pouch around my neck. Anyway, I imagine I could only have lost part of my spirit, as I still seem to have some left in me.

What I do know is that this is the longest walk I have made so far, and that I have changed. The five days walking, the miles, the geography, and the people I met along the way: the journey has changed me. I know this because outside the comptroller's chambers I laugh, a big silent laugh, slapping my knee so hard it hurts. It is the first silent laugh that has come out of me in over a week. Debbie looks at me, a little worried at first, and then she laughs too.

When I recognize the absurdity of our Kafkaesque situation, something else becomes clear to me; notoriety has become part of my persona, and as a public person I can do very little to prevent someone from taking a picture of me in a public place. If each time someone takes my picture I allow it to sadden me, I will be a very unhappy person indeed.

Right then I decide to embrace my condition, to grab the tail of the tiger and use the notoriety to further the cause of environmental protection. In this moment, I am transformed from a man expecting to live a quiet and idyllic life on the shores of Tomales Bay into an activist. I decide to use my life for change and to learn what this means.

A warm, euphoric feeling settles into the space of my stolen spirit. It fills me with purpose, laughter, music, and poetry. It follows me home. In the spring, that same feeling accompanies me on my search to understand this thing called "environment" that I now so passionately wish to defend. I make my first walk along the coast, 500 miles north to Oregon to begin my environmental education in earnest. There I explore the Siskiyou Mountains and from a high peak look into the rugged beauty of the Kalmiopsis Wilderness. I promise to return.

In October I am on my way back home, walking south along the coast. The forest and the Siskiyou Mountains are a fading dream. Just north of Point Arena I stop to camp. The autumn sun is setting behind the rolling hills of brown summer grass waving in a crisp breeze. I am waiting for the rain to come but still the sky is blue.

I rise with the sun in the morning, mend a sock, and move through the day in Point Arena. In the diner I have the "homemade" soup and bread, listening to some of the locals talk about the tall black man walking with a banjo, as if I cannot hear. I play a tune, letting the music flow from my fingers. They turn to hear this voice, tap their feet and smile. I accept their applause and kind words, then disappear down the yellow-dotted highway, the fog whistle blowing even as the sky is blue. Sometimes a car rolls past, with a face or two I know inside. The sound of the cars is comforting as they roll over the yellow reflectors, dot-a-dot, dot-a-dot, dot-a-dot, and continue on, tires humming.

I walk into the sky of evening stars; a warm wind blows from the sea. I stop and taste the air and watch the swaying trees, listening to the surf roaring from below. The air is sweet, a hint of summer mixed with guano and rotting seaweed. The trees dance, eucalyptus with slender limbs waving madly, cypress slowly bending; water tears apart rock and earth piece by piece. The scene is a feast and I savor each juicy moment as I make my way through the next town. The trees are silhouetted against the starry sky.

"We are the Milky Way." The words come to me out of the silence and walking, the journey through the hills and mountains and along the coast. "We are the Milky Way." The words turn to watercolors and then music. Tears well and spill from my eyes.

In the morning I wake up next to a gentle cliff beside the mouth of the Gualala River. The eastern sky is turning red with the rising sun. Behind some trees children are laughing quietly while they wait for their yellow school bus. The town is waking. The flag is now flying above the post office. I spend the day in just one spot, remembering up and down the road under the shade of the bishop pines. In the evening the fog moves in from the coast.

Three days later, I am walking the Seaview road that parallels a few thousand feet above Highway 1. It is quiet, isolated, and lined on either side by Douglas fir. There is little traffic and my spirit is full and at peace. I feel the meaning of every step and breath. As I walk I softly play "Life's Celebration" on the banjo.

The blue pickup truck passes me heading north, then returns, driving by slowly, then stopping just ahead of me on the side of the road. As I walk by the two men in the truck turn their heads as if to keep me from seeing their faces. The air is charged and my body tingles. The quiet is shattered and my music stops.

"Hey, boy, just a minute." It is the driver's voice, gruff and irritated.

Looking over my shoulder I stare back at the truck and now at the two men. There is something familiar about the long gray expressions on their faces. I think maybe they are people I have met before. I turn and walk over to the open window on the driver's side. It is an imported truck, small enough for me to place my left arm casually on the roof and peer inside into two wary eyes. Both men are blond, the driver with a short military crew cut and his passenger sporting medium-length hair which makes him look like a shaggy dog. The passenger seems nervous, hiding something beside his legs that I cannot see.

"Boy, are you lost or something?" He is almost friendly.

I shake my head and walk the fingers of my right hand over imaginary hills. I end by pointing down the road the way I am walking, south.

I shake my head and walk the fingers of my right hand over imaginary hills. I end by pointing down the road the way I am walking, south.

"Are you heading south?"

I nod yes and repeat the walking fingers over the hills, only this time a grin is forming at the corners of my mouth. I am not sure why, except that I am thinking maybe these guys are lost, and the thought is amusing. In fact I know they are not lost. We are all where we are meant to be. I know this from the very core of my being as the driver's right hand comes from beneath his seat, revealing the dark gunmetal of a .44 revolver, the barrel of which he places against my head. In this moment of crystal clarity I recognize the face of death. He is like an old friend I had forgotten, but who is always there, always walking with me in the forests, over mountains, over hills and into valleys, through the fullness of my journey to when the tears flow from my eyes as unquestioned rivers.

"We don't like niggers around here." Death says these words, but the words don't seem to matter. They are like a code that I have heard before but never understood. All that matters now is that we are here together.

Click. He pulls the trigger and the hammer falls.

I hear no explosion. My body does not slump to the asphalt road. My eyes are open wide, and I am looking past the gun into his frightened eyes. It happens so fast that I hardly realize the flash of light coming through. A rush of thoughts pass through me, but one gets stuck.

Damn, I did not make a painting for today. I almost say the words out loud. But now I am pulling back with a large smile, pointing at myself and walking my fingers across the invisible hills again, as if it is all I know. I give the sign that everything is "okay."

A puzzled look passes between Death and his companion. They look back at me. Time is standing still.

"Now get going."

I sign "okay" again and move slowly away from the truck, turn, and start walking down the road. A minute later I look back and the blue truck is gone. A little farther on I find a break in the trees and sit down beside the road. From here I can see in the blue distance the Point Reyes Peninsula, home. An ocean of brilliant white clouds hugs the coast. Only the highest hills, ridges, and mountaintops are visible. In this afternoon light I have to paint.

The painting is a meditation. It keeps my mind from spinning in continual replay and my hand from shaking. We are the mountains. We are the trees . . . but this reverie is short lived. A big white truck pulls up in front of me, blocking my view. The two men inside are both wearing white cowboy hats, and I do not recognize either of them. They must be the good guys, and just to drive home that point one produces a deputy sheriff's badge, a gold star he holds up so that I can see it. I feel a wave of relief.

"Hey, boy, are you lost?"

I shake my head no, and show him the unfinished painting of the road flanked by steep shoulders of summer grass, barbed wire fences, and fir trees heading down to the coast, crowded with fog, brown hills, and Point Reyes in the distance.

"Never mind that," he says, as he dismisses my journal with a wave of his hand. "The ranchers are all hot about you being up here."

I walk my hand in the air and point down the road.

"Whatsa matter with you? You deaf or something?"

I shake my head and cross my heart as if I were making a promise, and place my forefinger in front of my closed lips. He leans out the truck window across the lap of his passenger and takes a good look at me. He shakes his head and rolls his eyes.

"Well, it don't matter what you are. You do understand me, and you better not be sittin' here when I come back or there'll be some real trouble."

They wait until I pack my things and start walking down the hill. Once I do, the truck rumbles on up the road and disappears in the trees. I wave as they drive by again. Once they are out of sight I take a few steps more. Still barely in the sun, I stop again to finish my painting.

On my way down to Highway One I pass through the fog. After the warmth of the sun it sends a chill up my spine. I am both angry and afraid. Angry that life can still take such an ugly and familiar form, and afraid that death will catch me before I get home. I begin to shiver uncontrollably.

When I reach the highway some friends from Point Reyes are driving by. They stop and we embrace. They tell me that reports of my progress coming down the coast have been reaching home. I am so happy to see them that I begin to cry, big silent tears through a silly smile. They look worried and ask if I am all right. I hesitate and then nod yes, but for a moment I think of getting into the car with them where I can be safe. But there is too much for me to express standing there beside the highway. I can only wave to them as they drive on up the coast.

In the evening I camp beside the Russian River. I make a small fire and listen to the faraway surf and the barking sea lions. They can sound so much like dogs, but they never annoy me. Closer still is the lagoon and the mournful call of a common loon. In the stillness I think of Jerry Tanner, swept out into the vastness of the sea. I am still afraid of death catching me. But the fire warms me, and I recommit myself to the journey. In the morning I continue the walk home. Death will find me when death will. Meanwhile there is work to be done.

CHAPTER 5

The Bridge: Pedestrian's Point of View

By early morning the March rain stops its gentle fall upon the Inverness Ridge. On the mesa below, pale smoke from a stovepipe chimney drifts through the still-wet trees. Inside a one-room cabin nestled among the bishop pines, laurels, and tan oaks, I sit lingering before the wood-burning stove, sipping a cup of tea and listening to the fire crackle in the morning stillness.

I reread the letter I received almost two weeks ago. It is an invitation from Professor Sim Van der Ryn to be a guest lecturer at one of his classes studying energy, resources, and the environment at the University of California's School of Architecture in Berkeley. The letter explains that the class is interested in low-energy lifestyles and wants to meet people whose lives exemplify a movement toward independence from fossil fuels and harmony with nature.

I fold the letter and replace it in one of the pockets of my backpack that has slowly become a part of me. More than two years have passed since I started walking.

I've journeyed throughout Marin County, to San Francisco, Sacramento, and even into Oregon, but this will be my first walk into Berkeley. I begin six days before the class is to meet.

Rising from the chair, I lift the pack to my shoulders, adjust the straps, and reach for an almost full canteen hanging on a nail by the door. I pick up my banjo in the corner and, tuning it almost unconsciously, walk softly out into the cool gray day.

I follow the rain-soaked path through the trees to the worn asphalt roadway that leads down the hill to First Valley. When I reach the bottom, the air smells fresh and clean. For a while I stand on one of the wooden bridges that cross the valley stream, staring at the water rushing into Tomales Bay.

I continue across the bridge, playing a quiet tune on the banjo until I reach the post office in downtown Inverness, where I leave a forwarding address so I can receive my mail along the way.

I have been silent for nearly two years. Now I walk quietly down the road, accompanied by a muted banjo and several volumes of personal journals of pen-and-ink drawings, watercolors, and writings I have been keeping over this time. Inverness slowly fades away like so many roadside dreams in the seemingly constant process of walking.

By the time I reach Point Reyes Station, some four miles out of Inverness, it is late afternoon and beginning to rain. I stop to visit Jerry and Leila Corbitt, longtime friends, and stay for a late breakfast. Jerry and his band are performing at the Community Theater in Berkeley along with Jesse Colin Young, also a friend and neighbor. I am planning to be in Berkeley about that time so we make arrangements to get together. I always enjoy the music and look forward to the concert. But that is some miles and days away.

The rain is still falling as I depart Point Reyes Station, leaving the warm fireside at the Two Ball Inn, where George smiles from behind the bar and Shirley, who makes great cheese omelets, wishes me a good trip, a safe and quick return.

Now wearing foul-weather gear, banjo carefully wrapped in plastic and covered loosely by a small poncho, I make my way along the Point Reyes–Petaluma road, past Black Mountain looking like a huge fist erupting from the earth, past Lake Nicasio, full and spilling great white sheets into the creek below with a roar, past the Cheese Factory, counting mile markers beside the road, then melting into the green hills dotted with black-and-white cows ready to be milked, and on into the velvet night.

My intended route, approximately 75 miles each way, will take me through Marin County to Novato, around San Pablo Bay via Vallejo, then south through the towns of Rodeo, Hercules, Pinole, San Pablo, Richmond, El Cerrito, and Albany, and finally into Berkeley.

Nearly 12 hours pass before I emerge still dripping from the rain into the bright glare of the Novato streetlights. Struggling with fatigue and aching feet, I limp the remaining few miles in the solitude of the early morning. Quietly I slip through a familiar door, relieve myself of pack and shoes, and crawl wearily into the down sleeping bag I carry with me.

When I awake, it is almost noon and I find myself in a Novato home among close friends, a family. I stay there for the next three days, resting and watching the clouds roll over the hills and bay, feeling the pulse of spring's storm. Then one morning before the rain falls again, I pass over busy Highway 101 to the railroad tracks and disappear down the line, stepping carefully from tie to tie.

It is extremely windy and occasionally the sun shines through the spaces left by great white fluffy clouds that race madly across the blue sky. I stop often to enjoy the day.

Just before reaching Black Point, I leave the rails behind and return to the road (Highway 37) in order to cross the Petaluma River into Sonoma County. Soon a California Highway Patrol car pulls over just ahead of me. Leaving the car, a patrolman approaches, holding his cap with one hand, waving a greeting and telling me to stop with the other. He is saying something but I cannot hear it over the wind. I only see his mouth moving until he is almost in my face.

I am sure he sees the worried look on my face. Then he says something I never expected to hear from a California Highway Patrol officer.

"Say, buddy, it's pretty windy out here. Where are you heading?"

Even though this highway is only a two-lane road, I try to remember if I have seen any signs that prohibit walking. I point in the direction that I am walking, feeling a little silly at telling him the obvious. I am sure he sees the worried look on my face. Then he says something I never expected to hear from a California Highway Patrol officer.

"Don't be frightened. I just stopped to offer you a ride. I can give you a ride as far as Vallejo. How about it?"

With a smile, many signs, and a hastily produced letter, I decline.

"Okay, I get it."

I feel a lot more relaxed when he tells me the "real reason" for stopping me.

"Well, the real reason I stopped you is because it looked like you were carrying a banjo, and banjos are my most favorite instrument in the whole world. Is that a banjo?"

I nod yes.

"Can you play?"

I nod that I can and begin to unwrap the plastic bag protecting my instrument. Traffic continues to hurtle past us and the wind grabs at the plastic bag and flaps it like a flag in a storm.

"Wait, would you mind sitting in my patrol car so you can play it out of the wind? I won't drive you anywhere if you don't want."

A few minutes later we are sitting together in the parked patrol car, out of the wind's fury, and I play a couple of my favorite banjo tunes for an appreciative listener and captive audience of one. Afterward, we each go our respective ways, perhaps just a little bit happier.

Before I reach the Napa River another highway patrol car pulls off the road in front of me. The patrolman steps from his car and waves.

"Hey, don't be afraid. I just heard about you on the radio. Dobbs said that we just have to hear you play. He couldn't stop talking about you."

Along the rest of Highway 37 I repeat my performance, with slight variations, for two other highway patrolmen.

Beside the road, purple, white, and pink foxgloves are growing. The hummingbirds and then the bees discover them. I have never seen so many together at one time. I watch until they discover me— they are all over me, the bees crawling, the hummingbirds darting close to my head, the sound a loud buzzing hum.

It is a dream; I awake early in the morning from a sound sleep beneath the Napa River Bridge to the buzzing tires of the traffic passing overhead. It is a cold day, still windy, and large gray clouds threatening rain drift slowly in the sky as I make my way across the bridge and into Vallejo.

On the waterfront I sit in a Denny's restaurant and order breakfast; two eggs up and hash brown potatoes. The waitress is amused by my pantomime and returns with my order and an extra egg. I point to the plate and hold up three fingers.

"Oh, the cook has traveled with a backpack before and we thought you could use the extra nourishment."

I can. I thank her and sit for a while, studying the map while the rain makes circles in the parking lot puddles.

Before long I am sloshing across a muddy field, watching seagulls fly and a column of white smoke pour from the stack of a steel-gray ship at Mare Island. During the Second World War the Mare Island Navy Yard built and maintained the Pacific Fleet.

Vallejo's name comes from General Mariano Guadalupe Vallejo. He received the grant of the eastern Sonoma Valley and the foothills adjoining Carquinez Strait as a reward for successfully defeating the area's Indian tribes. In 1852, when the legislature gave the name to the community, it also made Vallejo the state capital. Unfortunately, the general was unable to keep his promise to raise $350,000 in gold if Vallejo were made the capital, so the legislature moved on to Sacramento.

On one occasion General Vallejo was transporting a number of his horses on a crude ferry across the strait from the Contra Costa shore to Benicia when the barge capsized. Some of the horses swam ashore and others drowned, but a prized white mare special to the general disappeared. Several weeks later, the white mare was discovered grazing on the hillside of the island across the channel from Vallejo. From that day, the island was known as "Mare's Island," shortened to Mare Island.

I make my way up to the access road that leads to the toll plaza of the Carquinez Strait Bridge. The sign on the side of the road reads pedestrians and bicycles not permitted. I have a bad feeling about being able to get to Berkeley. Up at the toll plaza I find it is illegal for pedestrians to be there as well. The traffic is heavy and dangerous. A toll collector watches me negotiate my way across the lanes and when I get to his booth he looks at me and laughs.

"Hey, what the hell are you doing up here, don't you know it's illegal?"

I point across the bridge and walk my hands in the air in front of me. Cars are piling up behind me. It is clear to me that I am not going to be allowed to walk across this bridge.

"No, no, you can't walk across the bridge."

I look as dejected as I feel. The cars continue to accumulate behind me, but no one is blowing their horn. My sad face must be working, as the toll collector takes pity on me.

"Listen, go over there to the office and see if they can help you." He points over to a low square on the other side of a line of lanes. "Be careful, watch the traffic."

I cross the remaining traffic lanes carefully and clamber across a metal barrier. On the other side is the toll plaza office. Inside the relative quiet assaults me. The guard on duty greets me.

"Hey, you finally made it."

I am surprised until he tells me that one of the highway patrol officers had notified them that I would be arriving soon.

"Can you really play that banjo as well as they say you can?"

I unsling the banjo from my shoulder and let loose with an upbeat traditional fiddle tune, "June Apple." When I am done, several off-duty toll collectors are gathered around me listening, and they ask for another tune. Music is bouncing off the institutional green walls and uniformed people are tapping their feet. The spirit inside the building has definitely changed from unaccommodating to cooperative. While I play my original composition, "Life's Celebration," the plaza guard passes his hat among the toll collectors, who fill it with bills and small change.

Afterward he pulls out a map and scans it thoughtfully.

"The problem," he says, tracing his finger along the red line of a highway, "is that all of the bridges, not including the Golden Gate, crossing San Francisco Bay and the Carquinez Strait bar both pedestrians and cyclists. Of the two alternative routes, the shortest is through Fairfield, to Rio Vista, where it's possible to cross the Sacramento River, then head south to the San Joaquin River, across the Antioch Bridge through Antioch, Pittsburg, Martinez, and some other towns. Hmmm . . ."

He stops and makes a quick calculation with a pencil on the side of the map. His eyes grow wide and he adds the numbers again and looks at me, smiling.

"The alternative route will add approximately a hundred and twenty-eight miles to your journey to Berkeley, making a total of about two hundred miles each way."

We cannot keep from smiling as we trace the Fairfield–Rio Vista route to Berkeley with our fingers in disbelief several times.

"Tell me again why you want to walk to Berkeley?"

I pull out the letter, showing him the invitation to lecture at the university. He studies it.

"I have never met anyone like you," he says. He looks over his shoulder as if someone might be listening and then signs for me to follow him. He leads me across the room to a window. He points.

"Look. This is a twin-spanned bridge, and as you can see there is no traffic on the south span. That's because it's closed for repairs. But a fellow could walk across it just fine"—he nods at me— "especially if I didn't see him."

I slip out of the door and head for the empty span. Seagulls are sailing in an invisible sea beneath me as I cross the Carquinez Bridge. It is wonderful to be alone so high above the water. I unsling the banjo from my shoulder and begin to play. I do not stop until I reach Berkeley late that night.

In the morning, I am able to keep my engagement at the university. With the aid of an overhead projector and someone turning the pages of my watercolor journal, "The Road, Friends, and Places," the class travels from Point Reyes along the northern California–southern Oregon coast and back again. I play the banjo all the while.

A few days later I am sitting in the Berkeley Community Theater listening to the music of my friends. I decide to do something about the lack of access to the Bay Area bridges. When I return to Inverness I write Governor Jerry Brown about the lack of pedestrian and cyclist access across the state toll bridges.

I receive an answer from Howard Ullrich, the state's director of transportation, who suggests I use the system of small vans, buses, and Bay Area Rapid Transit (BART) trains then in operation to shuttle cyclists and pedestrians across the bridge or under the bay.

My answer to him reads in part:

"Upon careful examination of these systems, you will notice that while the pedestrians or cyclists are partaking of this form of transport, they are in fact no longer pedestrians or cyclists, but have become consumers of industrialized transportation.

Painting or drawing a scene or a landscape helps us experience where we are more fully. You can begin with a small sketchpad or blank bound book and watercolors. Don't be discouraged by your first attempts. Tomorrow is another day. Turn the page, walk, and remember to have fun. You will be amazed at where you find yourself.

"While I am not against this type of transportation for those of us who wish to use it, I feel that especially during this time of concern related to environmental pollution and energy crisis, the lack of pedestrian and cyclist facilities only points out our lack of planning and concern for one of man's oldest nonpolluting forms of transportation.

"Still, I am encouraged that we have at least entered an era of awareness about this issue."

However, a few days later, the Organization of Petroleum Exporting Countries (OPEC) shocks energy markets by orchestrating an oil embargo. The awareness of our nation's oil dependence increases even more. In the Bay Area, for the first time, there are long lines at the gas pumps.

In letters, my mother explains to me how difficult it is for her friends and relatives to believe that I have given up riding in cars and stopped talking.

In letters, my mother explains to me how difficult it is for her friends and relatives to believe that I have given up riding in cars and stopped talking. Lucille Russell, one of her neighbors and her best friend, is the first person she tried talking to about "the change" that had come over her son. I imagine their conversations.

"Well, La Java, how is Johnny? Is he coming home for a visit anytime soon?"

"Oh, he is fine, and still out in California, but we aren't expecting to see him since he stopped riding in cars and flying in planes."

"What do you mean, 'He stopped riding in cars and flying in planes'?"

"I mean now he only walks. He walks everywhere, and he won't be coming to Philadelphia unless he walks."

"Girl, that's plain crazy. What does he say when you talk to him on the phone?"

"Well, now, that's just it, you see, I haven't talked to him . . . anyway not recently, not since he gave up talking."

Lucille's eyes open wide and she laughs.

"Java, do you really expect me to believe that? Why are you making up such a story? Is Johnny in some kind of trouble? Is he in jail or something? It's drugs, isn't it?"

The scene is repeated with variations throughout the neighborhood and with an assortment of family members. The general consensus is "Poor La Java. Johnny is in prison somewhere for selling drugs in California and she just can't deal with it."

But even I am surprised when, almost a year after my father's first visit to California, I receive a letter from my mother telling me that both of them are coming to visit and that they will be bringing a few people with them. At first I am happy at the prospect of seeing my mother. Then I become just a little nervous as I remember a story about a family putting their son into a mental institution because, as they put it, he had "lost touch with reality." I quickly make a mental assessment of my own situation and decide that I am on shaky ground. Over the next several weeks I feel out my parents' motive for their journey and pull together whatever resources I feel might help my case.

As it turns out, my parents are visiting with their social club made up of friends, neighbors, and relatives, who use their numbers to get the best prices for travel. I have nothing to fear. They are not coming to lock me up. Nevertheless, I make plans to meet them in San Francisco with evidence that I am not crazy, just an artist who is a little eccentric.

Before the busload of Philadelphia neighbors and relatives shows up in San Francisco I make arrangements to meet them at the KRON television studio.

A local news show has done a three-minute human interest story called "The Silent Minstrel of Inverness." It has already aired but I think it will be a good introduction to "the change" that has come over their little Johnny. The television producer thinks so as well and agrees to show it to my family in one of the studio screening rooms.

On the appointed day a chartered bus slides up to the curb in front of the KRON studio on Van Ness Avenue. I wave to the driver so that he knows he has the right place, and a minute later a line of familiar faces, voices, smells, and shapes pours down the steps, out of the door, across the pebbled sidewalk, and into my arms, their eyes laughing. Among them are my father and mother.

I have not seen my mother in more than three years. Back in Philadelphia she has become a special-education teacher in the public schools. In one of her recent letters she wrote about one of her students being blind and deaf, and learning sign language to communicate with her.

I also had the opportunity to study sign language in Point Reyes. The parents of a deaf girl gave free lessons to anyone in the community who wanted to learn so people could communicate with their daughter. The form is called Signing Exact English, or SEE signing.

Signing Exact English is a sign language system that represents literal English, to make visible everything not heard. SEE supplements what a child can get from hearing and speech-reading.

SEE is different from American Sign Language, or ASL, which is a language unto itself with its own vocabulary, idioms, and syntax. First made available in 1972, SEE is meant to supplement a deaf child's education in ASL.

My mother wrote that she is anxious to communicate with me in the sign language she has learned. Her letter was so enthusiastic about using her sign language skills that as I see her walk toward me all my fears melt away. She holds up her hand and signs, "I love you."

My dad grabs my hand again, but this time sun dances across the landscape of his face. Lucille stops and hugs me while she pats me on the back.

"It's good to see you, Johnny. Did your mother tell you we thought you were in prison?"

I look back at her in mock surprise, and laugh a silent laugh.

"But I really do not understand why you are doing this, and what you think you are going to accomplish."

I smile back and shrug my shoulders. For Lucille, prison would have been easier to understand. I walk with her arm in arm through the studio doors, following the rest of the crowd. Once inside we are all ushered into a screening room just off the lobby. The producer comes in and welcomes everyone and explains what we are about to see.

"You all must be very proud of John to come all this way to see him. The tape we are going to show you is from our new program that interviews interesting people in our viewing area doing positive things. I hope you enjoy it."

For three minutes on the large video monitor I paint watercolors, play my banjo, and walk over the rolling hills of Marin County, while the smooth voice-over of the reporter makes flattering comments. For a segment of the story I mime answers to the reporter's questions. When it is done, the screen goes black and there is complete silence. A few minutes later, I hear a few quiet words, and then a few more.

"That's nice, Johnny," I hear someone say. But some become strangely dumb and a few act as if they cannot speak, making tentative signs with their hands, old ladies and men with graying hair smiling and nodding. Uncle Carter, my mother's youngest brother and somewhat the family rebel, hugs me a long silent moment and then makes his way out to the bus with the rest. As they leave I know I will see them again. I wonder about the video and its effect. Do they think I am crazy? I decide it does not matter. At the very least they have another perspective to think about.

Later in the week I meet my mother and father for dinner in Chinatown, and in the evening we visit my dad's cousin Shep at Finocchio's, a famous female impersonators' club where he is the drummer for the house band. By day he is a guard for a downtown office building and, in his spare time, a fine furniture maker. Whenever I come to the city I stay with Shep and his wife, Pearl. As a musician he is sensitive to the creative process, and we share a passion for music. And so when they ask him his opinion of my lifestyle he is quick to grab me, pull me close to him, and say, "I dig it, man."

Just before my parents are scheduled to leave we make one last trip downtown to visit the mother of a friend working in an office building off Market Street. Both of my parents are impressed that I am always on time to meet them wherever we have to go, even when they are being driven and I am walking. But as we stand in the elevator during its slow climb to the third floor, my mother turns to me and whispers something in my ear.

"If you were serious about this walking," she whispers, taking me into her confidence, "you wouldn't ride in elevators either."

The next day she says good-bye. I turn to make the long walk back to Point Reyes. The feeling of her words stays with me. They are like a prayer.

Back in Inverness, Jean tells me she is selling her house and moving to San Anselmo to chase her revolution. I think to myself, It's time to walk north.

CHAPTER 6

All That Glitters: Discovering the Wilderness

John Muir was one of the first to look at the wilderness as a place where people, shaped by civilization, could go to be re-created and refreshed, not as a resource to be exploited for its minerals, timber, and wildlife. The words of Roderick Nash, a professor of history and environmental studies at the University of California, express a view shared by many contemporary wilderness proponents:

"Wilderness . . . is a profound educational resource schooling overcivilized humans in what we once knew but unfortunately forgot." (All the Nash quotations in this chpater can be found in *Living in the Environment: Principles, Connections, and Solutions*, orig. 1979, continually reissued.) This is the education I am seeking as I make my way north along the California coast once again.

Two months pass before I arrive in Brookings, Oregon. I check in at the Chetco ranger station. Dick Wessle is a big red-haired smoke jumper for the Forest Service. When he spots me inside the office amid the early morning bustle, he hurries over and buries me in a giant bear hug, lifting my thin frame into the air and then shaking me with his laughter.

"Well, you made it back," he roars, squeezing the breath from me before setting me back down. Typewriters stop clicking and for a moment everyone looks up from their work. Some of them smile and wave. I smile and wave back.

I had met Dick in 1974 on my first walk to Oregon. Now he has me by the arm and is telling everyone within earshot what a great guy I am and how I have walked all the way from San Francisco just to visit the wilderness. Some of them remember me from my last trip, so I spend a good part of the morning renewing old friendships before making final preparation for my wilderness sojourn. I am planning to be gone for three weeks.

It is the end of summer, and few other people are walking through. Everyone agrees that I will have a great time hiking. We are looking over a blue-on-white Forest Service fire map, and Dick is talking about the trail conditions, points of interest, and unusually high fire hazard due to summer drought when he stops mid-sentence and smiles.

"You're going to get to meet Perry and Ruth," he says. "That'll be the high point of your trip."

Dick goes on to explain that Perry and Ruth are gold miners who live on a placer claim they've been operating in the Kalmiopsis Wilderness Area for almost two decades.

"Oh, they're real characters," he continues. "Be sure to stop by their cabin and introduce yourself. Tell 'em I said hi too."

With that he puts a little mark on the map where their cabin is located.

"You'd be missing a real experience if you pass up seeing the Davises," says a ranger standing nearby.

I smile and nod my head. In spite of all they say, my idea of a wilderness experience does not include sitting down for a chat with a couple of miners. I have visions of unspoiled landscape and solitude—the fewer people the better, or so I think.

The coastal weather for the last several days has been bordering on rain, with brooding skies and morning and evening fog. But the mountains in the wilderness, about 30 miles away, are reported to be dry and hot. The fire danger indicator in Brookings as I leave, following along the Chetco River, points to high.

Two days pass before I arrive at the bottom of the Quail Prairie lookout tower (elevation 3,033 feet) on the western Kalmiopsis border. I can see the evening fog moving in from the coast, spilling over the mountains. Large thunderheads are rising in the sky. Slowly, step by step, I make my way up the stairway, maneuvering carefully with a 75-pound pack. As I move higher, I become increasingly aware of the fresh breeze moving the tops of trees just below me.

Once inside, I silently introduce myself to the lookout on duty, who is busy observing and reporting an incoming storm to the ranger headquarters in Brookings. It is a small room furnished with a little wood-burning stove for heat, a gas stove for cooking, a table, a few chairs, and a small cot with some storage space below. In the center of the room is a fire finder, a sighting device that enables the lookout to report the location of forest fires.

Not much is known about the fire history of the Kalmiopsis prior to the establishment of the national forest in 1907-1908. But charred stumps and blackened tree trunks give silent evidence that at one time most of the area was burned over. People speculate that fur trappers, traders, prospectors, and early settlers caused some of the fires; other say the damage was done by lightning. And as usual, both are probably right, in part.

The sun disappears behind dark clouds. Night has come during midday. The temperature drops, making me shiver. A few moments later the storm reaches us. Rain falls in great silver-gray sheets onto the metal roof with a deafening roar, and the sky turns blue-white with lightning, adding to the confusion of the elements. I am grateful to be inside, but our vulnerability is spoken without words by the lookout's face.

Small fires ignite where lightning touches the trees, sending plumes of white smoke into the stormy sky. At their camp near the Illinois River, the smoke jumpers are put on standby. In a matter of seconds, our visibility is cut to zero by the fog. The wind howls around us with gale force. More flashes of lightning are followed by rolls of thunder and driving rain. The tower trembles, and so do I.

"It's good to see natural powers and processes greater than our own," writes Nash. "The lessons of such experiences are precisely what are needed if the human-environment relations are to be harmonious and stable in the long run."

In a little while the fog is gone, giving us a clear view of the storm. The rain continues to fall for some time, extinguishing the fires, and the smoke jumpers are taken off standby. In the west there are no clouds, only the sun. Two rainbows arc across the sky and come down near Vulcan Lake. I watch the sun sink silently, crimson-orange, into the sea. This is my welcome to the Kalmiopsis Wilderness.

The next morning, as the sun peeks over the trees and the coastal fog sits thick like steamy milk in the valley, I descend the trail to Boulder Creek Camp. The day dissolves into the rushing blue water, splashing white among the shaded gray rocks, then seeking out the deep green pools where trout grow. The trees reach up steeply to the sky. In the heat of the afternoon I slide naked into the crystal water, headlong into a new environment. It is cold and my body shivers. Blue shadows dance all around and sunlight shimmers on the rocks and sandy bottom. The salamanders disappear and a water snake squirms to hide under a large submerged boulder. I break the surface and stroke for shore. Crawling up on the sandbar, I sit refreshed in the sun. Two kingfishers fly by doing their midair acrobatics. I try to think of all the places I have seen them before, but there are too many to remember, and they all melt into one as I sit by the flowing water.

In the morning I am up in the chilly air, thinking about another dip into the rushing water. I quickly dress and finish the last bit of tea from yesterday's tea bag. Soon I am stepping gingerly from rock to boulder, crossing the creek. Most of the trails are in good condition, but some sections are in great need of repair. Huge fallen trees create awkward barriers with dangerous slides that I negotiate with the greatest care. I pass through an area of *Kalmiopsis leachiana,* namesake of the wilderness. It is a small unassuming shrub somewhat resembling the rhododendron and is known to botanists as one of the rarest shrubs in the world. The plant's small red flowers bloom from mid-May through June and may be collected under special permits given only for scientific purposes.

Three days later I reach Slide Creek and make my camp among some abandoned mining equipment and a few fallen shacks.

Three days later I reach Slide Creek and make my camp among some abandoned mining equipment and a few fallen shacks. In the eastern and southwestern portions of the Kalmiopsis a few roads still remain that were constructed by miners as access to their valid claims. Most were built during and immediately after World War II for the excavation and stockpiling of chrome ore, for which there was great demand. However, Slide Creek and a few other places were especially known for their rich gold deposits.

The sound of horses startles me and brings me back from my fireside dreaming. The trails inside the wilderness are extremely primitive and are not recommended for horseback. I watch as four horses and riders pick their way nervously down the rock-strewn trail to the creek and rushing water below.

While the animals water, one of the travelers crosses the stream and approaches my camp with an extended hand, which I clasp in friendship. He speaks only his name; all else is communicated in hand signs and by drawing in the earth. They will camp tonight on the other side of the creek. Horses' hooves clop on the rounded stream rock; burning cedar emits a fragrant smell, and water rushes to the sound of crickets. All these voices mingle as the wind pierces the evening darkness.

The following morning my new neighbors awaken to discover that two of their horses have run off. I find another horse in a mild state of shock after it plummeted partway down the side of a canyon the day before. I learn from my friends that the section of the trail they have just traversed is quite dangerous on horseback. I assure them that if they venture any farther they will discover similar conditions . . . at least the way I have come.

In the company of another backpacker, who slipped into camp unnoticed during the night, a few of us spend the day sharing wilderness experiences and our views on wilderness preservation.

Early the next day two riders on horseback leave for Onion Camp, beyond the eastern border of the wilderness, via an old mining road; three others follow on foot. The horse they had hobbled escaped with its companion during the night. I am alone again and I drift back into a rhythm of silent contemplation. They leave some rice, flour, and extra salt, all of which will enable me to extend my wilderness adventure comfortably.

Sometimes the changes come from within
Seeing with no eyes
Hearing with no ears
We begin

September 23, 1975
Slide Creek, Kalmiopsis Wilderness

I somehow manage not to mind the silent clutter of abandoned mining equipment that lies rusting about—twisted cable, painted red-and-yellow motors with rods and pistons exposed—machines chipped to the bone. I become absorbed in watching the canyon wall, looking for the way I came just days before. The trail is now lost in earthy colors among the trees and rocks. The trees are clinging, holding on with roots knotted to stone, others slipping, falling to the stream below. A few of them I get to know. As Nash says:

"Forget size, terrain, the presence of wild animals, the absence of human technology—wilderness, ultimately, is a state of mind. If you think a certain piece of country is wilderness, then it is wilderness—for you. . . The dude from New York generally has very different criteria for determining wilderness than does the grizzled Idaho prospector. But every wilderness experience is worthy of respect."

The wilderness I have come to experience is how they dance, the trees with long green needles. How they stand in the wind, bending and swaying. And how they come to the water and drink there among the rocks like three sisters.

I see movement. Mixed among the variegated hues of green . . . ferns and grasses, bushes and small trees loaded with blue huckleberries and red chokecherries . . . a flash of gray, and the trail that is an invisible path is traced by a fat squirrel bounding with its tail high. It goes down steeply, switchbacks through the trees down to the river . . . not the way I imagine. But I do not really know the trail until I look back, until I catch sight of the gray squirrel on it. I relax into a simple experiential knowledge that unfolds within me. I am learning to see.

I watch the blue jays, 50 or more, that come down each day swooping easily from limb to limb with raucous laughter, feet curled under. And in the quiet I hear the voice of the river passing among the rocks and over stones, everywhere at once, making its way through steep green canyons to the sea. I try to catch the words mingling with the shushing of the trees. Perhaps this is where our speech began. Maybe long ago before there were words, there was only the river and the people listened to the water . . . and the quiet whispering.

I can only understand the laughter. I am still learning how to listen. Down by the water, a nameless little bird stands on the rocks near the rapids every evening, singing, its dark body bobbing to some silent music, then diving into the stream. I run down to the rocks to find it. Surely it will drown. But before I reach the stream there is another. I ask myself, could it be the same bird?

In the night, the canyon rises black beneath a starry sky, and on this soft velvet I paint pictures in my mind of what is hidden there, until the moon lifts above the rim and silver shadows dance down to the river and splash across the rocks. At Slide Creek I slow down to a stop, and all the hurried miles, the noise and smoky choke of the speeding roads and highways, finally slide away. I stay for five days.

Then one morning—the fish-scale sky hinting rain—I leave Slide Creek, stepping on five stones across the Chetco River, and continue south through the dense growths of poison oak. The trail greatly needs repair but I have grown to expect and accept it as part of the wilderness, as much as the large striped hornets, dark and menacing, that suddenly appear, grabbing moths from midair flight, and the threatening sound of a rattlesnake's tail shaking in the knee-high grass.

I was told that Ruth and Perry always welcomed wilderness travelers, and I would be no exception, even in my silence. But this greeting is unexpected.

Two days later I arrive at the mining claim operated the last 17 years by prospectors Ruth and Perry Davis. I do not intend to stop, but I find myself walking up the trail toward Emily Cabin. Perry is sitting in a rusted folding chair, shaded from the midday sun by a clump of maple trees. He is so intent on unlocking some mystery of a rock sample under the magnifying lens he holds, he does not notice me. I stand almost beside him, continuing to make the little whistling sounds I began when I first started toward him. No one likes to be startled from a reverie, especially in the quiet of the woods.

Alongside the stone-and-cedar log cabins spring water issues from a large rusty pipe stuck into the earth and supported by stones. The water splashes over moss-covered rocks and makes its way past Perry to the Little Chetco River a ways below. A fly buzzes around his ear. He waves it away and looks up. Our eyes meet for the first time. A sort of recognition passes over the lines of his face. Behind a push-broom mustache, the grizzled sourdough smiles.

"Well, what do ya say?" he exclaims in a crackly voice that matches his appearance. "It's been a long time."

I was told that Ruth and Perry always welcomed wilderness travelers, and I would be no exception, even in my silence. But this greeting is unexpected.

I smile and take the hand knotted by years of hard work and river panning that he extends in my direction. For a moment we look at each other a little harder than before and arrive at the same conclusion together. This is our first meeting, but no doubt we each saw something familiar in the other, though we could not tell what. We both laugh.

"No matter," he says, pulling at a shock of snow-white hair that hangs from under his worn felt hat.

He offers me the hospitality of the chair beside him. "It's just that I thought you were someone I knew."

Perry explains that his wife, Ruth, has gone to town for a few days to see the dentist. I hand him a recent newspaper clipping that explains about my walking and silence. He reads it slowly. When he is finished he tells me about a couple who had come the year before.

"Didn't say a word the whole time they were here. They were on some kind of word fast or something—just smiled and nodded—stayed pretty much to themselves, down there at the Copper Creek campsite. By the way, that's a good place for you to set up camp—water and a fire pit. You know how to handle fire, don't ya?" he asks while giving me the once-over.

I nod a reassuring yes that seems to satisfy him. Just the same he goes on about how the cabin and the whole valley could go up in smoke in a matter of minutes. He snaps his fingers to illustrate the point. Then his eyes smile from behind horn-rimmed glasses held together by wire and glue.

"What do ya say, why don't ya come on up later this evening after you set up your camp and have something hot to drink?" Perry likes to talk. He is not at all what I had expected.

At night I sit in the prospectors' log cabin at Perry's invitation. Warmed by the old wood-burning stove and the soft yellow glow of the oil lamps, I let the music pour from my banjo. To my delight, Perry, dressed in his faded and worn pants and jacket, is inspired to dance, strutting about and kicking his heels. I continue playing as he puffs thoughtfully on his pipe, sending sweet gray smoke curling beyond the reach of the lamp's glow.

"That music," he says, "reminds me of a mountain stream, a fast-flowing mountain stream."

He pauses, puffs again, and stares into the shadows.

"It brings to mind," he continues, "a peculiar little bird that lives near the rapids of such a stream."

The banjo falls almost silent as the words pass from his lips.

"A water ouzel," he says smiling. "Have you ever seen one?"

I nod my head and laugh, not quite silently, at the communication of the music, and dance around like the bird I had seen several days before, bobbing up and down, then diving into the invisible water.

I camp near the cabin for three days, visiting with Perry, drawing and painting while listening to stories about his life and the wilderness. He tells me about the grizzly he and Ruth saw a few winters back.

"Must've been the last one in these parts," he says. "It was in pretty bad shape. No one believed us, but we knew what we saw."

Born on an eastern Oregon homestead more than 70 years before, Perry was used to a ruggedly independent life. At five years old he was already helping his uncle string barbed-wire fences and taking the team and wagon 20 miles across the prairie to town for supplies by himself. "It seems as though I missed my childhood," he told me in a melancholy voice. He had spent most of his life on ranches or in the mountains prospecting, except for his time in the Coast Guard during the Second World War, and even then he was in charge of the shore patrols because of his knowledge of horses.

He married Ruth, his hometown sweetheart. After his military service and an undergraduate degree at Stanford, he went off to New York and earned a Ph.D. in physical education at Columbia University. It didn't take them long to decide that city life was not for them. They returned to the West Coast and bought a sailboat. It was a freak of nature, the tidal wave that picked up their boat and deposited it on the beach at Crescent City, in the northwestern corner of California. But to Perry and Ruth it was a sign. They sold what was left of their boat and a few years later moved onto eight abandoned claims in what was then still national forest, and began the arduous process of redeveloping the placer mine.

"All that glitters is not gold," Perry says, and smiles as if he knows some great secret and is about to let me in on it.

"You know that's been said before, but it's true," he assures me. The fire crackles, taking the edge off the evening chill. "There's gold here, ya know, plenty of it, but it's not just the kind ya find at the bottom of your pan. Oh, there's enough of that too," he says. "But the gold I'm talking about is the gold of just being here. If you look around you'll notice that we keep our mining to a minimum. We take only what we need and disturb as little as possible."

I have to admit that when I first arrived at the Davises' claim I expected to find monstrous machines, gouged and denuded earth, muddied streams, and signs reading keep out. What I find is just the opposite, bordering on the serenity of a garden. I am interested in what Perry has to say. In spite of being a "retired" professor, he likes to talk, and how he talks about things could easily be called lecturing. It must be my own not talking and the "word fast" of the couple he had met earlier that pique his interest in the subject of being silent. It is obvious in the way he questions me with his eyes that he has been giving the subject a great deal of thought. And then one night . . .

"Recapitulation."

That is what he says to me in the darkness of the cabin.

"That's what I think you are doing with your walking and not talking, recapitulation. Do ya know what that is?"

I shake my head.

"Well, it's like going back to the beginning of things and then working your way through all the successive stages of human development to where we are now. You must be going back to learn something. Recapitulation is a good teacher. Why, we all do it some way or another, especially before we're born."

He goes on to explain that the human fetus starts out as one cell that multiplies into something with gills, then develops a tail that disappears before it emerges into the world looking like we do.

"We're just goin' through all our ancestral stages on the way here. Somehow, whether you know it or not, you're doin' the same

Listen actively to learn. Be prepared to hear something new without judgment, and listen to what you have heard before from the place where you are now. Learning may come from a new understanding of what you already seem to know.

thing. I suspect one of these days you'll be riding in cars and jabberin' away again, but you'll be different. No doubt the world will be different too."

Ruth returns the day before I am planning to leave. At 70 she is thin and wiry with an outspokenness one expects of a pioneering woman. She thanks me for keeping Perry company while she was away, as if we had planned it in advance.

"Dear, did you talk this child's ear off?" she asks Perry in mock reproach.

Perry only smiles and puffs thoughtfully on his pipe. They have been together nearly 50 years, and it seems I had too little time to get to know her.

The next year I return and we spend more time together. Then during the following winter my friend Cherry and I snowshoe into Emily Cabin for a visit.

Cherry is 19, athletic, blonde, and likes to think of herself as a tomboy. I had promised her that she could walk to Oregon with me when she graduated from high school. After her graduation ceremony we leave from Point Reyes, walking along the California coast and into the Kalmiopsis.

Travel in the Kalmiopsis during the winter months is not easy, and Ruth and Perry are happy to have company.

"I'm getting too old for this," Ruth confides as she adds a few more sticks to the fire. "The winters are just too hard and lonely."

The Davises have no children of their own. They make up for it by adopting the backpackers who come through and sharing their vision of wilderness preservation. They take these hikers into their hearts and turn them into a family . . . and so it is with Cherry and me.

Ruth will not hear of us eating dinner alone at Hawk's Creek Cabin, where we have set up temporary residence. It is an old log cabin at the far end of their mining claim, about a mile from Emily. We stumbled onto it near nightfall after coming down from the snow the day before, wet and tired. To us the dirt-floored shelter with its little wood-burning stove is paradise.

"You kids are going to eat with us while you're here," she insists. "We have plenty of supplies."

We agree, adding what we can afford to the larder. On my birthday Ruth manages a yellow cake with white frosting and a couple dozen candles. It is a happy time.

"You two must love it here as much as we do," Perry says, after we finish washing the dinner dishes.

He is referring to my yearly thousand-mile pilgrimage to the Kalmiopsis, which now includes Cherry. He chuckles, not expecting an answer, but I know when something is on Perry's mind. His mouth opens slightly at the corner as if he is chewing on a straw. Ruth is warming herself behind the stove, smiling, pretending she is not listening, but she is. She is forever correcting or adding to Perry's lectures with an appropriate date or detail that makes listening more like hearing a duet.

"You know," now Perry is talking in a kind of gruff and authoritative voice, like he hopes to find courage in his tone, "a feller could do all right by himself living in a place like this."

I've heard him make this comment many times over the years when talking about his and Ruth's decision to make a go of the Emily claims. But this time he asks us a question.

"Would you two consider moving into Copper Creek Cabin next fall? We're getting too old to do it alone much longer."

It does not take long for Cherry and me to agree. We leave the next day for the 500-mile walk back to Marin County. We exit the Kalmiopsis by the east gate and head across the mountains through the Applegate Valley to Ashland. Filled with excitement, we head south through the Central Valley, cutting west around San Francisco Bay. It is spring by the time we reach Point Reyes.

During the early summer we spend our time in preparation. In the Kalmiopsis the snows are gone now, so I write a letter to Perry and Ruth to let them know that we will arrive in time to get the firewood in for winter. We do not have the usual time for resting. We can do that once we return to the Kalmiopsis.

Near the end of summer we are ready to walk north. We hurry this time, as much as you can hurry on a 500-mile walk. Cherry carries a mandolin so we stop to play music and we visit with the friends we have made along the way. It is familiar walking along the coast. We take the long way in, coming from Brookings, up the Chetco River into the mountains that are our home.

We arrive at Emily in the fall and move into the little redwood cabin next to Copper Creek. Before the snow comes, Perry, Ruth, and Cherry take the old Jeep out the mining road to

Cave Junction to bring in the last of the supplies. When the snow comes the only way out is by snowshoe or ski.

Around us grow the trees of my dreams, Port Orford cedars. They stand tall and straight with deeply grooved bark, green scalelike fronds in place of leaves, tiny white Xs on their backs, mingling with the Douglas fir, pines, maples, and spruce.

I talk with Perry about sailing and building wooden ships and he talks to me about the mountains, their gold, and things he feels are important. He sends me off to read *Walden*.

"It's what I've tried to model my life after," he says. "A feller could do worse."

It wasn't always that way, though, and he tells us about the time he was about to flatten off a mountain to make a wilderness landing strip for a plane he wanted to buy.

"Naturally the Forest Service didn't go for it." He chuckles. "I wouldn't think of doing anything like that now, though. Back then we didn't know any better."

He stops talking and puffs on his ever-present pipe.

Five years have passed, and each day together is like the first day we met. But I can see they are getting older now. The cold and the loneliness bother Ruth, and the time when they will have to leave is approaching. He says, "We're only visitors anyway."

Then one day he surprises us.

"You know, you and Cherry could buy this place from us if you want."

He quotes us a ridiculously low price of $8,000 and talks about us staying and taking over when they leave.

Selling mining claims is a common occurrence in the national forest. What is actually being sold are the mineral rights, but in the case of the Emily claims it also involves the transfer of historical landmarks and a way of life. Cherry and I talk about what taking over would mean. It is not a decision not to be taken lightly. It would mean a serious commitment and a lot of hard work.

Spring comes and we walk out of the wilderness to raise money for the purchase. When we return, Perry surprises us again, this time by telling us that in our absence they sold the claims to someone else, someone they didn't know.

But Ruth is speaking from her own experience when she says as sincerely as she can, as if she were sparing us from some great burden:

"We couldn't saddle you kids with all this."

We cannot disguise our hurt, nor do we try. Perry is convinced that he has done the right thing for us—that living in the Kalmiopsis is not really the gold that it seems.

"I know you don't understand it now," he says, "but one day you'll thank us."

We think it is just the rationalization of an old man who is losing his faculty for clear thought. After all, we shook hands in agreement to the sale. We feel more than disappointment, we feel betrayed.

It takes us a little while to see it from their point of view. After living an idyllic life in the wilderness for nearly 25 years, they are being forced by old age back into the world from which they had escaped. Their situation really shouldn't come as a shock to us. Disenchantment has become part of their conversations. The isolation, long winters, and hard work necessary to stay have become too great. If we were to take over we would eventually have to face these challenges too.

After living an idyllic life in the wilderness for nearly 25 years, they are being forced by old age back into the world from which they had escaped.

Despite my disappointment, I also feel relief. I have many dreams for my life. I want to finish school, and I still want to build boats and sail around the world. In all honesty, I am not ready to settle into a wilderness retreat, and I know it. Maybe Perry knows it too. For me, wilderness is still a place to visit, a place for being refreshed and renewed, and my time for this visit is drawing to a close. I can always experience the wilderness that is beside the road.

We are ready to leave when Perry calls me into his study. It is actually the original part of the cabin and more than a century old. He and Ruth added the kitchen and living room area during restoration. With only one window, covered in frosted plastic, the study is dark. From the shadows Perry retrieves a wooden case a little larger than a cigar box.

"Here," he says as he hands me the box, "we want you to have this."

Inside the brass-hinged case is the navy sextant that he salvaged from his own sailboat years ago. It is the instrument that helped them find their way on the open seas of the Pacific.

"You'll need it on your journey."

Water wells up in the corners of his eyes. It catches what little light there is and glistens. I am touched. I have seen the sextant only once, while listening to a spirited and emotional tale about their time sailing. It is all they have left of that time besides the memories and now, Perry is even losing those.

"Ruth never liked sailing," he says after I thank him. "That's part of the reason why after the wreck we moved onto dry land. Oh, it's been a good life all right, but the one thing you should do, John, is to continue following your dreams." Perry speaks in the most fatherly voice I can remember him ever using. I suppose he is right. The real gold is following your own dreams.

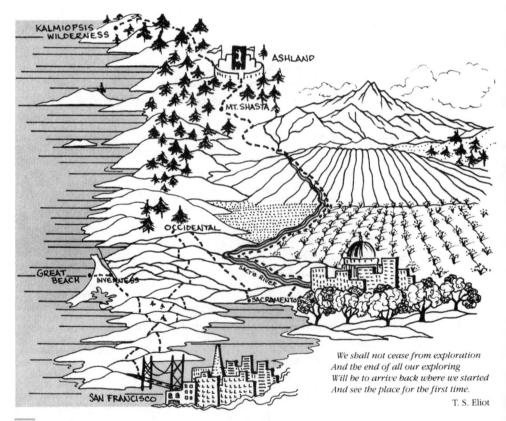

We shall not cease from exploration
And the end of all our exploring
Will be to arrive back where we started
And see the place for the first time.

T. S. Eliot

CHAPTER 7

School of Reflection: Gathering the Tools

Cherry returns by bike to Marin County to be with her family and I go on to Ashland, Oregon. I want to visit friends, so we make plans to meet later. Three years earlier, I had visited the town on my way to the wilderness.

The walk up the Sacramento Valley had been long and hot, and after climbing 14,000-foot Mount Shasta in Northern California, I looked forward to the stop for a rest. As I came down from the highway, I walked by the neat wood-and-brick apartments that were housing for married students at Southern Oregon State College (SOSC). How pleasant it would be to live and go to school here, I thought. That feeling was reinforced after I saw the rest of the campus. It was a small school with an enrollment of about 5,000. A tree-lined boulevard led into the center of town; multicolored banners with images of lions flew from the lampposts heralding their world-renowned Shakespeare festival. The town had a holiday mood. I stayed for a few weeks, making friends and playing music at the restaurants and in the plaza. I liked the town and the town liked me. This is the place I want to return to school.

Nevertheless, I am unsure about enrolling in a degree program while maintaining a vow of silence; this insecurity has kept me from attending school before. But as I sit in the registrar's office at SOSC with Mr. Davidson, my feelings begin to change.

He reads some of the clippings, interspersed with a few

scribbled notes that I have offered him by way of explanation. To my surprise he is receptive to the idea of my studying at the college.

"This is very interesting. *You* are very interesting," he says. "And you mean you haven't spoken in how many years?"

I look up into the sky and count the numbers off in my head, then hold up six fingers.

"Six years, yes. Well, you seem to be able to do all right even without talking." He stops, stands up, and retrieves some papers from his desk. "You may have to get permission from individual instructors to be in their classes without talking. You understand there may be some question about your motives or sincerity when it comes to your silence, but I'm sure you'll have no problem. You'll find we have some innovative programs here for the nontraditional student. The one I think will interest you is the Prior Learning Experience program, or PLE. It gives up to two years of college credit for demonstrating knowledge gained from life experiences outside the traditional college setting."

I am not sure why I am there, except that after having dropped out of college when I was younger, I want to finish.

He goes on to explain that the program requires a three-credit course in writing and documenting a PLE portfolio. The idea excites me. It is the first class I sign up for.

Ann Deering, our instructor, is a small heavy-set woman with ear-length blonde hair who loves horses and dogs, subjects she is happy to talk about for hours after class. During class she talks about discovering who we are through looking at where we have been and trying to see where we are going. There are about a dozen students in our class, from 25 to 50 years old. Most have jobs and families; they are returning to school for various reasons. Some hope to make job adjustments and career changes. I am not sure why I am there, except that after having dropped out of college when I was younger, I want to finish.

"What I want you to do," says Ann, drawing a horizontal line with yellow chalk across a green chalkboard, "is to imagine this line as your life. This is the beginning and here is where it ends."

The students groan and then there is an uncomfortable silence full of sideways glances.

"How long do you expect to live?" she asks the class.

No one answers.

"Sixty-five, seventy, a hundred years?"

A pall drops over the classroom. A woman about 35 raises her hand.

"What does this have to do with our prior learning?" she asks. "I have a family and I don't like to think about dying."

It is clear that she is upset and that she speaks for the rest of us.

"I know you might think this is a morbid way to begin a Prior Learning class, but the important thing here is to realize that our lives are finite; they have a beginning and an end. When making our short- and long-range goals, we have to keep this in mind."

What she is saying is an obvious truth, yet she is the only one who has much to say about it.

"Look," says Ann, "suppose you were born in 1935; that would make you forty-four now."

She scribbles the numbers beside the yellow line on the board.

"And let's say you live to be seventy-four; that would mean you would have thirty years to realize your long-range goal. It's nothing we have to dwell on, but it's something to keep in mind. If we can see our opportunity for accomplishment as finite we can start to make steps to reach our goal."

An older man in the class makes an uneasy comment about how he doesn't want to know when he is going to die.

"It's impossible for me to know anyway," he says nervously.

Ann is undaunted by the response and asks us to make our own charts at home as an exercise. Not many of us do it, though. Other projects she asks us to do are less threatening, like writing short autobiographies or chronological résumés, and identifying experiences that are similar to courses offered in college. But none is as powerful as the first, and no one is able to forget seeing his or her life as a dull yellow line scratched across a green chalkboard. I know I cannot, and for a while all I have done and all I want to do seem to lose importance. Once again I am forced to face death, and it makes me feel very small and fragile. My head fills with images of oil-soaked seabirds, bodies rotting on a California shore, Jerry Tanner lost in Tomales Bay, and the crushed body of a small robin on a Philadelphia street. But in facing death we experience the whole of life, and in that experience we find meaning and are obligated to act, often under great difficulty.

Attending classes without talking is difficult, though I have been preparing for it over the years. A few professors question my sincerity at first, but as long as I am able to do the work, they are satisfied. I communicate as I always have, with pantomime or, when all else fails, writing notes. Communicating in a specific class is easier than I thought. Since everyone is in the same mind set it usually requires little effort to ask a question or get a point across. But most of all I listen from within to the silence that has grown to be so much a part of my life.

Ann smiles as I hand her the black three-ring binder. It has taken me two years, while attending classes, to write and gather all the necessary supporting documents to complete my PLE portfolio. She reads my short- and long-range goals aloud:

"My personal and immediate goals are to finish school and receive a General Studies degree in Science/Mathematics with a concentration in biology and a minor in creative writing from Southern Oregon State College, continuing my self-directed study and involvement in the areas of environmental and related sciences.

"My lifetime goal is to sail and walk around the planet as part of my education with the spirit of hope that in some way I might help others and benefit the world."

She pages through the book, nodding after each credit request: General Science 9, Biology 18, Physical Education 6. She chuckles under her breath as she reads over my 15-credit request in Speech/Communications, which ironically includes a series of classes in nonverbal communication. She continues until she adds up more than 100 credits in my portfolio.

"This is an incredible accomplishment. You know that there's a limit of ninety-six credits that can be approved, but asking for more can't hurt?"

I nod.

"No one in this program has ever received more than nine credits, but if your portfolio is approved you'll have ninety-six credits, enough to graduate this summer after only two years of class work. That would be really remarkable."

Now a big smile spreads across my face as I realize that the possibility of attaining my first goal, finishing college, is within my grasp.

Finally, the school approves my PLE credit request for a record of 98 credits, of which I use 96 to complete my academic requirements for graduation. Immediately after my approval SOSC modifies its PLE regulations so that subsequent students will be required to pay tuition fees for each credit they receive. As for me, I am able to receive two years of college credit for a modest 75-dollar registration fee.

In June, my father arrives with his cousins Shep and Pearl, his older sister, Lucy, her daughter, Maud, and Maud's 12-year-old daughter, Maria. They are here for my graduation. It is the first time I have seen my aunt Lucy, Maud, and Maria since I stopped talking.

Aunt Lucy is a large chocolate woman with soft full lips and a large toothy smile. After moving from Philadelphia, she married a farmer in Stony Creek, Virginia, and became a teacher and principal at a small elementary school during the era of segregation.

Now she sits squeezed inside the breakfast nook of the 16-foot trailer that has been my home in Ashland for the past two years. She is talking in long, slow, rambling sentences about how proud she is about my graduation. Her voice carries the lilting sound of the West Indies. Nine years older than my father, she knows the value of a college education and he is obliged to listen when she speaks.

"Johnny, it sure is something to me that you are graduating college. You know that is important to me, because if it weren't I wouldn't have come all this way. I mean *really*."

I nod and turn to try to catch the eye of my father, who has somehow squeezed his large frame into the other side of the tiny nook. He is strangely silent, looking out the window at the vegetable garden that my friend John Seligman has planted in his backyard where my trailer is parked. Lucy prods him.

Silence is always with us. But we do not choose silence, silence chooses us. If you are called to be silent on your journey, recognize the invitation as a great gift. It is a gift to be shared with others. Your relationship to silence is one thing that will define the uniqueness of your journey.

"Doc, what do you say?"

My father comes back from wherever his mind has wandered and gives his big sister a smile. He lets go by quoting one of his famous sayings.

"Well, you know, you gotta learn to take the bitter with the sweet."

"There isn't anything bitter about Johnny getting his college degree, especially with him not talking. I think this is really an accomplishment."

"Oh, I agree with you, and don't get me wrong, I am really proud of him finishing school and all, but now what is he going to do? What can he do if he doesn't talk and ride in a car? I don't know how he managed to get through school without talking, but however he did it, that won't work out in the real world."

He turns and looks at me and asks me the question directly.

"Things are difficult enough for black folks without you tying a stone around your neck. What do you think you're doing? Man, just stop this foolishness and start driving and saying something, because right now you ain't saying anything."

I have nothing to say. I am thinking about how hard it has been to attend classes without speaking. Some professors have been skeptical, and I have not been exempt from classroom participation or required presentations just because I have chosen to not speak. I've sat in the front of each class to be close to the teacher, ready to act out, mime a question or an answer, hand in a note or scrap of paper, or scribble something on the green board.

Classroom presentations were more problematic. One assignment in natural history class involved making a presentation about map making. Putting together the slides and overheads was easy. Next I visited the county planning office with a tape recorder and a list of questions. Once the manager understood my problem his face brightened and he spoke into the microphone.

"So, you want to learn about making maps. Well, you've come to the right place. We use all kinds of maps in the planning work that we do here. Let's go speak with the cartographer."

The sound of footsteps on the hard linoleum floor ringing through the hallway adds texture to the interview. I played the edited tape in class while showing slides of mountains and other

landscape features. Working at my invisible drawing table, I produced an example of an unfinished and then a completed base map. At the end I stood there in the silence of Lincoln after the Gettysburg Address. Not knowing what else to do I bowed, and the classroom erupted into applause.

The graduation ceremony is followed by parties and goodbyes to friends and classmates. Some of them are going on to graduate school. Thinking about going to graduate school while I am silent gives me a headache and a tight feeling in my stomach. I am pleased with my accomplishment, but I think my father is right.

It is Sunday when my family piles back into Shep's powder-blue Ford station wagon and heads back to San Francisco. I wave goodbye as they drive down the main street and disappear in the traffic.

A half hour passes and I am in the grocery store when a friend runs up to me.

"Did your father find you yet? He's driving around looking for you."

I am sitting on a bench on the main street when Shep's Ford glides to a stop in front of me. There is excitement in the car as they call me over. The San Francisco newspaper is in my father's hand and his eyes are wide.

"You're on the front page, you're on the front page!"

He holds up the paper and I read the large bold print above my picture in cap and gown. "Bay Area Man Graduates in Silence."

"Man, look at that, you're on the front page!"

I give my dad an embarrassed grin. I do not feel comfortable with my image in my father's hand, not because of a stolen spirit, but because the image is so important to him, as well as the opinion of others. I wonder if it will ever be different. Lucy chides my father amidst all the congratulations pouring out the car window.

"You see, Doc, there is nothing bitter here. Now what do you think of Johnny?"

"Oh, I still think he's crazy. For sure that's why they put him in the newspaper. They are always looking for strange things to put in the paper. I just wish he would start talking now and give this craziness up."

We shake hands and they say goodbye again and drive away. I am left sitting on a bus stop bench. My friend Cherry finds me there and sits with me. She has ridden her bike up from Marin

County to be with me at graduation. She stays behind a few days and tells me of her own dream to go to college.

A year earlier I had written Bob Darr, a master boat builder on Tomales Bay. I told him of my goal to walk and sail around the world and asked him if I could be his apprentice. If I am going to sail, I want to learn how to build boats. He wrote back to say that he was starting a boat-building school in Sausalito, a little town across from San Francisco on the other side of the Golden Gate Bridge. He said there would be a place for me at his school when I graduated from college. I can hardly wait to begin.

I decide to ride my bike back to the Bay Area. I am strong enough to pedal all the way up to the pass. In the road cut I see fossils of sea creatures now exposed to the sun. I always stop to look at them and marvel at how life is changing, and how the sea covered this high place. Back on my bike I begin the long coast down into California. First there is the ease, and then the exhilaration of speed. I am keeping up with the traffic, and my speed is increasing. A passenger in a pickup truck beside me is smiling with big wide eyes, holding up six fingers. Sixty. I am not sure if the shaking is the bike frame or me, but I am gripped by fear. I imagine the front wheel collapsing into a tangle of wire spokes and then nothing.

I am breaking the sound barrier down Highway 5, past Mount Shasta in early summer white, into the valley heat, beside flooded fields of rice and yellow-faced sunflowers, along the Sacramento River spilling into San Francisco Bay.

I arrive at the Center for the Wood Arts in Sausalito. It has been only two weeks since I left Ashland. I am not fully here. Walking the 500 miles normally would have taken me about two months. A part of me is still on the road, somewhere around Mount Shasta, but all around me is the scent of freshly milled Port Orford cedar. Its pungent smell takes me to another place and time, back in Oregon.

Once I walked to Port Orford, a town on the Oregon coast about 60 miles north of the California border. I was looking for the cedar prized by many boat builders to build my own boat. I had dreams of felling a tree and milling the lumber by hand using a whipsaw or a pit saw. And in keeping with my nonmotorized lifestyle I wanted to haul the lumber back to Point Reyes using a horse and wagon. I would build a boat and sail around the world.

In Langlois, just outside Port Orford, I met R. D. Tucker, a gruff barrel-chested lumberman who took an instant liking to me because I had walked all that way to learn about his trees, and he liked the way I played the banjo. He showed me old pictures from when the cedars had lined both sides of the highway.

"But they're dying out," R. D. explained. Something was attacking the roots and no one knew what it was. He theorized that it was a virus transmitted in the water and talked about a recent flood that might have had something to do with it. For a week I camped at his mill and ate with his family, while he schooled me in what it would take to accomplish my project.

He told me that people in this country had stopped using whipsaws to saw logs into planks a long time ago. And the only place he knew to find them was in antique shops. Then in midsentence he stopped talking and scratched his head. He remembered that at an old abandoned homestead in the mountains he and his son had seen one rusting in an orchard. He drew me a map, and the next year I went there to search for it.

In Langlois, just outside Port Orford, I met R. D. Tucker, a gruff barrel-chested lumberman who took an instant liking to me because I had walked all that way to learn about his trees, and he liked the way I played the banjo.

I found the homestead tucked in a little valley in the Siskiyou Mountains. A few buildings were still standing and scattered among them I found a rusting plow, cultivating disks, and some other farm implements. As I searched the orchard I filled my pack with apples and hard pears, but I found no whipsaw. It was not until a few years later, as I walked a trail along the Rogue River just west of Agness, that I encountered Mr. Smithers, a grizzled 90-year-old prospector who had lived on his homestead perched above the river for more than 60 years. In his tool shop I saw my first real whipsaw, hanging on the rough plank wall. I offered to buy it from him. He thought about it for a moment, and then decided to make me a gift of the saw, saying he was tickled that I knew what it was, and that he didn't think he would be needing it anymore. I carried the saw balanced on my shoulder three days, all the way to the coast.

On my way south along the coast highway I met a deputy sheriff who offered to send my saw via freight to me in Point Reyes. I never saw it again.

Once again the cedar of my dreams surrounds me. Some of the planks are neatly stacked and stickered next to the walls, the rest form glistening skins of sleek marine bodies in various stages of progress. It is lunchtime and the shop is quiet. Bob Darr, the master builder, sees me standing in the doorway and comes over to greet me.

"John, you made it. I saw your picture in the Sunday paper and knew you were on your way, but I didn't expect you so soon."

I point to my bike, loaded down with four panniers and my banjo strapped lengthwise along the bike's frame. He smiles.

"Okay, John, you can start in right away. Your first project is to build a box for your tools."

> *Waiting for a blade*
> *Drying in neatly stacked rows*
> *The cedar smells sweet*

October 14, 1981
Center for the Wood Arts
Sausalito, California

My trailer arrives from Ashland and I set up my residence next to the center. Outside on the adjoining property are a few dozen shipping containers used for storage. As part of my agreement with Bob, I can attend the center without charge for being the night watchman. During the day, the work is arduous but satisfying. Our first project is to finish and launch a nearly completed banana boat, a three-station rowing boat of lapstrake construction. The boat was a learning project for one of Bob's weekend classes.

Our major project is building the *Renegade*, a 28-foot Lyle Hess cutter. It consumes us with all there is to learn, from lofting and making patterns for the frames to pouring the molten lead keel and molten bronze for the metal fittings. Each day we work on improving our woodworking skills. Bob is a master. Months pass and the cutter is nearing completion. My skills are improving and I have received my first order, for a rowing dory. One afternoon Bob comes from his office in the corner of the shop to find me at my bench, working on the *Renegade*'s black locust rudder.

"John, I just received a phone call from your cousin Shep in San Francisco." He speaks in a soft and ominous voice. At the sound of it a hand wraps itself around my heart and I wait for the bad news. "I'm really sorry to tell you this, but your mother called and it seems your dad is in the hospital and near death." I stand there and let the shock move outward from my heart to my hands and feet, and they are motionless. I try to think of something I can do, but I cannot.

"Your cousin wants you to come over to his home in the city as soon as you can," he says.

I nod my head slowly, and look at my watch. It is only four o'clock in the afternoon. By the time I get off work the bridge may be closed to foot traffic, a new regulation following a recent spate of suicides. Bob sees me thinking.

"I think you should just go, John—don't worry about cleaning up." We always put our tools away and clean up after our workday, which is one of the disciplines that Bob attempts to instill in us. But today I listen to his words, and a few minutes later I am on my way up to the bridge walkway. The winter sun has been set for nearly an hour when I reach the gate. It is open. As I cross the bridge, I can see the situation developing. I will be asked to give up walking. What will I do?

My cousin lives in the Silver Terrace neighborhood of San Francisco, close to Candlestick sports stadium. Inside the mood is somber. Shep's wife, Pearl, meets me at the door. Shep is behind her. We all embrace.

"Yeah, man." His voice is resonant. "Your mother called yesterday to say your dad went in the hospital with a fever and chills. She called again today to say that his fever is up to a hundred and five degrees. The doctors have no idea what's causing his fever. He comes in and out of consciousness but he's delirious, and he's been asking for you. Your mother wants you to come home as soon as you can. So what you gonna do, man?"

Without hesitation, I fly my hand through the air as if it were a jetliner.

"Well, look, let's call your mother now and see how your dad is doing. You don't have to talk, you just listen," says Shep, dialing. "Hi, La Java, how is John?" He listens in silence. "Okay, Johnny is here, you tell him. Here he is." Shep gives me the phone and I put my ear to the receiver and listen.

"Johnny, are you there?" Her voice is tired. "Listen, your father is very sick and has been calling your name all night, saying that he has to see you. I promised myself long ago that I would never ask you this, because I know that you are doing something very special. But I'm asking for your father. Please come home and see him. You know that he would do it for you."

I have to exert myself strenuously to keep from talking and telling my mother that I'll be on the next plane. I only allow myself a little humming sound in the affirmative, and give the phone back to Shep.

"La Java, he's going to fly out of here tomorrow. We'll call you in the morning to let you know what flight he gets on. Let Big John know." They talk a few minutes more and hang up.

We spend the rest of the night in preparation. I insist on riding to the airport on my bike. My idea is just to use the plane to get to Philadelphia, but once there I will use the bike. My mother has sent Dad's credit card by overnight delivery for me to use to buy a ticket. Before I fall asleep I think of how different things will be when I awake, a new adventure.

I have a quick breakfast in the morning with Shep and Pearl; my bike is packed and I am walking out the door when the phone rings and Shep calls me back. It is my mother. I listen to the receiver.

"Last night your father's fever broke and it's back to normal. You don't have to come. I only told him that you were at Shep's and that you were worried about him, but here, he wants to talk to you." She puts him on the phone.

"Hi, son?" His voice sounds weak, and he does not wait for me to answer. "Mother tells me that you've been really worried about me, and I just wanted to let you know that I'm all right. So don't worry, hear?" He can barely talk, but I know that he will be okay.

The fishing fleet sits
Far below the Golden Gate
Seagulls dive screaming

January 7, 1982
San Francisco, California

As my apprenticeship at the Center for the Wood Arts progresses, I revisit my lifetime goals as articulated in my Prior Learning Experience portfolio, "To sail and walk around the planet as part of my education with the spirit of hope that in some way I might help others and benefit the world." As I read the words, I realize that I have no idea of their true significance, only that I look forward to learning what they mean in the walking. When my apprenticeship ends, along with a group of friends in Point Reyes I found and incorporate Planetwalk, a nonprofit educational organization dedicated to raising environmental consciousness and to promoting earth stewardship and world peace through pilgrimage. My friends Cindy Ohama, a small-business consultant; Tegen Greene, a clothing designer; and Sim Van der Ryn, an architect and professor at the University of California's School for Environmental Design in Berkeley are Planetwalk's founding members and attend the first meeting.

Through my charades and the group's chatter, we come up with articles of incorporation and explore our visions of what "planetwalking" can be. In the end, we decide that the initial goals of Planetwalk will serve only as a framework. At its core, Planetwalk is a journey of discovery. We are filled with excitement and hope.

I set a date to begin my journey, and continue to prepare myself and gather resources to leave home. To create community on the road we begin to publish *Planetwalker*, a newsletter that will accompany me as I walk. I plan to travel on highways, roads, and trails across the country, through cities, small towns, and villages, forests and deserts. I will seek wilderness. Stopping, I will learn to listen. I will carry small slips of paper with a printed introduction:

Through my charades and the group's chatter, we come up with articles of incorporation and explore our visions of what "planetwalking" can be.

"This is to introduce John Francis, who left his home in Inverness, California, on January 1, 1983, on an 18-year pilgrimage around the world to raise environmental consciousness, and promote earth stewardship and world peace.

"John gave up the use of motorized vehicles not long after an oil spill in San Francisco Bay in 1971. Since 1973, he has maintained a vow of silence.

"For more information and a complimentary newsletter write: Planetwalk, P.O. Box 701, Inverness, CA 94937."

I begin my journey east by walking north.

CHAPTER 8

Walking Words:
The Road North

Outside the rain falls
Trying to find the right words
The morning I leave

April 27, 1983
Inverness, California

I leave Inverness walking slowly with a dozen friends. A warm rain falls from gray clouds tinted blue with morning sky. We hug the shoulder of the road, facing the oncoming traffic. Cars pass and the people inside wave, shout farewells and encouragement. I shift my pack to find the most comfortable position. It weighs no more than 50 pounds yet I am already thinking of things I can leave behind. This, I am sure, will be an ongoing process.

I know it is possible to get by with a lot less. Still, I am grateful for the Gore-Tex suit I wear. The rain gear has been donated by Sierra West, a small backpacking equipment manufacturer in Santa Barbara, California, in exchange for the use of some of my drawings and watercolors in their new catalog.

When we reach Point Reyes Station the rain stops. A rainbow bends down from the blue sky and touches the soft green hills. The cows, black and white, caked with mud, nod and swish their tails as we pass. Only Tegen Greene, Planetwalk's project coordinator, accompanies me the few miles down Highway 1 through the hamlet of Olema and over Tocaloma Hill, leaving the Point Reyes

Peninsula behind. We say goodbye, knowing we will see one another again soon. But with the hill between me and the other side of my life, I feel the weight of a thousand goodbyes. I turn onto the new bicycle path, a narrow band of asphalt that snakes its way along Lagunitas Creek and through the redwoods of Samuel P. Taylor State Park.

It takes five days to cover the 45 miles to San Francisco. Once there I stay a week, visiting with family and friends before tearing myself away. I hear the sound of tender roots snapping as they are pulled from moist earth.

> *Walking on the Bridge*
> *Caught in sunset's golden light*
> *We watched the tide run*

May 8, 1983
Sausalito, California

For the last time
I walk across the
Golden Gate Bridge.
Tegen, who met me
in the city, makes
the crossing
with me.

For the last time I walk across the Golden Gate Bridge. Tegen, who met me in the city, makes the crossing with me. Alone again I follow the back roads and railroad tracks that continue north through Marin and into Sonoma County.

In Petaluma, I meet Alan Scott, a friend and neighbor from Point Reyes. Not satisfied with merely saying goodbye, Alan suggested we get together at the Blue Mountain Center for Meditation and sit with his teacher, Eknath Eswaran. Alan has walked 25 miles to get there.

After meditation, Easwaran speaks to me about my journey and invites me to his home in India. He tells me that Gandhi, whom he knew, was a great walker. He remarks that my practice of yoga silence is unusual in Western culture. With only a few words and the touching of our hands I am drawn into his family. I am reminded that I am on a pilgrimage, a sacred journey, that we all have our own journeys and we are all part of each other's.

Afterward Alan walks me to the home of his friends, where I am welcomed to spend the evening. In the night sky the diffused white light of the comet Kohoutek, a little larger than the moon, captures our attention on its way around the sun. It has been in the night sky for several days. Alan thinks it is a sign, a propitious beginning to my pilgrimage.

I stay in Petaluma several days and oversee the printing of the spring issue of *Planetwalker*. A few days later I reach the Farallones Institute (now the Occidental Arts and Ecology Center) Rural Center in Occidental. Located on 80 acres of rolling meadows and forestland 10 miles from the Pacific Coast and 70 miles north of San Francisco, the institute was founded in 1974 for participatory education and appropriate technology—technology that is efficient, low-cost, locally controlled, and adapted to local needs. I had visited and worked as a volunteer at the center before and it seemed to be an ideal place to meet the film crew from the Brazilian television network El Globo, who want to interview me. The interview is conducted in sign, English, and Portuguese, and aired to 25 million people in Brazil. I am struck by the reality of the "global village."

Before I leave, Tegen arrives with a letter out of the weekly newspaper, the *Point Reyes Light*. Someone back in town feels I am moving a little too slowly to make it around the world in the 18 years I have given myself—or in this lifetime. Weeks have passed and I have only reached Petaluma, which is barely 25 miles from Point Reyes Station.

After reading the letter, I feel as if I should strike out immediately and knock off a quick 25 miles, but my three-miles-per-hour sense prevails. While the destination is desirable, the journey and being in the present each moment is the meditation my walking has become. If my goal is to return to the place I have begun, I surmise, I have already left where I want to be and I am already here where I am going. In walking there is a constant sense of place.

I make my goodbyes and after pinning a thank-you note to the kitchen bulletin board, head down the road into town. I send a few unnecessary garments back to Point Reyes and add a few others, convincing myself that the pack is indeed lighter. I take the Occidental Road, climbing steeply past the old Druid Cemetery and into the hills. The road winds its way through orchards, vineyards, and green fields of grass brushed with splashes of yellow wildflowers, all behind rusty barbed-wire fences. By the roadside golden poppies grow. The fragrance of mock orange blossoms makes my body tingle with spring memories.

I make the decision to bypass Sacramento and head straight into the valley. I travel east. In the morning the temperature rises with the sun and drips salty sweat into my eyes; my feet ache. Big trucks pass, oversized, with flashing lights. Lizards and ground squirrels scurry as I approach, making their own dust devils and rattling noises. It is refreshing to walk in the cool of the evening, caught between sunset and moonrise. I spend the next week sleeping outside, something I have become used to during my years of travel. Toward the end of each day I begin looking for an out-of-the-way spot to set up my small tent. Sometimes I can only find a place close beside the road.

When I reach Chico, the thunderclouds that have been gathering the last few days above the mountains finally burst and roll into the valley with high winds, lightning, and heavy rains. I stay at the house of an old friend, Tom Peterson, who is attending the state university. Waiting for me amid a joyful reunion is a letter from Brother John Paul, the guestmaster at the New Clairvaux Abbey, a Trappist monastery in Vina. I have been writing him since last August in an attempt to schedule a retreat. Up to now my indefinite travel plans have made that difficult, but this most recent letter explains that due to a cancellation a room will be available for a two-day retreat beginning June first.

In Chico I meet with several people at the university active in peace work, and the local newspaper interviews me. I leave two days later, the morning after a night storm passes.

The buildings gradually thin out until I leave Chico behind. In front of me the road runs straight through fields of waving grass, golden brown and green with hints of mauve, on into the beautiful day. Clouds play in an azure sky fading into milky blue on the horizon. To the east the foothills rise gently, and hovering in the hazy distance I can see snow-covered Mount Lassen.

The monastery gate is open when I arrive. Brother John Paul, dressed in blue denim overalls beneath a brown-and-white habit, does not look like any monk I might have imagined. He greets me in a booming voice from a vintage Schwinn two-wheeler.

"Welcome to New Clairvaux, John Francis. I didn't know if you were coming since I just sent the letter last week and was not sure it would find you." He gets off his bike and we shake hands. His are enormous and I wonder if in another life he is a boxer.

I nod in answer to his question, reach into a cargo pocket, and take out the letter to show him as he walks his bike along beside me. A little in the distance I am surprised to see two monks working on a roof and hear strains of the Rolling Stones drifting in the air, Mick Jagger unable to get any satisfaction in the midst of the sound of banging nails. I give a sideways look at Brother John Paul.

"Oh, they haven't taken their final vows. You know, over the years the strict code of silence here has been somewhat relaxed, and the monks are permitted to speak to one another during the course of the day, but long conversations are still frowned upon. I'm very curious about your silence, though. Have you ever thought of becoming a monk?"

I make a silent laugh and nod my head. I hold my hand at about the level of my shoulder.

"Oh, when you were younger. I must say, your letter was very interesting. It was hard to believe you were going to be walking here from where you live. We wanted very much to accommodate you if at all possible. How long have you been silent?"

I show him all of my fingers and smile.

"Oh my, ten years. I didn't realize that it had been so long."

I hardly believe it myself as we walk along the shaded path and through the quiet shadows of the monastery.

I think back to my thirty-seventh birthday five months earlier. It was ten years to the day since I had stopped talking. Every year on my birthday, I asked myself if it was right for me to continue or end the silence. It was no different this year when I walked into George Ludy's new Driftwood real estate office, smiled hello, and shook his hand.

"Did you bring this rain with you? And when are you going to start talking, you good-for-nothing son of a bitch?" George always teased me that way, so when I indicated that I wanted to use the phone he gladly gave it to me, knowing this was all part of the gag. I would pretend to call someone and then he would laugh and take the phone back and we would continue our visit.

This time I actually dialed the phone, and while it rang I watched the grin disappear from George's face.

"Hello, Mother?" My voice came from ten years of silence, rushing from me like the south wind on Tomales Bay, and a big tear welled up in each of George's eyes and he began to cry.

"Yes, Dwayne, what do you want?"

"No, this isn't Dwayne, it's me, Johnny."

"Okay, Dwayne, stop playing and tell me what you want."

"No, Mother, this really *is* me." I guessed that my brother had played this joke before. "Ask me something only I would know."

"Well, if this is Johnny . . . " She thought for a moment and then continued, "Tell me what I told you in the elevator in San Francisco."

I was silent for a moment. At his desk, George wiped away his tears and was now intently listening to one side of an unfolding drama being played out in his office and over his phone.

"You told me that if I was serious about what I was doing I would not ride in elevators."

"Oh Lord, Johnny, it is you! Let me get your daddy." Suddenly her voice was filled with excitement. "John, John, pick up the phone, Johnny is talking!" In an instant my father was on the other phone and we exchanged our first words in ten years.

"I wanted to talk to you," I said, "to let you know that you will be hearing some things about me soon. I am going to begin a walk around the world. I just want you to know that I am all right and that I love you."

"We love you, too," they answered in unison. In my family, to give voice to expressions of love was, at best, unusual. That I could say the words and they could acknowledge them and answer in kind together was this side of a miracle. We talked a bit more about when I would start walking, and if I would continue talking. I told them I already had started walking and that they should not expect me to continue speaking.

In part, breaking my silence after ten years was my attempt to keep the decision a living one, and to avoid talking not out of habit and instead out of choice. After hanging up I spoke with George, who was starting to cry again.

"I am so glad you talked to your folks, and that you did it while I was here. I won't tell anyone you spoke if you don't want," he said sniffling.

"George, you can tell anyone anything you want," I said to him. Often people asked me if I talked when I was alone, as if my silence were something directed at them, or only done when they were around.

"Well, I hope you'll be okay," said George. We talked a few minutes more. He thanked me for speaking to him now, as he did not believe he would be alive when I finished my journey. He took my hand in his and we said goodbye. By the time I reached Point Reyes Station I was again deep in silence, as if I had never left.

What had started as a way to escape arguing, and continued perhaps as an experiment in communication, has grown into something deeper. It has brought me to the edge of silence, and through its practice into a landscape of spirituality, communion, and contemplation.

Sitting in the guesthouse, Brother John Paul is speaking in a whisper: "When you're finished walking around the world, you should come back and join us here. You should become one of us. There is a lot a community like this can offer you."

Already I feel the great relief of being at home in the monastery, where silence is still a large part of the monastic life and is believed to be perhaps the greatest single contributor to spiritual growth. I feel my experience of silence deepen and the choices I have made are accepted without question.

I feel my experience of silence deepen and the choices I have made are accepted without question.

Meanwhile, traditions endure—rising for vigils in the quiet before dawn; morning, afternoon, and evening prayers interspersed with the labors of the day. In my brief stay I find new meaning in the words "silent contemplation." Then one morning I shoulder my pack and find the road, continuing through the valley.

Just past Red Bluff the secondary roads I follow abruptly end and Interstate 5 is all that is left. It stretches out before me, rising and falling gently on its way north. The highway patrolman who stops to inform me that pedestrians are prohibited on the freeway is courteous. After giving me a citation he even shows me on my map an alternative route that adds only 12 miles to my walk.

A 12-mile detour seems quite unreasonable to me, especially since the same restriction will exist farther on while the distances of the detours will increase to several hundred miles. In effect, enforcing this law closes the northern section of the Sacramento Corridor to foot traffic (bicycles are permitted). Threatened with arrest, I acquiesce and leave the freeway and follow a dry creekbed. Climbing barbed-wire fences and scrambling cross-country I reach a small road that leads to the railroad. I follow the tracks to the next town.

Not long after embarking on my journey I begin hearing about others. The Bethlehem Peace Pilgrimage, a group of 18 pilgrims led by Father Jack Morris, is on its way across the United

States to the Holy Land. C. B. Hall, with several pilgrims on the World Peace Walk, is in Europe and on the way to Moscow. And a group led by Columbia University students comprising the Ploughshares Pilgrimage is nearing the Pantex plant in Amarillo, Texas, where the nation's nuclear warheads are assembled. The promotion of world peace and related ideals such as human rights, environmental sanity, and social justice are the unifying themes connecting these modern-day pilgrims. Their hope is to create social dialogue and effect social change. They all capture my imagination and inspire me.

But as I tour the New Morning Peace Center in Anderson, California, a photograph of a silver-haired woman with a determined look, striding down a country road, catches my attention. Across the dark tunic she wears are two words, "Peace Pilgrim." My host, Robert Traush, is talking about the center's vegetable garden project when he notices me stopped in front of the picture.

"You know about her, don't you?" he asks.

I shake my head as I try to take in more details of the woman's image.

"That's Peace Pilgrim. I'm surprised you haven't heard of her," he says. "She's walked across the country about half a dozen times."

He carefully removes the picture from the wall and hands it to me. It is actually the folded cover of a book, *Peace Pilgrim: Her Life Works in Her Own Words*. On the back cover is a smaller photograph and a few paragraphs explaining that she walked more than 25,000 miles, penniless, carrying a simple message of peace, and that people were inspired by her lifestyle because she lived what she believed.

I immediately feel kinship, and at the same time humble. It is the first time I have heard of anyone who has given up the use of automobiles not just for a few months of walking, but also for a lifetime. In Peace Pilgrim I think I will be able to see a clearer reflection of myself. That she has walked nearly three decades with only the clothes on her back makes me question more the contents of my pack.

"She has passed through Anderson several times," explains Robert, "and it just so happens that one of the people she stayed with is here at the center." He introduces me to this woman.

"Oh yes, Peace Pilgrim was a remarkable woman . . . a true saint."

I cringe at the word "saint." People have used that word on occasion to describe me, and I do not like it.

"It's too bad you won't get to meet her, though," she continues. "She was killed in an automobile accident a few years ago."

Shaking my head at the irony, I feel the loss and leave that afternoon, walking north, wondering who Peace Pilgrim was. What life experiences delivered her onto the path of a pilgrim? What message might her life hold for others and for me?

I leave Anderson, following the frontage road that becomes the Old Oregon Trail. Historians estimate that about half a million people headed west from the 1840s through the Civil War. They generally agree that Oregon was the destination for about a third of the emigrants, California for another third, with the remainder bound for Utah, Colorado, and Montana. This migration lasted until the coming of the railroads.

The trail is now blacktopped, with houses scattered here and there by its side. An elderly gentleman standing beneath the shade of a large tree in front of one of the more elaborate dwellings hands me a cold drink as I walk by.

"I know this is something you want." He smiles.

The asphalt trail gives way to more freeways and I am again forced to break the law. It has become an act of civil disobedience for me. I make up my mind that if need be I will go to jail.

A highway patrol officer's car comes to a stop in front of me. The red lights begin to flash. He approaches with his citation book in one hand and his hat in the other. I am sure he is not interested in hearing me play the banjo but I have it ready just in case. He says that he heard about me walking on the freeway a few days earlier, and yes, it is illegal for me to walk on this section of the freeway. I show him the map and he understands my situation. He declines to arrest me, saying that he can't speak for the officers I might run into up ahead. I leave feeling a little relieved. When I can I climb down to the tracks. They snake through the valley, cross the Sacramento River on steel bridges, then climb gentle hills and tunnel under heavy stone mountains. That night I sleep by Lake Shasta. Mount Shasta lies ahead.

In the morning I walk to the Old Stage Coach Road, a gravel affair that makes its way into Mount Shasta City near the base of the mountain's western slope. Margy and Harry Ling, two friends who have invited me to stay in their home, come out on their bicycles to meet me. I met Margy several years earlier while preparing to make my first climb of Mount Shasta. Her husband, Harry, is now in the process of developing a small ski area on the mountain. The old one was destroyed by an avalanche, and with it much of the area's economy. It is a complex situation: multiple land use mixed in with economic and environmental considerations. Harry's group seems to be doing a good job and I am interested in seeing the results of their labor.

More mail catches up with me when Tegen and her traveling companion, Don, pass through on their way to the Planetary Congress in Toronto, Canada. Along with personal correspondence from other walkers, C. B. Hall and the Ploughshares Pilgrimage, there is a notice for me to appear at a justice court in Red Bluff. The charge is being an illegal pedestrian on the freeway. Ten dollars would satisfy the court but instead I write a letter to the clerk. I explain that there is no reasonable alternative for walking north up the section of the Sacramento Corridor in question. I further explain that California transportation officials in the state capital assured me that when such cases occur it is permitted to enter the freeway. In any case, because I do not ride in cars I consider it a hardship to return to Red Bluff, nearly 100 miles in the opposite direction.

At the last California rest area, 16 miles before Interstate 5 crosses into Oregon, I stop and "speak" with a highway patrol officer about walking on the shoulder of the freeway.

"Hmmm. Yep, that's the only way." He scratches his head. When I refer to the sign prohibiting pedestrians, he simply dismisses it by pointing to the sergeant's stripes on his uniform. "I'm in charge of this district and you can be sure no one is going to stop you." I thank him and continue on.

The highway rises slowly and for a short while follows the Klamath River, which eventually swings to the east and runs through a summer-green valley.

It is near sunset when I cross the Oregon border. Here pedestrians are permitted on all roads and bridges. I walk more at ease because of this attitude. I fall asleep on a grassy knoll away from the noise of the traffic. In the morning I climb to the summit of Siskiyou Pass and make my way down into Ashland.

Having lived in Ashland for two years while attending Southern Oregon State College, I find myself returning home. I arrive at the beginning of the summer term. It is enjoyable and most rewarding to sit in on Professor Frank Lang's class, Conservation of Natural Resources. The course covers the history, biological principles, and practices relating to the use and abuse of our natural resources, with emphasis on the interdependency of these resources and the impact of humanity on them, analyzed from an ecosystem viewpoint. Even though I had taken the class during my senior year at the college, I still have much to gain from review and exposure to new information.

A high point of the class is a viewing of the Canadian Film Board's documentary *If You Love This Planet* with Dr. Helen Caldicott, the national president of the group Physicians for Social Responsibility, speaking on nuclear war. It leaves us all speechless.

While the film has been awarded the Academy of Motion Pictures Arts and Sciences Oscar for the best short documentary, the United States Justice Department designates the film "political propaganda," which subjects it to a number of regulations and sanctions that Edwin A. Rothschild, the current general counsel of the Illinois American Civil Liberties Union, says fall just short of censorship.

In my mail, mixed in with new subscriptions and *Planetwalk* letters, is an answer from the Red Bluff court clerk. The judge has turned down my request and ordered me to post bail or appear in court. If I fail to comply, a warrant will be issued for my arrest.

CHAPTER 9

The Road North: Along the Coast

In a summer sky
Amid stars' diamond sparkle
A silver moon smiles

August 12, 1983
Ashland, Oregon

I leave Ashland. The morning blue sky turns cloudy gray. My pack feels heavier, though I am sure it is several pounds lighter. The few months spent without it on my back have taken their toll. Once again, I find myself thinking of other necessities I can leave behind. A vision of Peace Pilgrim rises in my mind, that gray-haired lady who crossed the continent on foot several times in the name of peace with little more than the clothes on her back. Tightened muscles relax and my body warms with the motion of walking.

I plan to spend the evening at a friend's home in Jacksonville, which is 20 miles away, so I walk at a brisk pace, paying little attention to my throbbing feet squeezed inside a pair of new wool socks. The road passes into valleys, over rolling green hills and through miles of pear orchards nearing harvest, before I realize my feet are in trouble.

The family whose door I knock on seem only a little puzzled at me standing there, weighted down in their front yard. The daughter, a high school student, fills my empty water bottle while her parents ponder the address and directions I have scrawled on a

piece of crumpled paper. They finally figure out what I already know: I am lost!

"Oh, you've gone about six miles out of your way," says the girl's father, brushing some hair from his shoulder onto the ground. I have interrupted his monthly trimming. "Well, I'll just drive you over there and we'll find it." He goes inside to get his shirt and I go into a pantomime about not riding in cars.

I explain about Planetwalk, and they telephone my friend David, who gives them a new set of directions for me. The man hangs up and starts to say something about sewers and how the county is making him hook into them, and how that makes him want to walk with me. In the end, we all shake hands and I continue on my way.

The gray sky shudders with thunder and drops cold rain, while lightning dances on the mountaintops, occasionally reaching the power lines that run beside the road. The sun is setting and my progress has diminished to a slow limp when David and Merike, his other dinner guest, pull up onto the road's shoulder in front of me. They are able to convince me that it is quite all right in the scheme of things if they ferry my pack the last six miles up to the house.

With only a small daypack to carry, my feet feel much better and I make good time. When I reach town the streetlights are off. The last great bolt of lightning has taken out the power. The house is still several miles away. I am more than tired and want to get out of the storm. I fumble for the flashlight in my pocket. When I find it, I enter a local restaurant and make my way in the darkness through a shadowy maze of patrons, into the lounge for a cold soft drink.

I find an empty seat at the bar. A face appears, illuminated by candlelight.

"Hey, aren't you the guy my friend saw walking in all that rain a few miles down the road?"

I nod in mute agreement. They had even stopped and offered me a ride, which I declined, right at the height of the storm. His friend comes over to where we are sitting. They are visiting from out of town.

"So how come?" He asks as if nothing I can say would make it all right. He leans a little closer. I can feel the moisture of his breath. "So how come you're out there walkin' in the rain?"

I laugh, almost aloud, realizing that I asked myself that question earlier. I reach inside my daypack, retrieve a damp copy of

a San Francisco newspaper clipping, and hand it to them with the flashlight. They both read it slowly and when they finish, they thank me as if they understand. But I can see in the candlelight that questions remain.

Jacksonville is still in darkness as I climb the hill to Dave's house. No cars are on the road and the rain has finally stopped. Stars peek brightly through spaces between the clouds, and in the quiet of the evening, walking the last few weary miles, there are no questions.

I arrive in Applegate two days later and stop at the wayside park to sit in the shade. People of all ages are cooling themselves in the Applegate River, some wading knee-deep near the sand beach while others float in big balloon inner tubes. The more daring jump from high rocks on the far shore into a deep green pool. The water explodes with laughter. Crossing the steel bridge, I turn off the main road and head up Thompson Creek.

The house is empty when I reach the farm of my friends Chris Bratt and Joan Peterson—one of my usual stops. I make myself at home. I find out later that everyone has been working up at a new pond site. I learn that the pond will eventually furnish irrigation, food, and energy for the 160-acre property, as well as fire protection for the surrounding countryside.

Joan, a responsible environmentalist, along with her husband, Chris, and a group of local residents, has successfully challenged some of the questionable forestry practices of the Bureau of Land Management (BLM) and the U.S. Forest Service in their area.

Joan, a responsible environmentalist, along with her husband, Chris, and a group of local residents, has successfully challenged some of the questionable forestry practices of the Bureau of Land Management (BLM) and the U.S. Forest Service in their area. The pond site needs minimal excavation, yet they do it with thoughtful and careful planning.

Here I meet Orville Camp, a backhoe and tractor operator who is helping Chris and Joan with their water project. In addition to being an artist in his use of heavy equipment, Orville has developed a natural selection forest management system. It evolved, he tells me, through his many experiences and dissatisfactions with traditional forest management practices starting in 1950. About 20 years later, he began to effectively address some of his many concerns about forest management.

Today Orville's management goals are intended to meet the needs of forest and people, a philosophy that I can remember hearing in Dr. Lang's Conservation of Natural Resources class back in Ashland. After receiving a number of county awards for small woodland management, Mr. Camp is writing a book to share his ideas with others. During my stay, I have time enough to listen to his words and walk with him through the trees on the farm. He speaks of the forest as a friend.

I leave one evening, catching the moonrise in the darkness. Music greets me up the road around a crackling fire with the neighbors. I play awhile, and then fall asleep as voices sing familiar folk songs and the yellow-orange flames dance in the night.

It is a four-hour walk up to Krause's Cabin, seven miles to where the all-weather road gives way to a scramble of earth and rock where the trail begins. Located in the Rogue River National Forest, the log cabin was used by cattlemen for nearly a century. Built at the edge of a verdant alpine meadow, it is an especially beautiful place to stop for the day.

In the evening the sun sets suddenly behind a distant peak and gray clouds press onto a line of red sky. After my meal I sit by the fire and let my fingers touch the banjo's steel strings, then listen to the thunder roll across the heavens as I fall asleep.

It starts raining about four in the morning. I am sleeping on a picnic table, using an old canvas mattress that I found in the cabin. Behind the clouds the moon is a pale pearl set above the mountains. The fire is dead, the coals cold. I haul my pack into the shelter and try unsuccessfully to return to my dreams. They come at sunrise.

I take my time leaving. At first the rain falls hard, then tapers off into showers. The sky turns pale blue and then gray. I start slowly through the meadow. Sometimes my spirit soars as I climb the several thousand feet over the mountain, simply following the path before me. Other times, it slogs along with me through the mud, brushing against the wet grass and the purple and gold wildflowers.

On the road, over time, the natural world will reveal itself to you. Observe the moonrise and the sunset long enough and you will be able to predict a lunar eclipse. Watch the clouds gather and listen to the songs of birds and you will be able to foretell the weather.

When I leave the trail and follow the creek down the side of the mountain I remember that Joan said that Oregon Caves National Monument is just a half day's walk from the cabin. Only 480 acres, the monument is rich in bio-diversity. Above ground, the monument encompasses a remnant old-growth coniferous forest, and below ground is an active marble cave created by natural forces over hundreds of thousands of years in one of the world's most diverse geologic realms.

The sun is setting when I finally stumble out of the brush and onto the Monument Road. Camping is not permitted within the monument, so I set up my tent just outside the boundaries and visit a ranger friend before returning to my tent for the night. I fall asleep listening to the patter of the rain.

I walk the 15 miles into Kerby the next day, on the eastern edge of the Kalmiopsis Wilderness. I spend the night at Dorothy Moore's home. Perennially in the midst of cleaning and other household projects, she clears a space for me among the clutter of her current endeavors. It is good to see her. She fills me in on all the happenings—births, marriages, and deaths, when the mill shut down, and about the people who want to mine nickel from Eight Dollar Mountain. Many of the residents in the valley oppose it, but because of the community's poor economy, some believe it to be a godsend.

I leave in the morning, taking a most familiar walk up the rutted road of red earth, serpentine, and clay. I climb over the pass and drop down to cross the first creek, using the stones to get across. In the winter it is a torrent and anyone wishing to get to the other side has to use the hand trolley strung overhead.

Inside the cabin
Filled with musty memories
A small candle burns

August 25, 1983
Peterson Claim
Kalmiopsis Wilderness, Oregon

No one is at the Peterson cabin. The mice run free, eating the old mattress cover, piling nibblings away for a nest. I sweep away the droppings, split some wood, and bring in water from the spring.

While dinner cooks on top of the woodstove I bake unleavened bread in the oven. The fire takes away the chill of the evening, and in the warmth of the oil lamp's glow, I listen to the silence.

In the morning the blue jays come and squawk. I leave through the Darlingtonia bog beside the river and pass Copper Creek cabin, where Cherry and I once spent a winter. Ruth and Perry are gone now. Ruth died in the spring, as I was preparing to leave Point Reyes. I remember our first meeting years before when she pointed out the rare plant for which the wilderness was named, *Kalmiopsis*. "You see these gold specks on the underside of each leaf?" I can almost hear her voice.

It takes me only three days to cross the Kalmiopsis—following the trail seems so natural, and I have taken the cross-country route up to Vulcan Peak several times before. I know it by heart.

Clouds are gathering when I come down the mountain road. It is the weekend and deer hunters are about. They wave as they drive past in their Jeeps and pickups. I wave back, happy to see some people again.

Twenty-five miles down from the mountain I stop to camp at Musser's Bar. Here the Chetco River spreads thin over the sand and vehicles are able to make the ford. As I approach the camp I hear the buzz of chain saws. Leaning over a wind-fallen oak is Cal Musser. He is just about as surprised to see me as I am to see him. We both try to count how long it's been while we sit on the tailgate of his truck and share a lunch.

Cal worked at the mill in Brookings. It was a cooperative where the employees owned shares. The arrangement was good for him, and with all his children grown and on their own he considered himself and his wife fortunate people.

There isn't much left for us to do after lunch. We finish cutting the firewood. He leaves with his truck full and my promise that I will come by for dinner when I get to town.

The clouds that came and went during the day come and stay at dusk. The rain follows. I scramble beneath an abandoned tarp and spend the night. In the morning, while the rain still falls, I walk the last 20 miles downhill to Brookings on the Oregon coast. The muted sun is setting in a slate-colored sea.

I stay in town with some friends, waiting for a break in the storm. It seems that Brookings has grown in my absence and its

economy is doing well, quite different from the other side of the mountains in Kerby and Cave Junction.

Having worked for the Forest Service as a summer employee in the Kalmiopsis, I take time to stop in at the district office. I ask about the Bald Mountain logging road, which many people oppose. I find out that a federal court has ruled against the Forest Service and temporarily halted construction. Opponents claim the road is being built illegally; even some forest rangers voice this opinion. The legalities, economics, and politics became ironic when the construction company filed suit against the Forest Service. The company contended the USFS was to blame for the halt in construction, leaving the company without work or compensation. In any case, lives have been changed, and protesters have been arrested over a road going nowhere. The conflict seems far from over.

Meanwhile, I am invited to attend a meeting of a local chapter of the Citizens Action for Lasting Security (CALS). It is a statewide organization working to promote public awareness of world peace and security issues. The group's newsletter says they believe that nuclear war is not inevitable—that people working together can prevent it.

At this meeting, the group of mostly older adults discusses plans to hand out thought-provoking leaflets at the end of the film *War Games*, due to open at the local movie house in a few days. The message of the film is that "no one wins a nuclear war." Still, when the topic is raised of building trust between the people of the world, no one has ready answers. Dick Draper, a sociologist and retired research administrator from Eugene, says that he has thought about writing letters to individual citizens of the Soviet Union, but they are still trying to figure out just how to do that.

Prior to the 1980s, the concept of "mutual assured destruction" (MAD) kept the threat of nuclear war remote and created a stalemate between the United States and Soviet Union, because MAD would mean the destruction of all the participants in an all-out nuclear exchange. But, increasingly, statements about "limited nuclear exchanges" sent tremors of foreboding throughout the world. In 1983, President Ronald Reagan announced the Strategic Defense Initiative (SDI), known to critics as Star Wars—a plan to build a shield against a nuclear attack on the United States. Most people understand that SDI would destabilize the MAD policy, and fear of nuclear war in many communities has become palpable.

I leave in the morning after breakfast—just a few goodbyes, and then out into the wind rushing from the sea. I walk north along the coast.

> *Standing on one leg*
> *Feathers ruffled in the wind*
> *A gray seagull waits*
> *For me to throw a scrap of food*
> *Or for a chance, I think*
> *To dive into my pack*
> *But when I walk*
> *He follows me around the beach*
> *A small gray cloud*
> *His shadow in the sand*

September 4, 1983
Nesika Beach, Oregon Dunes

I find a place out of the wind behind a barricade of shrubs and driftwood shoved against a sandy cliff. I fall asleep by the fire, listening to the waves and watching the heavens turn and fade.

It is difficult to walk in the sand and I think I have made a mistake in coming this way because I get tired quickly walking against the wind.

At dawn the seagull flies away the moment I awake, as if a dream escaping memory. I wish we had been closer friends so he would have followed me. I laugh at myself and continue down the old beach road.

The Labor Day weekend ends and schools are open again. In the morning and afternoon the roads are filled with yellow-orange buses with flashing red lights and animated faces pressed against their windows; sometimes the children wave as they pass.

A few mornings later, just south of Bandon, I stop in the Two Mile Café for breakfast. I enjoy listening to the men talk about the arrival of cranberry season. Nearly everyone is preparing for the harvest. There is a definite feeling of excitement in the air.

I stay in Bandon for the day, exploring the Old Town section next to the docks, playing music in the streets and at Andrea's Restaurant for tips and something to eat. I make some new friends and run into a few old ones.

In the evening at the city hall I go to a public meeting attended by about 40 people concerned about nuclear war. It is a cross-section of the community, a group without a name. I imagine groups like this meeting in small towns and cities throughout the country—perhaps even around the world.

Afterward I make my way to the Sea Star Hostel to spend the night. The national office of American Youth Hostels has donated a three-year pass to me in support of the ideals of Planetwalk.

Downstairs in the men's section I have a hot shower and visit with several fellow travelers, sharing experiences, thoughts, and ideas on a variety of subjects. When it is time for sleep I opt for the floor. The bed, I think, is too soft. I sleep soundly and rise as morning spills through a large picture window. In the bunks next to me are the sounds of a few weary souls snoring softly.

The walk to Coos Bay takes me two days. The wind has been blowing from the south, turning the undersides of the blackberry leaves so they show silver-green. I play music at the Knave of Cups, a coffeehouse near the community college, and am offered a place to spend the night. In the morning I visit the Ken Keyes Jr. Center, which offers a supportive environment and consciousness-raising programs that are intended in their own way to bring about a world capable of loving itself and living in peace. Ken wrote the little classic *The Hundredth Monkey*, which deals with the theory of formative causation, a possible mechanism in the process and dynamics of social change. I am delighted when the center offers to supply Planetwalk with complimentary copies of the book for friends and subscribers.

The next 40 miles take me through the sometimes desolate and cinematic beauty of the Oregon Dunes, a national recreation area with large freshwater lakes that practically touch the sea. The geology of the area is not yet understood, but some geologists believe it is the most stable part of the coast. I linger in its solitude, conscious of the changing weather.

I continue north, stopping in the small towns to play music, to meet and be with people. Rain starts falling as I turn in from the sea. I feel the season changing when I reach the monastery in Lafayette. The monks welcome me, as do the people of Portland two days later along the same road.

Letting go the trees
Golden leaves fall autumn rain
Softly to the ground

October 10, 1983
Portland, Oregon

When I arrive in Portland, I stay at the home of Planetwalk supporters Devon and Larry Holmes. Larry works as a surveyor for the Department of the Interior's Bureau of Land Management, under the directorship of James Watt.

Watt's policies are controversial, as they open protected federally owned lands to exploitation by large corporations. His guiding principles appeared to me to be based on a belief that there is no need for conservation because the end of the world is near. Whether we despoil the earth or not doesn't matter.

In the evenings, we talk a little about the department's policies and how they affect the BLM and the rest of us. We talk more about the forests, trees, mountains, and rivers we have met, while their new son, Lorin, cries, giggles, smiles, and frowns as he plays with the toys scattered on the living room floor. During the days I walk downtown to explore.

Watt's policies are controversial, as they open protected federally owned lands to exploitation by large corporations.

Situated at the confluence of the Columbia and Willamette rivers, Portland is Oregon's largest city, with a population close to half a million. The downtown business district, just west of the Willamette River, is connected by nine bridges to the part of the city where I am staying.

On my way into town, I often stop over the murky water of the river to watch the freighters being loaded with grain. Dreams of far-off places hide in their names and flags. Clouds of yellow dust drift up from their holds and settle on the ground. Sometimes it takes several days before they are full and heading back out to sea, sitting low in the water.

Across the bridge and a little farther on, morning meal lines form in front of the shelters and guesthouses and quickly stretch the length of a city block with hungry people waiting to be fed. In the evening, other lines form with homeless people looking for a bed. Some of those who aren't able to find their way into one of the free shelters find a covered space beneath a freeway bridge. By night, all the good spots are taken.

I carry my banjo with me, playing as I walk along the streets. At the Food Goddess, a small vegetarian restaurant in town, I am invited to play for food and tips. I am surprised when Nancy, the owner, tells me that when the restaurant started, once a month all the employees except one would keep silent for the day. The one who spoke would answer the phone. The Food Goddess reminds me of my friends at Mount Eddy Bakery and Café, back in Mount Shasta. Here, too, exists a local center for the exchange of ideas.

I spend several days visiting Portland State University. There I meet Stephen Kosokoff, a professor in the school's speech and communications department. He has just returned from the People's Republic of China, where he was teaching English, and I am very interested in hearing about his experience, since I hope to be there someday myself. He is just as interested in Planetwalk, and especially in my silence.

The year before, he was a member of the committee that received and approved "Perspective on Speechlessness: A Case Study." The paper addressed the "problem" of speech disruption when an individual abruptly and without explanation stopped speaking to those around her for a year. I meet with the chairperson of the department and later leave the university with a copy of the thesis tucked away in my daypack, convinced that it will make interesting reading during the winter.

I have been in Portland little more than a week when I meet Mary Jane Bagwell. She and her dog walked across the country a few years earlier with a group of Japanese Buddhist monks. Upon her return she organized another walk along the Columbia River as a protest, to inform people of the possible environmental hazards of the nuclear industry along the waterway. She speaks about the joys and hardships of long walks and the path.

When she invites me to visit the Pacific New School, where her niece attends, I readily accept. We walk the 40 blocks together.

The school occupies a corner of an old stone church in the middle of one of Portland's residential neighborhoods. We arrive just slightly out of breath and wait on a wooden pew in the hallway. Children scurry about at the prompting of a few teachers. It is near the end of their day and they are in the midst of the daily cleanup.

Inside the classroom, we sit on the floor together and Mary Jane tells the young people gathered around us about Planetwalk.

There are a few gasps, and then I let the music and pantomime say the rest. The children love it. Applauding, they ask questions between each tune.

"Where do you sleep at night?"

"What do you eat and how do you earn money?"

To answer the last question, I ceremoniously pass my hat around to demonstrate that age-old custom. Children giggle as they add invisible coins.

"Gee, your hat must get overflowing." A little girl sighs. I smile and play another tune. After performing the last piece I pull a small globe from my pocket to trace my route around the planet. Children gather around closer to ask more questions.

"How will you cross the oceans?"

"Do you play any other instruments?"

"How old are you?"

When we are preparing to leave one little boy raises his hand to be heard. I nod toward him. He mumbles something that I cannot hear so he repeats it, taking care to form his words.

"Do you play the *thethesiser?*" he asks with a lisp, eyes cast down.

"He means the synthesizer," someone calls out. I shake my head no.

"I didn't think so," he mutters, just under his breath.

We all laugh and say goodbye. The room has quietly filled with parents and relatives who have come to take their children home. I stop to meet a few of them before stepping back out into the street with Mary Jane. We hardly "speak" at all on the way back into town. My hat is overflowing.

The weather is still mild. Some days it rains warm rain, which leaves the air fresh. Outside Devon and Larry's house, sidewalks are carpeted with brown and golden leaves. I think of writing the next newsletter but production of the summer issue has been delayed. I decide it would be best to wait.

When Tricia Vigilante, a friend from California on her way to Port Townsend, joins me for a few days, she brings some of my warmer clothes, mail, and the new Planetwalk cassette tapes. It is the first time I have seen the tapes and I am really pleased. With the support and cooperation of the good people at Windham Hill Productions, I recorded a collection of original banjo music at the

Inverness studio of my friend and neighbor Jesse Colin Young. Having just completed his own album *The Perfect Stranger*, Jesse is on tour and is due to give a concert in Portland before I plan to leave.

The music is still with me as I leave the city behind. It has started raining and my mind races ahead, wondering where I will spend the wet night. The miles pass slowly. I have made friends and touched hearts, and again leaving is not easy.

I awake in a bed of jimsonweed by a small stream beneath a concrete bridge. The rain has stopped and the morning traffic is buzzing overhead. I make my way up to the road. Trucks loaded with cabbages, soft lemon-lime green, rumble by in the early morning grayness.

I reach the town of Saint Helens, about 40 miles northeast of Portland, and find the home of Mark and Bonnie Hill. They had been hosts of Mary Jane's Columbia River walk and welcome me just as warmly into their home. In the evening I go with Mark to a meeting of a disarmament group in the basement of a local church. The group is trying to get the approval of the school board to present a program on world peace and nuclear disarmament. Initially they ran into some difficulty, but it appears to be working out. Some of the members are obviously frustrated by what seems to them to be stalling tactics by the board, and are themselves contemplating a more forceful approach. An older woman in the group reminds them, "We have to work for peace in our hearts, even when we are rebuffed."

The moon is full and the walk back is quiet and filled with the smell of wood fires. During the day the sweet fragrance of burning leaves reminds me of my childhood in Philadelphia and the smell of fall.

It is late when we get home but Bonnie and the kids are still up, waiting for the banjo concert I promised. The music is a good release.

In the morning I am the last to leave. Locking the front door behind me, I wander lost into a few dead-end streets before I find the road leading to the highway. I take the tracks instead and then a bike path, to be alone with my thoughts and not with traffic or the people inside the cars and trucks that scream by.

Gray clouds stack upon each other and threaten rain. A huge cooling tower of the Trojan nuclear plant sends a billowy gush of steam into the sullen sky as I walk by, following a path through the lush wet grass beside a still pond. Picnic tables beneath a grove of well-kept trees invite visitors on sunny days.

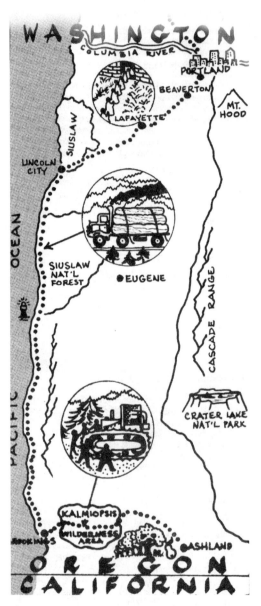

In the information center near the main gate elaborate displays and exhibits help the layperson understand the miracle of nuclear fission. But miracle or not, many in the energy field believe nuclear energy is a fading dream. While a number of economic obstacles hinder the development of nuclear power as a major energy source, safety is also an issue and public mistrust of the reassuring statements by proponents of nuclear power is growing, especially after the 1979 partial meltdown and radiation release from the Three Mile Island nuclear plant in Pennsylvania.

It is a slow 20-mile day and when I reach the small town of Rainier the sun is setting. I put up my tent in a sandy spot surrounded by tall weeds close to the tracks, still within the city limits, and then find a diner, where I have some tea and write. It starts raining and continues through the night.

CHAPTER 10

La Java: Tea Leaves and Sympathy

Beneath the steel bridge
Horns blow and boxcars rattle
A freight train passes

October 10, 1983
Portland, Oregon

Just north of town, the Lewis and Clark Bridge crosses the Columbia River into Longview, Washington. I wait until the rain stops before breaking camp and making my way up to the bridge. At midspan a sign hanging from the superstructure welcomes me to the Evergreen State, as a formation of migrating terns flies overhead. Industry stretches along both shores, smoking. Logs are stacked neatly in sprawling yards.

I find the post office and mail a few letters, then wander on through town. My pack feels easier to handle. I think it is because the sun is beginning to peek through the clouds, or maybe it is because I stopped and had a good breakfast. No matter, I do not question it very long. Feeling the bite of adventure, I turn off the main route north to the ferry road which I hope will follow the Cowlitz River. It does, but after a few miles the asphalt ends in a gravel road and signs that read not a county-maintained road and keep out in Day-Glo orange. My pack feels heavier again and I begin to wish I had kept on the main thoroughfare. Then there is no road at all, only a house at the end of a dirt drive.

I knock on the door and explain my plight to the lady who answers. She directs me to a path along the river. I follow it, passing through a grove of maples still dressed in fall colors, until I emerge once again on the main road. Before long I reach a bridge crossing a small creek that promises to provide shelter for the evening. I set up camp but the sight of cattle grazing nearby persuades me not to use the water from the stream. My canteen is empty, so I set off for the nearest farmhouse, a quarter of a mile away.

I knock on the door and an elderly lady answers with a warm grandmotherly smile. I make some silent gestures to tell her that I do not speak and hand her a tattered copy of a newspaper clipping as further explanation. The smile never leaves her face. When she finishes reading, I produce my empty water bottle and pantomime filling it from an invisible tap. She nods, takes the bottle, and disappears into the house. When she returns and hands the thing back to me I stand for a moment in disbelief that changes slowly to mild amusement. Inside the bottle is not water but a folded dollar bill. I try to explain but she is set on me having the money.

Inside the bottle is not water but a folded dollar bill. I try to explain but she is set on me having the money.

"No, no. That's for you," she says in the sweetest voice. What can I say? I thank her and walk back to the road, not sure of the emotions I feel. Still in need of water I write a note and present it to the people in the next house: "Could I have some water please?" They oblige.

Before dawn, a waning moon rises and disappears above the fog that seeps into the valley. In the distance, machines grumble and clank, pulling sand and gravel from the river. I restuff my pack, make my way up to the road, and head north.

The sun breaks through, and to the east, past fecund fields and fall-colored hills, Mount Saint Helens glistens. The memory of its eruption a few years back is still fresh in my mind.

It is nearly noon and I am just south of Vader when I hear a truck drive up and stop behind me. As I turn, the driver switches off the motor and the quiet of the country road returns.

"Do you have a radio?" calls the gray-haired man sitting behind the wheel.

I nod yes. I carry a small transistor radio affair, which I sometimes listen to in the evening or just before starting out in the morning.

"Have you heard the news today?" His voice is soft and on the edge of sadness.

I shake my head no.

"There was a bombing of the U.S. Marine post in Beirut. Over two hundred people were killed. I've seen you walking the last few days and I thought I might be able to talk about it with you."

That I don't talk back does not seem to matter. He needs someone to listen to his sadness. He invites me home for lunch. And I listen.

Afterward, I continue into town and stop to watch some men plow a small field with a team of mules. Just off the main street, farther on near the rail crossing, a helicopter lands and waits for another load of pesticide. Lights blink red and warning bells clang as a train passes—the Superliner—in a smoky silver flash. I follow the tracks until I find a place beside a fenced pasture to spend the night. A fire takes away the evening chill. The rancher who comes to check on the pasture gate leaves me with a few fence posts to burn and I thank him.

The temperature drops, the fire dies, and by morning, hoarfrost covers my sleeping bag and the grass around me. Truck lights appear at the top of the little dirt road that crosses the tracks. It is Frank Higueras, the rancher from the night before. He is coming to feed his cattle and has brought a thermos of hot coffee and some fruit Danishes. We shake off the cold and stand in the morning quiet together. A formation of geese flies overhead through the diaphanous clouds that streak the sky. They honk and Frank points. As a question, I aim an invisible gun into the air. He shakes his head no and casts an invisible line from an equally imaginary fishing rod and smiles yes. I nod and smile as well. When it is time to go he shakes my hand, gives me a few dollars for the journey, and says goodbye. His truck jumbles and bounces up the road and disappears in the misty distance.

Further on in the day I stop for lunch at a little café near Napavine. I overhear some of the customers talking about an $8 million monthly coal bill to fire the steam-generating plant in nearby Centralia. One of the employees is convinced that nuclear energy would be cheaper even though he personally does not like the idea of having it around. As I listen I try to remember all I have learned about the hidden or external costs of nuclear energy that are passed on to someone else. Many of the environmental problems we face today and will face tomorrow are due to external costs that degrade the environment, creating, for example, poorer health and the need for more expensive pollution cleanups and controls. It is a lot to think about, but more and more people seem to be doing just that.

That night I camp by the tracks again, not hurrying into the next town. I am up with the passing of a freight train, slow and lumbering. I wave at the engineer while I warm my hands over a rekindled fire and sip hot tea, enjoying the quiet of the morning.

Two days later I pass through Tumwater, the end of the Oregon Trail. Ahead is Olympia, the state capital. I visit the governor's office and leave some newsletters with his aide. A short time later, a man approaches me on the street and offers food and a place to stay. He takes me to the Applejam Folk Center, where I join the local talent for an open mike performance. It is near Halloween and many people are on the street.

I spend a week in Olympia, but all too soon I find myself on the road again as the first winter storm moves in from the sea. I make my way up the Olympic Peninsula, walking through the rain and 50 miles of cold night before I stop to find some sleep along the Hood Canal, a crooked finger of water joined at its north end to Puget Sound. It is more a fjord than a canal. In the time of the British explorer George Vancouver, the Hood Canal watershed was the domain of the aboriginal Twana tribe. These people maintained nine plank-house winter villages along the western shore and upper southern arm of the canal. They called it Twana's salt water.

Fishermen at dawn
Come silently to the shore
To set silver nets
Morning comes too soon
Stars fade quickly

November 5, 1983
Brinnon, Washington

My ankle aches—the recurrence of an old injury. The rain has started falling again. Port Townsend is only three days away. I move slowly now, perhaps because of my ankle, or perhaps because I anticipate the end of the summer's walk.

In Port Townsend I share a large, comfortable house with my friend Tricia, who arrived by car a few weeks before me. The house is just above Fort Worden State Park, overlooking Admiralty Inlet, the entrance to Puget Sound. North and beyond, a white apparition, Mount Baker, rises nearly 11,000 feet above its surroundings. In the yard there is a vegetable and flower garden as well as two redwood transplants that somehow have managed to grow in Washington soil and are now towering above the cedar shake roof.

All day freighters, tankers, and barges towed or pushed by powerful tugs pass in and out of the inlet on their way to nearby ports or back to sea. Sailboats, motor yachts, and fishing boats of all descriptions also ply these waters. Port Townsend is a center for commercial fishing and boatbuilding and the home of the Pacific Northwest School of Wooden Boatbuilding. My plan is to build a small rowboat in Port Townsend and row across the sound to continue the Planetwalk the following summer.

Occasionally a nuclear submarine slowly passes on its way to Bangor Naval Base on the Hood Canal, subtly reminding me of another reality. As remote as the Olympic Peninsula may seem, it is within the "ground zero" radius.

About 30 miles from Port Townsend, the Bangor Naval Base is the staging area for what has been reported to be one of the world's most lethal and accurate missile systems, the Trident submarine. It is also the final destination of the White Train, which carries nuclear warheads from the Pantex plant in Amarillo, Texas, where they are assembled. Next to the chain-link and barbed-wire fence that surrounds the base is the Ground Zero Center for Nonviolent Action, the starting point for many of the walks across the nation and around the world protesting war and the use of nuclear weapons. No one lives at the Ground Zero Center. Jim and Shelley Douglass have dedicated their land as a meeting place for people interested in nonviolent approaches to world peace.

A group of Buddhist monks from Japan have begun construction on a peace pagoda but they stopped work when county officials revoked the center's building permit. The decision to complete the project now rests in the hands of the courts. Each day the monks come to chant and pray around the skeleton of the unfinished pagoda.

In Port Townsend numerous people work toward peace in their own unique ways and the Port Townsend Peace Coalition attempts to foster that work and bring the different views and approaches together—not always an easy task. There are many meetings, gatherings, and vigils. A few residents have participated in a walk across the country or through Europe to the Soviet Union. Others have traveled to Central America, a region now in great turmoil as a result of popular revolutionary uprisings against repressive governments, to work and witness with people in the villages and on farms. (In El Salvador that year there is civil war. According to Amnesty International, people suspected of opposing the government become victims of human rights violations, including arbitrary torture, "disappearance," and execution.) They returned with a special understanding that they shared with the community. Some people have taken part in the protest and attempted blockade of the first commissioned Trident submarine on its way to Bangor, risking arrest and their lives. Not everyone agrees with each other's methods, but I am impressed with what seems to be a great level of tolerance—an important quality if we are to live in peace on the planet. Even more important is the quality of acceptance.

I am pleasantly surprised to find that a number of old friends from Point Reyes have moved to the Olympic Peninsula. Along with the openness of the community, this familiarity makes me feel at home. Though a thousand miles apart, the two places share many similarities: the water is one and the mild weather another. Port Townsend is located in the rain shadow of the Olympic Mountains and the weather is a bit drier than that of the Point Reyes Peninsula.

It has been windy, cold, and raining for weeks.

Though a thousand miles apart, the two places share many similarities: the water is one and the mild weather another.

"It's usually not like this," says Gabriel, looking into the gray cloud-torn sky. On a metal tower at the edge of the bluff overlooking downtown, two orange weather flags wildly flap a storm warning. The water in the sound seethes. Gabriel is a friend of nearly fifteen years who lived on Tomales Bay before moving north with his family to settle in Port Townsend. He had been a bank employee in San Francisco, commuting 50 miles to the city. Now he is one of the moving forces behind Bay Shore Enterprises, a community outreach program that trains and employs people who are physically and mentally impaired. The change seems to have done him wonders. He is the picture of health and happiness.

"Yoga," he answers matter-of-factly to my tacit inquiry. I listen as he recounts this recent transformation and how he has become a yoga instructor. My summer walk ended, I figure I can use the exercise.

I take the class he offers for the next month and a half, riding my bike through all the vagaries of weather on this peninsula. When the temperature drops and the lagoon freezes, a steady stream of latent and neophyte skaters tries out the ice. Someone brings a box of skates to fit all sizes. My ankle has not yet recovered completely from the long walk, so I decide that yoga is enough. Since walking is my primary way of getting around I must be very careful.

The kids dragging their sleds behind them through an inch-deep snowfall say it is a rare thing. They race down the hill behind the school, shouting and laughing in muffled voices. I laugh too and wonder if my old Flexible Flyer sled is still in the basement of my parents' house in Philadelphia. The air is cold and crisp. I stack some wood and walk to town, enjoying the unusual weather and the rare day, leaving large white footprints behind me.

> *Gray sky touched the sound*
> *Quietly the ferry crossed*
> *To the other side*

January 2, 1984
Port Townsend, Washington

It is a new year. A thousand miles away on a Point Reyes beach, friends are gathering to celebrate the planet's journey around the sun. A year ago I was with them, taking the first step of my own journey. Today I walk down to the water, to the yellow-and-brown building out on the pier. Inside are the tanks of the Marine Science Museum, filled with a variety of tidepool life.

Two local women who wanted to share their hobby started the museum. It developed into something much larger. Now it's in the high-use area of Fort Worden; people come in waves to point and stare and learn about the environment that is so close to them. I come to do the same, but the museum is closed. The water laps at the beach of the underwater park just offshore. No spear fishing is allowed. In the summer visitors can swim with masks, fins, and snorkels to see the hidden wonders.

I teeter on an old driftwood log and look into the shallow wilderness that drops off suddenly into a cold deep blue. A cormorant dives and then surfaces, its long slender neck glistening in the pale light of the day. Out on Puget Sound a ferry crosses, white against the blue-gray of distant land.

My boatbuilding tools arrive by UPS and I begin building a dory. Besides needing it to cross the sound, I am building the dory for my friend Ingrid, who commissioned it and has given me a down payment. During my apprenticeship I learned boatbuilding from the design phase through selecting, felling, and milling the timber. This 13-foot design is the first I am attempting to build on my own. I spend many hours in the company of more experienced builders, seeking help, advice, and information concerning particular problems that always seem to come up.

Bob Darr, the director of the Center for Wood Arts, continually stressed the use of local woods as a more practical and environmentally sound practice than importing foreign lumber, which contributes to the deforestation going on in many developing nations. I have been left with an appreciation and respect for the resources around us, many of which go unused because of certain prejudices passed down through the years. It is with this sensibility that I acquire the locust, fir, cedar, and oak for the dory.

The work is slow and every day some part of the project consumes me. Today it is lofting, drawing out the plans of the dory full size on the floor. After deciding on a design and obtaining the offset numbers, I really begin to build the boat, at least in my mind. During this process I draw and fair the lines of the boat so that I can begin to visualize what it will look like in three dimensions. To me boatbuilding is as close to a metaphor for life as I can get.

A week later I am still imagining. Then Cindy Wolpin, a community activist, asks me if I would visit a school and share my feelings about the environment, peace, and my pilgrimage with the children. I happily accept, and enlist the aid of my neighbor, local storyteller Jeanmarie Anderson, to help me design a program for the children at the Swan School. The Swan School is an alternative school in town for five- to seven-year-olds. The spring term's focus is on global peace.

Jeanmarie goes right to work. She has wanted to write something about peace that would be of interest to children and adults. The result is an engaging fairy tale depicting my decision to stop

talking and to become a Planetwalker, complete with a faraway kingdom, aloof king, mindless giant with no heart, and, of course, children. Complementing Jeanmarie's vibrant narration I play the banjo, dance, and mime all the roles. The mindless tongue-wagging monster elicits howls of laughter from my audience.

In the story, as the monster roams the land, several children see a strange man wearing a hat of many colors and a pack with a peculiar five-stringed instrument. The stranger plays music and tells the children with a note traced in the air that the instrument is a banjo. He is relieved the children can read because he has given up speech until he finds peace. In the end, the children and the peace walker defeat the monster and the children tell the minstrel that they, too, wish to walk with him for peace. But he says to them, "No, that is my way. You must look into your hearts and find your own way to peace."

When the foghorn blows all night it invades my sleep. Dreams form around its mournful wail. Tankers collide and oil spills; sometimes I solve a knotty boatbuilding problem, joining the stem to the keel, wood to wood, or finally calculate a certain bevel. I try to remember them when I wake, but at the front door I greet the cold wet clouds hanging from the sky. The seagulls laugh and the crows, shadowy phantoms, pick at the compost in the garden. The tide is out; the wild black geese feed in the shallows while I walk along the shore to town.

At the Salal, the local cooperative café, it's not yet crowded. The solarium is cold and stark except for the latest local art, multicolored mandala weavings, hanging on the wall. I sit by the heater catching bits of quiet conversation about dreams, ships, and God. Outside the ferry comes and goes, its whistle blowing. A pilot whale breaks the surface of the bay, sending a warm, misty spray into the air that takes my breath away.

Near the end of February, Tricia accepts a nursing position aboard a crab-processing ship off the coast of Alaska. My lofting now complete, the project moves from the floor of the small greenhouse to the covered porch that is the front of the house. I lay the keel across three sawhorses; the sawn locust frames give the boat real shape. For every way to build some part of a boat there are at least a dozen other ways that are just as good and maybe better. I engage a constant stream of curious and helpful folks with all the ideas and suggestions I could ever want. The trick is to settle on one of them.

Spring is approaching. The dory is far from finished. Jeanmarie and I still have rehearsals and scheduled performances of her peace walker story at various schools and community centers, and in preparation for my departure from Port Townsend I have weekly rehearsals with flutist Ann McClure and bassist Alex Fowler for a Planetwalk benefit concert sponsored by the Peace Coalition.

I have not seen my mother for more than eight years. Her letter says that she and Aunt Jean will be coming to visit. "How wonderful," I think to myself, wondering why everything always seems to happen at once. It is June when they arrive, after a three-and-a-half-day bus ride across the country. I know they will have talked the whole way. Aunt Jean is one of my mother's best friends, and is not an aunt by blood. It makes little difference; she treats me as a favorite nephew, I treat her as a favorite aunt. She is a slight woman, unlike my mother, with wispy gray hair and a voice that is a high whisper playing slow and careful to the ears. They can talk for hours about almost anything and absolutely nothing; it is their vehicle for sharing. Their last ride reaches Port Townsend by way of the Seattle ferry. I meet them at the bus station in town. The two little old ladies are the last ones off the bus, disheveled from their days on the road. They are still chatting away and hardly notice me enough to smile and say hello.

"Johnny, you look so good," says Jean. "Java, don't Johnny look good?"

"Yeah, he looks good all right." Already my mother is teasing me. She kisses me on the cheek. The smell of two unwashed ladies is overpowering. I pinch my nose and frown.

"Don't you be turning your nose up at me," my mother jokes. "It's been three days we haven't had a chance to wash."

I smile and pat her gently on the back. I introduce them to my friend Cindy, who drives them to the house so they can wash and rest after their trip. I ride my bike home and find them sitting peacefully in the living room. They are reading devotional prayer books, their daily habit. My mother looks up, smiles, and returns to the page.

My friend Dick is waiting outside on the porch. He has come over to help me fasten the stem, a long narrow curving affair that makes up the bow at the front of the boat, to the keel. Later we fasten the transom, at the rear, which is the stern. I had made some errors in my earlier attempts, but now we make them right and the dory sits waiting for the bottom and side planking to go on.

Building a boat was one of my childhood dreams, one my mother had lived through in the basement of our Philadelphia home. What is unusual is that I have nearly finished this one on the porch. The ones I built in our basement remained only pieces of wood across two of my father's sawhorses, fashioned, shaped, and held together with the glue of my imagination. At Christmas the sawhorses held the table for the electric trains that ran figure eights and circles in the dining room under a translucent skylight.

"I didn't know you were really building a boat," my mother says, clearly impressed. Some of her words are in sign language, and I am impressed as well. We take long walks together. We talk about everything that is important to her, about my father and their relationship, our family, my younger brother, Dwayne, and spirituality. My parents have been married more than 40 years, and from listening to my mother I gather for the first time that their marriage has not always been easy, but will go on another 40 years. On one of our walks she tells me that she worries about my brother.

Building a boat was one of my childhood dreams, one my mother had lived through in the basement of our Philadelphia home.

"And me?" I ask with my eyes, pointing at myself and then biting my fingernails. "Do you worry about me?"

We are almost back to the house, and I can see the nearly finished dory behind the railing on the porch. La Java stops, looks at me, and then at the dory. We walk up the stairs to the porch and squeeze past the boat.

"I still pray for you every day, but I worry about you less and less. I know for sure you must be doing God's work, or for sure God is working through you. All right, you know, at first I thought you were crazy sure enough, but you see, I know you, and what you are doing is bigger than you. That you could stop talking for . . . so many years is enough. But I see how you are with people and I see how they are with you. I see how you are with yourself. You're different, not as selfish. That's why I am here, and because you are my son."

Friends come by now and then and take my mother and Aunt Jean for day tours around Port Townsend, but mostly they stay at home with me, reading their devotions and watching the dory take shape. Now the planks are cut from thin fir boards and riveted to the sawn frames. My mother and Aunt Jean stay for a week before they board the bus for the ferry to Seattle and the long ride home.

Jerry Gorsline, one of the founding members of the Salal cooperative, accepts the position of guest editor for the next edition of the Planetwalk newsletter, and that makes things a lot less hectic. I find myself looking forward to the simple pace of the road, but when I look out on the porch, the dory is still a long way from being finished. I know I cannot leave until it is done.

Irene Hinkle moves to Port Townsend to help and to become part of Planetwalk. I met Irene as I was passing through Olympia, and her parents took me in. A few years earlier Dick Hinkle and his wife, Ramona, made their own three-month walking sojourn from Olympia to Lake Tahoe, California, where they were raised. They were now involved in a number of social welfare projects they had started. It is good to have Irene's help and her family's support.

The Planetwalk concert is a huge success. Doug Milholland, who had been "witnessing for peace" in Central America, opens the evening with a few words on peace within ourselves and among our neighbors, and includes a minute of silence. About 200 people gather in the Fort Worden Chapel to hear Jeanmarie's stories and the music of our trio.

In June the house is sold and at the invitation of Jeanmarie and her husband, Lowell, Irene and I move ourselves and the unfinished boat into their yard across the street. Two weeks later the dory is finished and a group of friends come to carry it the half mile to the water. We celebrate and everyone goes for a row. The dory's name is *Twana*.

Irene and I spend the next few days out on the bay, getting used to handling the boat and watching the weather. We agree that she will accompany me on the walk for the next month before moving to Bellingham to help with the newsletter and other Planetwalk projects.

Foghorns moan all night. Just the same, we are up at dawn packing away the tent and storing the last few things for Ingrid to take. Ingrid arrived a few days earlier from California and is buying the boat. She plans to take the ferry and meet us on Whidbey Island.

Just outside Point Hudson harbor is a wall of cottony white

fog. We wait for it to lift at Bjorn and Gunda's house. Bjorn wants to row his boat part of the way with us when we leave.

Irene calls the weather station for an update and to ask about the tide. They laugh when she tells them what we intend to do.

"Hey, these guys are gonna row over to Indian Island," he shouts. I can hear his voice come out of the receiver from across the room. There is more derisive laughter as Irene attempts to correct him.

"No, it's Whidbey Island," she says. Whether he hears her or not does not matter. It is still foggy. He gives her the tide information and hangs up.

The weatherman, of course, is not entirely unjustified in his feelings about rowing across to Whidbey Island. It is common knowledge that the currents in Puget Sound and especially in the inlet and the Straits of Juan de Fuca are nothing to trifle with. If you start out in the wrong direction or in the wrong tide you can easily be swept out to sea. Meanwhile the fog is lifting and patches of blue begin to appear in the sky.

To be on the safe side we go looking for Kit Africa. Kit is another boatbuilder, a sailor from the San Francisco Bay Area, who has built more dories than anyone in town. He has also explored most of the San Juan Islands in his own rowing dory and knows the currents as well as anyone. We find him at home.

"That's great!" he exclaims, when he learns that today is the day. He tells us what we need to know. The fog finally dissolves into a clear blue sky. We leave on the incoming tide. About a dozen of our friends wave from the dock. Bjorn follows us in choppy water out past the red bell buoy, and then turns back and we are alone.

CHAPTER 11

The Journey East: Washington to Montana

Sky rockets whistling
Above the ocean's dull roar
Then a sharp report

July 4, 1984
Whidbey Island, Washington

Beneath a milky blue sky, Port Townsend slowly spreads out behind us. On the cliffs reaching up from the shore, old Victorians stand against a backdrop of the Olympic Mountains. The lighthouse winks. Mount Rainier glistens to the east. The inlet is calm blue glass, lifting and falling ever so gently. Close by, a seal breaks the water's surface and stares at our passing, at the oars dipping and pulling. We reach the channel and the incoming tide grabs our little boat and silently takes us on its way.

We watch for the tankers and freighters common to the shipping lanes. We don't see any—only the afternoon ferry loaded with cars and trucks churns by. A few passengers crane their necks to see what speck the captain has given such a wide berth. The horn makes a mournful blast and we swing our craft around to take the worst of the ferry's wake and then continue on.

Three hours and several ferries pass before we realize that the current is taking us beyond our intended destination. We're heading for a spot next to the Keystone ferry dock on Whidbey Island, the second-largest island of the continental United States, about 50 miles west of Skagit and Snohomish counties and midway up the length of Puget Sound. Whidbey's western shore faces the Straits of Juan de Fuca. The sun is setting, and the wind is rising. The steeply rolling sea turns the cold blue-black of gunstock steel.

In the hands of a competent seaman a dory is a seaworthy vessel. Dories proved themselves in the 1890s when they were used principally in the New England fishing industry. Just the same, we reach for the life jackets and Irene scoots into the bottom of the boat to help lower our center of gravity.

As I row, *Twana* dips and rises with each wave and swell. The oarlocks groan and creak—a comforting noise, but I can hardly imagine the survival of a small rowboat caught in a winter storm. We are within sight of land, yet we are plenty anxious about our safety. As I struggle with the oars, Irene directs our course and makes encouraging talk, but for a while we make no progress. On each shore of the bay we enter, the landmarks we choose seem out of reach. Then slowly, the little red barn, the trees, and the hills begin to move, begin to slip slowly by us as we work more with the direction of the sea than against it.

As I row, Twana *dips and rises with each wave and swell.*

A short time later we pull onto the stony beach, to our great relief. We load the boat onto Ingrid's truck without much fuss for the trip to California.

We find a campground nearby and set up our tent. Night is close. We eat in the darkness. By candlelight we escape into the pages of the paperback books we carry. The ground still rolls beneath me with the motion of the sound as I drift off to sleep—into a sailing dream—rising and falling gently, thinking how fragile it all is.

> *Sitting by the warmth*
> *Of a smoky night fire*
> *Moonrise through the trees*

July 5, 1984
Oak Harbor, Washington

Dawn comes and we stay in the tent listening to the soft patter of rain. Outside on the little gas stove, water boils for an oatmeal breakfast with bananas and local strawberries.

We make our way back through the trees and the tangle of

brush that had hidden us from the road. The sky is overcast but for a clear blue streak above the western horizon. We can see Port Townsend, much smaller now—a picture postcard—across the watery distance. As we head north toward Deception Pass, Irene points out the few San Juan Islands that she is able to recognize. There are more than a hundred of them blocking the entrance to the Straits of Georgia. Some are barely large enough to appear on navigation charts. Many of the islands are forested in evergreens; they are said to rival any group of islands in the world for their beauty. From this vantage point I begin to understand for the first time a little of my geographic relationship to our most recent home.

The mild temperature and the slight breeze at our backs make our first day walking a pleasure. Our packs are light—under 30 pounds.

Beside the road that makes its way along the coast and through the summer countryside, the purple and yellow thistle and mustard mix with the hunter greens and golden browns of the hills. Garter and glass snakes slithering into clumps of dried grass make rustling and shushing sounds as we approach.

Just north of Oak Harbor, the island's largest town is Ault Field, a naval air station. At the main gate a sign reads, pardon our noise, it is the sound of freedom. The "sound of freedom" is a deafening roar as a steady stream of jet aircraft, dull blue-gray like the sky, take off and land in slow motion on their practice missions. They are close enough that we can see the pilots inside. They do not wave. Beneath the wings of some bristle an array of missiles and bombs.

These are the planes that flew over the house in Port Townsend, appearing instantly and then disappearing almost as fast over the strait. Sometimes, like a kid, I would stop whatever I was doing and run outside to see them fly in ones and twos—a sort of deadly grace. But up close I can barely stand the noise.

A brindle cow chewing her cud looks up from the green pasture at our passing, seeming not to notice the cacophony overhead that shakes the earth. A hawk circles in the air, then lands on a high branch above the cow and waits.

Next to the road a man pushes his mower in a long straight line. Sweet green grass, cut and shredded, spews from a metal chute.

We wave but he does not notice. We cross the highway and take a back road to the pass. The hawk lifts silently from the tree. Another jet is landing.

> *Walking down the road*
> *Flowers gather all around*
> *Summer's sweet bouquet*

July 7, 1984
Bay View State Park, Washington

At Deception Pass State Park the head ranger learns about our walk and offers us a campsite without charge. We stay an extra day, exploring the beach and the woods.

The next day, the morning clouds are already dissolving into a sunny blue sky as we reach the Deception Pass Bridge.

The early Spanish explorers of Puget Sound thought Whidbey Island was connected to the mainland. Vancouver's contemporaries later discovered the narrow and intricate channel, which divides it from the continent.

We watch from the dizzying heights as the water attempts to squeeze all at once between the two shores of the passage, making fierce eddies, upwellings, and whirlpools. Powerboats of all sizes struggle against an obstinate current to negotiate the troubled stretch of water. We move on slowly. The profusion and variety of roadside flowers increases. The day turns hot.

Irene's shoes are giving her blisters, and she falls a mile behind me on a little-traveled road that parallels the highway.

Several miles farther on the same road I stop in a tidal flat. Off to one side stand a dozen or so plywood fireworks stands decorated with shimmering brightly colored signs—temple of boom, thriller, the dragon slayer. Occasionally a rocket whizzes and whistles into the air, leaving a wispy trail of gray smoke that ends in a feeble pop snatched away by the wind. It is the post–Independence Day sale. Everything is half price. A few cars pull up; some kids from Canada spill out of one with cautious smiles to buy a year's supply.

Irene arrives and after a short rest we find the highway and cross the next bridge over the salt marsh and the waterway that comes up from a small bay. On the other side we follow some tracks, stopping at the turnoff that leads north through a field of green grain to Bay View and the next state park.

We are sitting by the railroad crossing when an old Ford station wagon, dented and scratched with tattered curtains across cracked and foggy windows, pulls up beside us. The bearded driver shouts something I cannot understand at first. I smile.

"Hey, you guys want a ride?" He cranes his head out of the window, his eyes open wide and his expression wild.

I shake my head no.

"Well, how about something to eat, then?" Not waiting for an answer he begins rummaging through the clutter inside the car and hands me a half dozen small chocolate bars from a plastic bag. The girl sitting beside him says nothing, but looks on in amusement.

I thank him and off they go, rattling and bouncing down the road in a cloud of black exhaust. We polish off the chocolate without another thought and follow. We arrive at the park at dusk and search the numbered spaces for a place to set up camp.

"Well, there you are. What kept you so long?" The voice seems to come out of nowhere.

I raise my hand to acknowledge the greeting. It is our friends from the crossing. The contents of their car now clutter the picnic table and the ground around them.

Burning tree limbs and branches protrude haphazardly from the steel fire ring. A column of white smoke from the unseasoned wood rises into the arbor.

"Hey, we've got plenty of room . . . Here, have a seat," he says excitedly, clearing a space at the picnic table. "Have something cold to drink." He produces a bottle of beer from a Styrofoam container.

Irene joins me on the bench while our host, dressed in worn faded army fatigues, goes about axing small trees and shrubs to add to the now smoldering fire.

"Damn fire going out," he curses, and opens a gallon can of something marked Flammable with the bayonet that hangs on a cord around his waist. He tosses the contents on the smoky heap that now contains bottles, rags, and other household trash. He curses again. The liquid splashes. The flames shoot up with a roar, singeing the leaves of nearby trees.

I take a gulp of the beer. My eyes roll.

"Are we going to spend the night here?" Irene whispers.

My head shakes no almost imperceptibly as the park ranger's truck pulls to a stop in front of us. It is our cue to make our break. We thank our host, though by this time he is involved in explaining things to the ranger. I would have liked to hear what he had to say, but we move off to find our own spot.

We spend the night in a quiet campsite a dozen spaces away from the conflagration. We leave early the next day. The park wakes up with the muffled voices of children and their parents discussing breakfast menus and vacation plans.

We stop for lunch outside Edison, a little town not big enough to show on our map. A European visitor there speaks in sign language. She is a teacher of the deaf in Germany. Irene has studied in Germany and has a good grasp of the language. My own two years of German in high school are only slightly helpful. The sign language, however, is a different matter, and we jabber and sign away for a few hours before returning to the road.

In the evening we set up camp on a cliff overlooking Bellingham Bay, above the trails that snake along the shore into the city. The tide goes out, exposing the mud. A peculiar odor mixes with the smell of the salt sea air, like something rotting.

"There was good clamming here," Irene says, "before the pollution. A lot of industrial waste was dumped into the sound, and the effects are just beginning to be realized." She speaks with the emotion of someone mourning her home. A freight train passes as the sun sets, and the moon rises, sparkling the incoming tide and making a school of silver fish shimmer on the water's surface.

In the morning we step from tie to tie, the smell of creosote rising with the summer sun. Only eight miles to walk today, following the tracks in our own quiet solitude that moves along the bay. Clouds turn away and the sky stays blue. The stones crunch beneath our feet as we pass the beach, where nude bathers sun themselves and raise their heads at our intrusion. The San Juan Islands, set in liquid blue, stand out emerald green against the sky.

We stay about a week in Bellingham with the family of Irene's sister and brother-in-law, Dawn and Billy Sodt. They all work at Fairhaven Communication Company, the print shop owned by Billy's parents, which is donating the printing of the next several issues of the newsletter. I learn it is not an unusual thing for them to do. They are very active and donate much of their time to work on peace and human rights issues. In addition to donating printing services to nonprofit endeavors, Dawn has just finished coordinating a successful "crop walk," raising money to feed the hungry, and Billy's mother, Rita, has her own radio program that addresses, for all to hear, the thorniest issues of peace and justice.

When Billy finishes the last page of *Planetwalker* it is collated and stapled, and sent on its way. Then we collect our maps and make food-drop arrangements before leaving on the next leg of our journey. It will take us by trail around Mount Baker, across the northern Cascades, and through the Pasayten Wilderness into Washington's Central Valley.

When Billy finishes the last page of Planetwalker *it is collated and stapled, and sent on its way.*

Outside Bellingham we stop by the Nooksack River in view of Mount Baker. A horse comes to our camp in the night, stamps and snorts on the other side of a barbed-wire fence. It wakes us each from dreams. Irene mumbles that it is a unicorn like the one she wears on her T-shirt, and then drifts back to dream of centaurs. I lie awake for a while thinking of bears. The high wispy mare's tails have gone. Clouds gather piebald, hinting rain.

Three days pass before we reach the Glacier Ranger Station. We arrive just one minute before closing time, with ice cream cones we have bought at the general store. The ranger comes to the door laughing and lets us in. She holds an impossible-looking contraption, painted with the words "Ice Cream Holder."

"It's just a joke," she explains, still laughing, as we look on more than a little bemused. "You see, you'd have to put the cone in upside-down." We nod.

Helen White is a graduate student from Chapel Hill, North Carolina, with a sturdy frame and a friendly manner.

"You're number 430 and number 431," she exclaims, as if we have won the North Cascades Grand Prize. She locks the front door with great satisfaction. It doesn't take long to figure out it has been a busy day. Donning heavy-framed glasses, she walks us through the process of filling out backcountry passes. The passes regulate and monitor the usage rates in the park. Filling them out gives the ranger a chance to acquaint the hiker with rules and regulations about wilderness and national park usage.

In our Western culture, the concept of cherishing wilderness is really quite recent. The Old Testament mentions "wilderness" about 200 times, always as something unpleasant, a trial or something to be avoided. The same change in thinking can be found in literature in reference to mountains.

There is, of course, an "easier" way to cross the mountains. Highway 20 winds through several passes, a thin band of dark asphalt with variegated streams of traffic. The thought of a quiet trail wins out. We reach the trailhead a few days later and begin the slow climb toward the first pass.

> *In the blue distance*
> *Mountain peaks in brilliant snow*
> *Rise into heaven*

July 24, 1984
Below Hannegan's Pass, Washington

It starts out as a stone-lined path through a fairyland of wildflowers, then rises moderately as it wanders in and out of timber. The cedar has been logged long ago and now tall firs provide what shade there is from the sun.

It is not quite noon when we reach the first snow bridge. It arches precariously across a 40-foot-deep gully and a rushing stream. Back at the ranger station Helen had warned us about the danger of falling through a bridge because it is so late in the season and the snows are melting. We are just about to take the long way around when we hear a commotion on the trail. Two burly hikers, coming down from the pass, appear on the other side and without a second thought bound across the passage. Throwing caution to the wind, we follow suit.

Hannegan Pass is about 5,000 feet above sea level. It is not a difficult climb even with our loaded packs, but just the same, we look forward to the walk down into the next valley to our designated campsite. Due to overuse, camping is not permitted at or near the passes. But while we are there we stop to rest, and meet a group of hikers from Canada who have struggled up the other side. It is a good excuse to unwrap my banjo and share a bit of Planetwalk over lunch.

The gray jays come to perch in the trees and eye our food

hungrily. They are used to people, and soon they are feeding from our hands.

By the time we arrive at Big Beaver Camp on Ross Lake, we have lost nearly 4,000 feet in elevation. Three quiet days and 55 forested miles have slipped by. This is the eastern boundary of the 674,000-acre park complex. When we finally meet the dozen people who are scheduled on the trail with us, it becomes apparent how effective the backcountry pass system has been in regulating hiker flow and campsite use.

Twenty-three-mile-long Ross Lake was formed by Ross Dam in the upper regions of the Skagit Drainage. The hydroelectric facility there furnishes power for Seattle City Light. Objections were raised when the company proposed raising the dam's height to increase the flow of power to Puget Sound. British Columbians objected to the suggestion, citing the loss of several miles of fine angling streams as well as the drowning of the adjoining forest. Fortunately, City Light decided not to raise the dam.

Several canoes land along the shore, and their occupants spill out into the last few waterside camps. The sun is preparing to set when a seaplane touches down with a splash and roar that breaks the evening stillness. I wonder if seaplanes are allowed to land on the lake, but I join in the holiday mood, waving and taking pictures with the rest of the campers as the blue-and-white craft motors up onto the beach.

The pilot and his passenger smile and wave. Someone in the crowd mentions *Fantasy Island*, and we all laugh.

"Hey, it just took us an hour to get here from Bellevue," one of the men shouts as he climbs out of the cabin. He waves a white Stetson hat and poses on one of the plane's struts. A few cameras click.

Music is an amazing communicator. Find an instrument that you can carry easily. In the spirit of the wandering minstrel, you can tell the story of your journey with the help of your instrument. Music can soothe a tired soul and heal an injured spirit. A great companion on your walk, music can be a vehicle for profound change.

"I guess we all have our idea of fun," a man beside me says in a soft voice.

In the morning a ranger arrives to investigate reports of an unauthorized seaplane on the lake. It is all very friendly, but the little Seabee is definitely in violation of some regulation, and the ranger dutifully writes out the ticket. And that is that.

But as the ranger heads back to her patrol boat, she stops and squints from behind dark glasses in my direction. I make a kind of nervous "How do you do?" nod, and then a little wave.

"Is that John Francis?" she asks warily. I break into a big smile as I recognize Christine Fairchild, a classmate from Southern Oregon State College and friend from my home back in Point Reyes. What a surprise reunion.

"Is that John Francis?" she asks warily.

> *Walking down the trail*
> *Deep blue-green the lake glitters*
> *Through the forest trees*

July 28, 1984
Ross Dam
North Cascade National Park

Christie invites us to spend a few days with her at the Ross Guard ranger station, so we hurry around the lake and across the steel and concrete dam.

The guard station sits on pontoons just offshore and a hundred yards or so back from the dam's spillway. It consists of two wooden cabins, one an office and living space, the other a shop and storage area. Moored alongside one of the floating docks is the *Skagit,* a work tug owned by Seattle City Light.

No one is at the station when we arrive, but the key and a note are waiting for us in the derelict washing machine—never used because of the problem of storing and transporting the wastewater. We make ourselves at home. When hikers amble down the steep trail from the highway and knock on the door, we hand out the appropriate maps and answer questions as best we can.

The owners of the camping and fishing resort across the lake are prepared for our visit and in the evening they bring a canoe for us to use during our stay. Jim DuRose, one of the park's maintenance men, suggests we take the canoe up to Lightning

Creek Trail. Another guard station is planning a potluck send-off.

The day before we leave, Irene's family arrives with a box of food and clothing. The next afternoon we pile our packs into the canoe and begin the 20-mile paddle, which we figure will take us two days. The sun is setting as we put ashore on Little Jerusalem, one of the tiny islands that dot the lake. The breeze is quickening, and rain seems imminent.

We put up our tent and settle down to a quiet meal beside the fire. A mouse searching for a bite to nibble jumps from my open pack down onto my shoes and scurries across the dusty earth. Having had several packs ruined by rodents trying to get into an empty side pocket, I always leave my packs open for easy entrances and exits. Our food is hanging between two small pine trees.

A mouse searching for a bite to nibble jumps from my open pack down onto my shoes and scurries across the dusty earth.

Two troops of scouts are camped a few miles beyond us on the lake shore. When I was younger I had wanted to be a scout, but my stay in the sanitarium kept me from joining. Instead I joined vicariously through the exploits of cousins and uncles, friends and *Boy's Life* scouting magazine. We can see the twinkle of their fires as night falls. Back at the ranger station, Christie laughed at our notion that it would be fun to camp with a troop of Boy Scouts. "They get pretty noisy," she said, and recounted the story of the last rowdy pack on the lake.

They had already gotten a few complaints about the noise, but when the rangers went to check on the scouts they found mayhem: trees cut to make furniture for some sort of merit badge, and the scoutmaster all wrapped up in splints and bandages. He had broken his neck diving into shallow water, and had to be evacuated by helicopter.

"I don't think anyone got a first-aid merit badge either. No," she mused, "we'll keep you away from the scouts this time."

The rain arrives during the night. Great rolls of thunder shake the ground and flashes of lightning briefly illuminate the landscape. I rescue my banjo from under a tree and tuck it in a safe corner of our tent. We stay awake listening to the storm rage—such a beautiful symphony. It lulls us to sleep.

On deep green water
A golden leaf sails slowly
In a deep blue sky

August 3, 1984
Devil's Creek

In the morning the lake is glass. In the sun insects swirl in golden-brown clouds above the water before being swept away like dust by the rising wind. Above us the mountains rise, traced in the lacy white of last winter's snow.

Tracy Morrow, the ranger on patrol from Lightning Creek, stops by our camp to visit as we are preparing to leave. By the time we push off, the lake is dressed in whitecaps. Fortunately, we are paddling with the wind. Along the shore, Girl Scouts drying out from the night's rain wave enthusiastically as we speed by.

Another thunderstorm is approaching from behind and we point our craft toward the shelter of Devil's Creek Canyon. The water is calm here, and we paddle in the quiet between two steep canyon walls covered in delicate ferns. Farther upstream we pick our way through a logjam to waterfalls Christie has told us about. Electricity is in the air.

By the time we drift back to the main body of the lake, the storm has passed. We reach Lightning Creek late that afternoon. Tracy puts us up for the night in her cabin. Like the rest of the buildings on the lake, it floats so as to remain level during periods of high or low water, now the lake is high. Along the shallows near the shore, however, stumps of the logged forest can be seen just below the surface.

Tied next to the Lightning Creek float is the *Ross Mule,* the park service boat, a little like a barge or World War II amphibious landing craft with a bow that opens into a ramp. It hauls guard station garbage and wastewater the 25 miles up the lake to Hozomein trailhead. From there a truck transports the waste to a disposal site in Canada. The *Skagit* also collects waste from the sealed chamber outhouses at the waterside campsite. Maintaining the lake's water quality is a costly proposition, but the reward of clean water is definitely worth it.

The following morning a fierce wind is still whipping up whitecaps on the lake. We have our breakfast with Tracy out on the dock, enjoying the sun. A little roly-poly brown bear takes his daily walk across the footbridge over the creek and up the trail. As for us, we write letters, and then take off for a day hike to the top of 6,000-foot Desolation Peak. From this vantage we can see into Canada and gain another perspective on Ross Lake, the mountains we crossed, and the wilderness we are about to enter.

All the rangers and the owners of the Ross Lake Resort show up at Lightning Creek Station with their own special dishes, to wish us well. Conversations range from wilderness trail conditions to solutions to world and regional environmental problems. Christie promises to write for the newsletter. When the sun sets it is time for music, something soft like "Night Rain" on the banjo. It is prophetic; before the sun rises the next day the rain begins to fall, chasing all who stayed late into a shelter of hastily arranged tarps.

It does not last long, only a minute or two—not enough to dampen the dusty trail. Reddish-brown clouds kick up as we struggle up the hillside under heavy packs; we walk an hour, then two and a half more before we stop at Deer Lick Camp on the western edge of the Pasayten Wilderness. The log cabin is empty except for some kindling and an old wood box. The shingled roof is in good repair. We decide to stay.

When Irene has gathered enough wood for the evening she goes down to the creek to try her luck with the fish. I stay behind and prepare our supper just in case the fish prove luckier. I do not hear the splash over the sound of the rapids, but Irene comes back soaked to the skin, without fish. She has slipped off a log sticking out into the stream. I have enough sense to refrain from any comment.

The trail from Deer Lick follows Three Fools Creek to the next shelter, which is no more than a three-sided log structure with a roof. Not far from the shelter, in the shade of the trees, a figure reclines. I whistle, not wanting to startle anyone in the backcountry by appearing suddenly.

We make a new friend. Averaging 20 miles per day, Charlie Hickenbottom is built for speed, a wiry fellow with a full blond beard. He is also the former editor of *Sign Post*, a northwest hiking magazine. We have a lot in common, especially when it comes to wanting to protect and enjoy the wilderness. During the winter Charlie drives a school bus; he enjoys the kids. During summer vacation and school holidays he hikes, stocked with his own special concoction of trail mix and dried fish. He has been several days on the trail this trip. Coming from the south, he has turned west and is now heading for Ross Lake. We trade information about snow levels and trail conditions.

The route we plan to take is the Boundary Trail, about a hundred miles of peace and quiet in the deep wilderness skirting the

Canadian border. Because the trail is not easily accessible by automobile, we do not expect to have many human encounters, but we have been warned again and again to watch for grizzlies.

We leave Charlie by the creek to begin the steep climb to Freezeout Mountain. He says only that we should take lots of water, and how glad he is to be going the other way. He does not mention the ferocity of the mosquitoes and the deerflies. Irene has to don a makeshift veil to obtain relief. Four days pass before we see another soul.

We arrive at the Pasayten Airport not certain what to expect. Our map indicates an airfield and a ranger station. Our food cravings begin: pizzas, milk shakes, and french fries. The airstrip turns out to be a rectangular patch of green along the Pasayten River dotted with young trees. Built by the Civilian Conservation Corps around 1935 to supply backcountry stations in the event of wildfires, it has been mostly closed since 1968.

At the south end of a field, off to one side, the heavy log cabin is unlocked and unoccupied. It is one story with glass windows in each wall. Inside, pots and pans hang behind an old Monarch woodstove. At one end of the cabin's single room are two bunk beds. Stacked in a cupboard is a healthy supply of gothic and Western paperbacks. We decide to stay the night. We are engrossed in our reading when a pack train snorts up the trail and stops beneath the pine trees next to the cabin.

The train has arrived to resupply a group from the National Outdoor Leadership School (NOLS) camping a mile down the trail. About two dozen students from different parts of the country and a couple of instructors are on a monthlong trek across the wilderness. They have already been out for more than a week. In the evening some file into our camp to sit by the fire, swap stories, and listen to a little music.

We readily accept their invitation to dinner the next day. It will be at least another week before we emerge from the Pasayten and reach the next town. Though we have been catching fish along the way, our meager food supply continues to shrink. At their request I promise to bring my banjo, and we both agree to bring healthy appetites.

"We really like to cook," one of them says. "You'll be surprised."

The following evening we arrive at their camp amid the organized confusion of a dozen cooks practicing chemistry around hissing gasoline stoves, murmuring pots and kettles, and a smoky fire. The first group unveils their noodles and sauce, the second burritos. Around one pan covered with glowing coals there is a conversation tinged with frustration and then hope. When they unveil the dish our mouths drop open. It is a pizza. I guess we are impressed.

For dessert there is cheesecake and music around the campfire. The moon rises above the trees as we make our way home up the trail; moonlight on the field of grass looks like snow.

Before we leave, the NOLS group and their packer give us a few supplies to add to our dwindling stores. For the next several days we talk about cheesecake and pizza. We wonder what other wishes might come true. Ice cream…

The wilderness is still with us when we reach the little town of Twisp two weeks later. Friends of Irene's, the Dorans, are among a growing number of ranchers working toward a nuclear freeze. We arrive just in time for the Nuclear Freeze Square Dance being held at the Community Center. I am invited to play with the band when the dancing gets to be too much.

Dan Doran, the elder member of the family, is a former naval officer who participated in early nuclear testing. While preparing a training course, Survival in Nuclear War, he came to the conclusion that survival was improbable. He has devoted himself to spreading that message ever since.

Dan arranges for some neighbors and other ranchers to come by for an evening of music and nuclear freeze talk. People have lots of opinions on how to achieve a freeze, but everyone there agrees it must happen. Dan leans toward writing letters and exerting political pressure—and against tactics like bodily blocking the White Train, which reportedly carries assembled nuclear weapons for deployment in the Unites States. The government is prosecuting some members of the Twisp community for such blockades.

From Twisp Irene heads back toward Bellingham, where she plans to help with the next several issues of the newsletter. I continue across eastern Washington to Spokane.

The rough mountains gradually give way to gently rolling plains covered in golden grain. It takes ten days to cover the 150

The following evening we arrive at their camp amid the organized confusion of a dozen cooks practicing chemistry around hissing gasoline stoves, murmuring pots and kettles, and a smoky fire.

miles to the city. On the way I stop to take a dishwashing job for an evening at the Methow Café. Some of the musicians from the square dance in Twisp are playing and they ask me to sit in again. Music is always a welcome break.

In Spokane I first stay with retired paint contractor W. D. Hottel and his wife, Alice. They are the parents of Bill Hottel, who works at the paper in Twisp. Later I stay across the street with Michelle and David Zambrano, a younger couple who have recently moved from Colorado. David is just starting out as a photographer and Michelle works for a mining consultant. They set me up in their living room with a typewriter to work on the next installment of the newsletter. When I finish, the Hottels organize a neighborhood dinner in my honor. "Good Luck, John Francis" is scrawled in yellow frosting on the cake.

> *Softly the rain fell*
> *Tires whispered on wet streets*
> *Slick with green-red leaves*

> September 26, 1984
> Spokane, Washington

For 15 miles I follow dirt roads into Otis Orchard, a little community near the Washington-Idaho border. The sun makes long shadows as Ted, a brown-eyed 11-year-old, rides up on his BMX; for a while he pedals beside me in silence and we smile at each other. Then curiosity gets the better of him.

"Where you walkin' to?" he asks.

I go through the familiar pantomime and when he understands he takes off down the road to tell his mom. He returns a few minutes later deep in thought, and resumes his place beside me.

When we run into his classmate Joey, words begin to fly.

"I don't believe it!" Joey says more in amazement than disbelief.

I go through the same gesturing, producing a news clipping and newsletter. More expletives and signs of amazement pass between them.

"Oh, you just got to come home with me and meet my dad," begs Joey.

The rails cross the road and lead off behind the houses into a field where I can see some sheltering trees in the distance. I point to the trees, then lay my hands as if a pillow and tilt my head alongside of them.

"You can sleep at our house," Joey assures me.

"Joey's dad is a nice man," Ted chips in. "He's our baseball coach. He's tough sometimes, but he's real nice, loud but not rude."

It is getting late and I am a little tired. Any misgivings I might have I put away in service of a mission of Planetwalk, "friendship through personal contact," and follow Ted and Joey home.

Joey disappears into the house while Ted and I wait in the yard. I am a little nervous. Joey's dad, Barney, is a big man. He comes to the door with his wife, Nancy, who is busy trying to glean something from the newsletter their son has given them. Stretching his hand out, Barney clasps mine in a warm bear grip and invites me in for coffee so he can read the clipping and look over the newsletter.

"That's very interesting," he says, handing the worn clipping back. I am invited to stay for dinner and the night.

After dinner we move to the living room for more conversation and some TV. On the mantelpiece the softly clicking clock chimes. Hanging on the wall around it are an old cowboy hat, spurs, and other rodeo paraphernalia. A disassembled shotgun, parts carefully placed and ready for cleaning, sits on the coffee table. Charlene, their 12-year old daughter, who is wearing a Michael Jackson T-shirt, says she has taken a gun safety class and is looking forward to skeet shooting, or maybe even hunting.

Barney was All-Marine Rodeo Champ for ten years. Raised on a ranch near Sweet Hill, Montana, he has been in rodeos most of his life. A logging accident several years ago left him with five fused vertebrae; it hurts him to ride now.

"I'd be afraid to walk through Russia," Barney says. "They might yank me into jail. I had enough of the communists in Vietnam." Nancy nods.

"We're a love-the-USA family," she says.

The kitten playing on the rug suddenly begins crawling up my pant leg. It tickles and I make a little laugh as it squirms to get back out.

After the rest of the house retires, Barney tells me how glad he is to be able to offer me his hospitality.

"A few years ago I couldn't have done that," he says. "You see, I was prejudiced."

I look into his eyes and try to understand what has caused such a change in this 43-year-old ex-Marine and rodeo champion. With a questioning look, I ask him.

"I had a talk to work that out with the Lord, and I realized how much I had been limiting myself with that attitude."

CHAPTER 12

Hello, Goodbye: Leaving Montana

The days start out cold
Until the sun rises high
Into a blue sky

September 29, 1984
Coeur d'Alene, Idaho

Sometime in the morning I cross the state line, passing from Washington to Idaho, but the countryside remains the same. Only the license plates change on the cars that glide by, and as I walk farther on, the mountains that are so far off close in to make a valley.

I follow the directions scrawled on a crumpled piece of paper to find Pandora's Books. It is a small two-story wooden house near the edge of town where they sell metaphysical and science fiction publications. Someone has called ahead and made arrangements for me to spend a few nights. Karen, the proprietress, is a round, happy woman who welcomes me warmly, inviting me to stay as long as I like. I fall asleep on the floor of the prayer and meditation room.

The next day Karen hosts a crystal workshop and I climb to the second-floor living room with 20 others to hear about the psychic powers attributed to various types of crystals. Some of it I have heard before in the context of healing stones, but the woman conducting this workshop also talks about using them for visualization, astral travel, and a host of other supernatural endeavors. I like crystals, but the only memorable experience I ever had with one was when my dad and I built a crystal radio set, and it worked. That is still a mystery to me, so I try to keep an open mind.

I stay in Coeur d'Alene for three days, getting to know a little about the town through the people who come into the store. When I leave, I am given the addresses of several places I can stay along the way. Idaho is only about 75 miles across at the panhandle and I have a place to sleep each night.

Three days later I reach Lookout Pass at the Idaho-Montana state line, after a 13-mile climb. There is a ski lodge at the top and I am supposed to spend the night at the caretaker's cabin, but no one is home when I arrive except a dog locked on the other side of the cabin door. I go off to look at the lodge and the chair lift when I hear the car horn; a few seconds later a light green Volvo pulls into the driveway. The dog is barking as I limp over. It is a familiar car, one that I have seen several times during the day. The two men I had waved to as they drove by earlier today are the same two who are standing on the porch by my pack. One is holding a large nickel-plated revolver.

"Oh, it's you," he growls. "I could have shot your head off."

The look he gives me tells me he means what he says. He is a heavy man with a full dark beard and his stance is nothing less than menacing.

"What you doin' up here?" he asks.

The pistol is cocked but pointed in the air. I ask myself the same question, remember the letter I am carrying in my shirt pocket, take it out, and hand it to him. He glances over it quickly and then everything changes.

"Aw, shucks, you're all right," he says. "Any friend of Dan's is a friend of mine."

It may sound trite but he means just that. He puts the gun into a holster and extends an open hand. Everyone relaxes.

"I'm sorry about the gun," he says, "but there's been some vandalism and shots fired into the window."

He points at several bullet holes to make his point and goes on to introduce me to his friend, Paul, and a tail-wagging black Lab.

Rick Keck turns out to be a warm, friendly man. He tells me I am welcome to spend the night.

"It's a good thing you came when you did," he says. "Deer-hunting season begins in a few days and I'm goin' up to the hunting camp in the morning to get things ready."

He is going to the camp to be the cook, and you can feel his excitement.

"You'll pardon this mess," he says as he gathers the dirty laundry from the corners of the room.

Then the color television, the fishing rods, the butchering tools, and whatever else he values make their way out to the car. His partner, Paul, reads a newspaper clipping while the Padres play the Cardinals silently on the black-and-white TV that remains.

"I don't want to leave any of this stuff here while I'm away," he explains.

I throw a mattress on the floor of the first-aid station, which is attached to Rick's cabin. It is cluttered with sleds, a few hospital beds, benches, desks, and broken skiing equipment. I do not mind the chaos. I drift off to sleep to the sound of the rain that falls during the night.

Mountain on fire
Smokeless gold and crimson flames
Fall from every tree

October 10, 1984
Idaho-Montana Border

Twinkling stars fade with the dawn. Rusty red and pink clouds blend into a light blue sky, setting off the golden larch along the road and the hillsides. Parked at the summit are two tractor-trailer trucks, engines running, windows fogged, drivers sleeping. I wonder if Peace Pilgrim came this way on her journey, where she slept, and what she felt climbing the last hill. I do not listen to the nagging voice inside that says my feet hurt too much to walk. I take some aspirin and ignore the pain and move slowly onto the highway. There is little traffic. I cross into Montana.

A crew of truckers moves earth along the four lanes. Back and forth they pass until we all become familiar and wave to one another as the day progresses and the miles pass. A few people stop and ask if I want a ride, but as usual I decline. Ten miles later I reach Saltese. Rick has given me a note and the name of a friend who runs the café there, so I stop for breakfast. It is too early to stop for the day so I continue on.

I make 23 miles and find a place away from traffic noise. There is no need for a tent. I sleep in a fragrant bed of pine needles beside the river. A small fire of broken ties blazes hot. For a moment the burning creosote makes thick black smoke darker than the night. I read until late, chasing away the mouse that scurries around my head. In the quiet I listen to the river talk, and jump at the splash of a falling rock. In the night sky, the stars move slowly . . . they always do.

> *The clouds that gather*
> *Cast a shadow from the sun*
> *Leaves begin to fall*

October 24, 1984
Missoula, Montana

When I arrive in Missoula, I stay in an old school bus belonging to friends I have made along the way. Then one day, with some apprehension, I head for the school. It has been about two years since I was accepted into the University of Montana's graduate environmental studies program (EVST). At the time I applied I thought that since my pilgrimage is based so much on concern for the environment and world peace, it would be a good idea to stop and study those subjects along the way. But I am struggling with inertia.

Inertia is the law of physics that says if a body is in motion it wants to keep on going, and if it is at rest it wants to stay that way. Well, it has not started snowing yet, so I think I should keep walking and maybe reach Wyoming, and pass the winter with some people living in a community of yurts who are expecting me. If I stay in Missoula for school, I don't know where I'll get the money for tuition—I have just enough to repair the snowshoes my friends Steve and Verdan have sent from California.

I find the EVST office located in an old two-story red brick building. It is named after Jeanette Rankin, a Montanan, the first woman to be a member of the U.S. House of Representatives, and the only congressperson to vote against the United States entering the first and second world wars.

I stand outside on the steps, feeling the warmth of the afternoon sun on my face. The campus is spread out at the base of a mountain, and I watch a slow procession of people making their way along the switchback that leads to a large M embedded in the mountain.

"Uhh . . . you must be John Francis."

I hear the voice stutter and nod in its direction.

"We've been expecting you. My name is Tom Roy. I'm the chairman of the EVST department."

We both smile and shake hands. Once inside he tells me how happy he is to see me because the next day is the last day to register for the fall quarter, and if I had missed the registration I would have had to apply all over again. I explain about my dilemma, whether to continue to Wyoming or to attend school here in Missoula, and the fact that I do not have tuition.

"We'll work something out," he says. "Come and see me tomorrow afternoon."

The next day Tom hands me an envelope with enough money to register for an independent study class in water problems. Slowly the idea sinks in that I am going to stop in Missoula and attend the university. A few days later I write my friends in Wyoming. It does not surprise me when they write back and tell me they are closing down the community for the winter. There are other laws besides inertia. The first snow has already fallen.

I share the house of a retired literature professor, John Moore, and his housekeeper. It is inexpensive and only three blocks from campus.

Study begins slowly for me, and that is a good thing. After spending the summer on the road walking through the North Cascades, it is probably best that I start off easy. My first academic endeavor is to identify water resource and management problems in developing countries throughout the world, but especially in Central and Latin America, where I plan to be walking in a few years. I am to procure an initial list of people working on water projects that I might visit and work with as part of Planetwalk. I begin to realize that the breadth and depth of Planetwalk depend greatly on the breadth and depth of my own education, both formal and informal. I vow to take every opportunity during my pilgrimmage.

By the time the second quarter rolls around I have begun my EVST program in earnest. One of the strengths of the program, and of environmental studies generally, is that it requires students to include a number of disciplines in their course selections. And after taking the class War, Peace, and Western Society I begin to better understand the connections between peace and the environment. In the words of Middle Eastern philosopher Seyyed HosseinNasr:

"Many labor under the illusion that only war is evil and that if it could be averted man could go on peacefully to create paradise on Earth. What is forgotten is that in both the state of war and peace man is waging incessant war upon nature."

I also take the more traditional courses, which include Forest Hydrology, Toxic Substances, Resource Analysis, Man's Role in Environmental Change, and Geography of Water Resources. In addition I study Philosophy of Ecology, Chemical and Biological Warfare, and War in the Environment. A special lecture series that explores the environmental problems and solutions of other countries is most interesting. It is the first time that I am able to meet with various diplomats and discuss environmental issues and the interests of Planetwalk.

I also receive the Erasmus Award to complete my studies, which includes a scholarship. So I make the decision to stay without much difficulty.

As spring approaches my thoughts drift to the road again, but I have nearly completed my coursework and have already picked a topic for my professional paper: "Pilgrimage and Change: War, Peace, and the Environment." I also receive the Erasmus Award to complete my studies, which includes a scholarship. So I make the decision to stay without much difficulty. Besides, my schoolwork is not the only consideration.

During the winter I take on the responsibility of supervising two interns for Planetwalk from the university, Tom Benevento and Amy Yakle. Both are interested in the environment and peace. Tom's Planetwalk project is to set up the Pilgrimage of Central America program, in which students and people from the community would have the opportunity to visit Nicaragua or Guatemala. Amy's project is to organize the construction of a community peace quilt to be delivered to the Soviet Union. They will also be doing Planetwalk community outreach, canvassing door to door and distributing the Planetwalk newsletter.

By the time summer arrives, I have begun working on my paper and occasionally sitting in on an Upward Bound class. The summer program is for Native American high school students who are planning to go on to college, and includes some Southeast Asian students. We spend most of the time just getting to know one another, exploring the differences and similarities in the ways we think and feel. I am in no hurry to strike out on the road. My writing goes slowly.

Fall comes, and then winter. With the Erasmus scholarship, I am guaranteed a teaching assistantship, so I prepare to be the first nonspeaking discussion leader at the university. I was politely turned down for such an assistantship the year before because of my silence, and there is still some concern among administrators and others that perhaps a discussion leader who does not talk is not such a good idea.

That is not the concern of professor Ron Erickson, whom I will be assisting. The class is called The Conservation of Natural and Human Resources in Montana. Ron had been the director of the EVST program when I applied three years earlier, and we maintained a correspondence as I made my way north and to Montana. He has the highest confidence that it will be a learning experience for all concerned. I do, too, but in my lowest moments I do not share his optimism.

I have 12 students in my section, mostly education majors taking the course because it is required, but also some students from forestry, music, the humanities, and recreational management. We meet once a week to discuss the lectures from the previous three days. For our first meeting I ask my roommate, Sara Miller, to interpret my sign language to the class.

Sitting in a circle, we introduce ourselves and say a few words about why we are there and what our plans are. I save myself until last.

"This is the only time I'll speak to you this way," I explain through Sara.

The students glance sideways at each other and their mouths fall open and stay that way as Sara speaks. I can feel the shock and disbelief that runs through them, yet I continue signing my introduction, explaining why I do not talk and about the oil spill that prompted me to walk. When I finish, I answer questions about the lifestyle I have chosen and then we move on to the class material.

During the next class I hand out a five-question quiz. As I

explained at our first meeting, I will use these questions to make up my section of the final exam. After the 15-minute exercise I gather the class into a circle and begin a pantomime in their midst. All eyes are on me dragging my hands back and forth through the air.

"What is he doing?" says one student.

"I'm not sure—I think he's sawing down a tree," says another.

I nod my head and continue. Now one arm is standing straight upward into the air. I listen to what they say.

"Yes, he is sawing a tree. It's about clear-cutting."

"No, he's using a hand saw so I think he's communicating something about selective forestry."

"Hey, you can clear-cut with a hand saw!"

Sometimes I do not mean what they are saying and sometimes I wish I did, but the learning goes both ways.

"Yeah, but I think this is from our last lecture and more than likely has to do with selective forestry."

At this point my strategy is to step back and let the argument go on, stepping in only to keep the discussion civil.

At the end of the quarter I receive the highest teaching assistantship evaluation. When the students are asked how they felt about having a discussion leader who did not talk, one answers: "I was shocked. At first, I did not think it was fair that our leader did not talk and all the other groups had ones that did. But all that has changed, and I feel that I have learned a lot more than I would have otherwise." In the end I feel the same way.

My father has never been to Montana before, but he comes to Missoula for my graduation. This time he comes alone. He is in a mild state of disbelief that I actually can finish a master's degree program. Nevertheless he is proud of my accomplishment and brings those sentiments from my mother, who is unable to come because she is teaching.

"Now don't get me wrong," he starts, "your mother and I are very proud of you. I mean, you have come up here and . . . " His voice trails off to a whisper. ". . . gone to school . . . " He looks around and sees me listening.

I know what he is going to say. I wish that he did not have to say it, but he does.

"I just don't understand this not talking. You have to talk. What are you going to do with a master's degree? What kind of a job are you going to get? You have to drive a car and you have to talk." He shakes his head and then laughs at the little storm that comes down from the mountain without any rain and disappears into the desert.

At my mother's request, he takes photos of me in my graduation cap and gown. The local paper does a story about me. He buys a few copies and catches the plane back to Philadelphia.

Walking through the streets
To say the last three goodbyes
Until the sun sets

July 1, 1986
Missoula, Montana

I spend my last evening in Missoula at the home of my neighbors, Steve and Mary Pat, graduate students at the University of Montana. Steve is studying education and Mary Pat is studying speech and communication disorders. She also teaches one of the sign language classes offered at the school. We sometimes practice signing together. Their basement holds the cardboard boxes containing Planetwalk papers, clothing, camping gear, art supplies, and books, part of my recent academic life that has to be stored away. They agree to send them to me when I stop walking for the winter.

There are no sad goodbyes between us. We have plans to meet a few months later in the Teton National Park to do some camping and climbing together. Three months earlier I underwent corrective surgery on both feet for hammertoes, a painful condition that had my toes bending under themselves. The trauma is still with me. I wonder if I will be ready for any serious climbing; for that matter, I wonder if I am ready to continue my journey. I fall asleep in their guest room and dream of walking and the road.

In the morning I cross the street and knock on the door of the other house where I had lived the previous two winters with John Moore. Frances, the housekeeper, a small, delicate woman with gray hair and intense gray eyes, fumbles with the latch, and finally lets me in.

"I thought you had already gone," she says, and apologizes for the locked door. She had usually left it open during the day when I lived there.

Inside I am assaulted by the familiar musty smell of the old house, laced with the fragrance of pine disinfectant. I move down the darkened hallway over the creaking floorboards to the softly lighted back room. Old John, sitting in bed, looks up from his paper. His body is frail; years of smoking have taken their toll. He adjusts the plastic tubing to fit more comfortably below his nose. Not invisible, the tube takes a circuitous route across the landscape of the scrubbed linoleum floor, through a bottle of bubbling water and valves attached to a large green tank of oxygen quietly hissing in the corner. Our eyes meet.

Some researchers claim that up to 90 percent of what we normally communicate is nonverbally transmitted. Occasionally, however, I come across people who have difficulty interpreting the most elementary hand signals, though in communications both sender and receiver share in the responsibility. Old John is not one of these. In the silence, volumes pass between us. Sometimes he talks, and I listen. Other times he shares with me one of his recently written poems about Halloween, TV, death and dying . . . something from inside. The quality of our communication is extraordinary. So when he looks up at me from behind thick glasses, I feel the symphony that moves across his face reaching a penultimate chord in the clicking of false teeth. I turn and leave before cloudy eyes well into a storm.

Old John, sitting in bed, looks up from his paper. His body is frail; years of smoking have taken their toll.

"God bless you, John," he wheezes. I close the door behind me.

At school, summer classes have begun. My desk has been emptied and another graduate student has moved in. Tom Roy, the environmental studies director, finds me in the office writing a thank-you note to Vivian, the department secretary.

"So, when are you going?" he asks, a broad smile stretched across his face.

I look up and answer in sign, making my gesture most immediate. Usually Tom is good at reading my signs, though sometimes I go to scribbling notes on scraps of paper or on the blackboard.

"Right now?"

I nod my head.

"Right now? But . . . " The smile slowly dissolves from his face, to be replaced by an expression of shock mixed with disbelief and concern. He waits until I finish the note, then follows me outside onto the steps.

"You mean you're leaving right this minute, and you're going to walk to Philadelphia to attend the University of Pennsylvania next fall?"

At first I am a little startled by his surprise. He knows about Planetwalk, and that I took nearly two years to walk from California to Montana. We have talked for months about my leaving after graduation and my interest in the appropriate technology program at the University of Pennsylvania. I asked all the questions as I worked my way through academic and administrative requirements to earn a graduate degree. Today it is Tom's turn.

I smile and nod yes, like it is just a matter of fact and the most natural occurrence in the course of the day. Inside, however, I know what he is feeling. It is a reflection of my own feelings . . . my own doubts and anxieties.

There is a pause and awkward silence. He turns to Raz, a friend who is going to spend the first few days walking with me.

"How's he going, by bike?" he asks hopefully.

I walk a pair of fingers through the air in front of his face, but he ignores my answer and concentrates on what Raz is about to say. He shakes his head. I shake his hand and wave goodbye, leaving him there on the steps where we met a year and a half before.

"How can he just leave like that after all this time? I couldn't do that," Tom says, as I walk off. He seems stunned to be witnessing the event.

"I told him I guess you are an anomaly," says Raz, as we walk the highway headed out of town. "He repeated it as he went back into the building, 'Yeah, I guess he is an anomaly. Yeah, that's it, an anomaly,'" his voice trailing off.

As the traffic passes we both laugh. I do not feel like an anomaly, but leaving does not grow to be any easier after becoming part of a community. It tears up tender roots. It feels like putting on a winter coat that has somehow become too small or grown too large. I wear it anyway. But inside heavy boots, the trauma remains and my feet are killing me.

In the evening sky
New moon makes a sideways smile
Above the river

July 11, 1986
Salmon, Idaho

Raz and I head south through the Bitterroot Valley, taking the back roads and train tracks when we can. The air is filled with moist smells of green hay and summer rain. Stopping to visit friends and camping beside the road in the evenings, we both limp along. Blisters develop on one tender foot, then another.

A few days later Raz calls it quits and returns to Missoula. I continue through the mountains and into Idaho.

Now I am camped on the edge of the Salmon River in a little island park in the town of the same name. My ankle is swollen. I put it into the cool flowing water, sinking in the soft mud up to my calf. Afterward I pack it in the ice I got from a nearby store. Ten herons rise and paddle lazily through a pale blue sky, almost aimlessly, then in unison. They disappear over a stand of cottonwoods behind me.

I study the wiggly red line on the map that snakes south, then west through forest and mountains before finally turning east across the Arco Desert, outlined with a broad pink border. East is the direction I want to go and this route assigns an extra 1,000 miles to an already tardy summer journey. But I am looking forward to the pleasures of the wilderness that creeps close to the side of the road, and to the prospect of visiting my friend Jon Marvel, whom I have not seen in nearly 20 years.

My ankle does not seem to be improving and I think about the possibility of having to give up walking for a bicycle. It is a discouraging thought. I enjoy riding bicycles; while living in Missoula, as in other towns, I used them to get around. But it is not the same as walking, moving slowly on the ground, feeling every rock and stone.

In the evening a man dressed in ragged cut-off shorts and a blue denim work shirt saunters over to my camp. A green bandanna circles his head over closely cropped sandy brown hair. He stops short, interrupting my riverside reverie, and stares hard at my pack.

"Wow! I thought your pack was a motorcycle and I came over to see what kind it was."

We both break into laughter; I am nearly rolling on the ground.

"Well, that's another one of life's great illusions," he manages through an explosion of guffaws. I think to myself, Yeah, that's just what I need, a motorcycle. We laugh some more.

Tim Gazda lives in an old blue bus parked in the tall grass not far from where I am camping. He has been traveling around the state for the summer, stopping every now and then to work. After his surprise at my not talking wears off, he tells me of his own "word fast" in Colorado, and how he had been riding horses north to his home in Priest River after ending a stormy relationship and running into trouble with the authorities. It was his attempt to find what was important in life, but several weeks into his trip he discovered that the homemade packs didn't fit properly on the animals and were causing serious withers infections, and he had to abandon his journey.

I rub my ankle in sympathy.

"Nature is a teacher, and being out in nature like that is healing, and saved me," he explains. "Besides, I had a violent temper, always getting into fights and trouble with the law when I was living in town.

"But me and God made an agreement, so I don't fight anymore. And one day I'm gonna take another ride, maybe up to Canada." He laughs. "But right now I got my bus. I'm free and happy. All I need now is a woman and a dog." He smiles at himself and his loneliness.

I touch my ankle and think again about the option of biking. I smile. It is an attractive option, one in keeping with the spirit of my beliefs, but for now I opt for the slow and deliberate encounter of life around me that is walking. Today it includes a painfully swollen ankle and sitting beside the river with Tim.

The mountain rises
Behind two rusting tractors
Clouds and broken dreams

July 21, 1986
Stanley, Idaho

Jon comes down through a stand of pine trees to meet me on the road. Behind him the Sawtooth Mountains rise jaggedly into the sky. We have not seen each other since we both lived in Chicago, where he and his wife, Stephanie, attended the University of Chicago. I was working as a community organizer, leading rent strikes in East Garfield Park on the west side of the city with the

American Friends Service Committee through VISTA (Volunteers in Service to America). Since then, Jon has become a successful architect with two homes, one at the foot of the Sawtooths and the other just south of Sun Valley in Hailey. Stephanie has become a weaver, and they now have two children. In our short embrace, the 17 years of separation begin to disappear.

The acrid smell of a recent fire is in the air . . . a lightning storm. Jon is philosophical about the destruction visited on his garage and the loss of family treasures. "Our most loved possessions can be taken without notice. At least we still have the cabin," he says, "and no one was hurt."

I remember the rain that had fallen and the thunder and lightning that had accompanied it as I huddled one night in my tent 100 miles away. I could not have imagined how connected I was to the event and its effects.

Jon looks much the same as when I last saw him. At 39 he has grayer hair and he is perhaps a bit heavier. After my time in school, I am a bit heavier as well. On seeing him and hearing his voice, I am flooded with memories of youthful searching and rebellion. We stay up while the household sleeps, regarding each other across the dining room table. We are as amazed at our survival as at the seeming incongruence of our chosen paths.

We look at ourselves through each other's eyes. Jon does not hide his concern for my safety, if not for my sanity, with all this walking and especially my silence.

"You're getting too old for this sort of stuff," he says. "Look at you, you can barely get around." He shakes his head in mock disgust and laughs.

He is at least partly right. My ankle is still giving me trouble and when I walk it is more of a hobble. What really bothers Jon is not the walking; he can understand that more or less as an environmental statement. It is the not talking that causes his brow to wrinkle.

Several days later at his Hailey home we continue our visit.

"I find it strange," he says. "People just don't stop talking."

I remind him of when he was so impressed with Meher Baba, an East Indian sage who had given up speaking, that he and some friends had planned a pilgrimage to India to visit him. Baba's death in 1964 ended their plans. Jon smiles as he remembers an earlier time.

"Well, that was different." He laughs. "You're no sage, you're just John." Our talks are filled with laughter; Jon's gentle jabs and jibes to see if he can get me to speak out loud after so many years are all in fun, reminding me of the danger of taking oneself too seriously.

In the end Jon doubts that my silent pilgrimage will have any great effect on the fate of the world, but he acknowledges that doing something is better than doing nothing. At least I am, in his words, "contributing to the diversity of human life."

Our talks are filled with laughter; Jon's gentle jabs and jibes to see if he can get me to speak out loud after so many years are all in fun, reminding me of the danger of taking oneself too seriously.

"Though there is a certain freedom to walking and pilgrimage, it's not something I would do," he says.

I wonder if I will ever have a family. For the time being I take comfort in the words of Thomas Merton, the Trappist monk who was no stranger to solitude and silence: "There are always people who dare to seek on the margin of society, who are not dependent on social acceptance, not dependent on social routine, and prefer a kind of free-floating existence under a state of risk. And among these people, if they are faithful to their own calling, to their own vocation and to their own message from God, communication on the deepest level is possible. And the deepest level of communication is not communication, but communion. It is wordless. It is beyond words and it is beyond speech, and it is beyond concept."

It is a good visit with my friend. It leaves me with much to reflect on as I continue.

CHAPTER 13

The Desert:
Carrying Water

Pink in morning sky
Desert blooms beside the road
So I stop to watch

August 3, 1986
Arco, Idaho

I awake in some grass between the highway and the railroad tracks. The moon is just a smile and the morning star an eye. I pack my things and linger over breakfast in a café. Across the street a sign on the face of a stone building reads in proud electric letters, welcome to arco, the world's first atomic city.

I am surprised by this information. There does not seem to be much in the way of industry around here to warrant a nuclear power plant, just agriculture and tourism. Then the shaded area with the wide pink border begins to make sense. It is just east of town, the Idaho National Engineering Laboratory (INEL). I look more closely at my map and read the small print, U.S. Atomic Energy Commission Reservation. It looks as if it takes up half of the Arco Desert, and I have to walk right through it.

I remember someone mentioning the laboratory before as the site of antinuclear demonstrations. All I can think about is where I will be able to get water.

A waitress at the café tells me that after the rest area at the edge of the desert, it is 50 miles to the next water, in Idaho Falls. If there is an easier way, I know I would take it.

When I leave Arco for the Big Lost River rest area, my last chance to get water for the day, it is afternoon. I pass through Butte City: a few houses, a bar, and gas pumps. Several people stop and offer me rides. I thank them, and before they drive off I hand them my little printed introduction.

Some nod their approval or show their amazement. Then I watch them shake their heads as they disappear into the desert.

The land flattens. Storm clouds move overhead all day, but the rain falls behind me. I play the banjo as I walk, sweat pouring down my face behind silvered sunglasses. About 100 yellow, white, and silver air-conditioned buses marked INEL, carrying off-duty workers, pass me on their way back to town. Near the day's end, as my shadow stretches out in front of me, I grow discouraged. I have been walking for hours and wonder if my map is wrong and there is no rest area, only the site of the first nuclear reactor.

INEL is also the birthplace of the nuclear navy. It seems odd to be thinking of submarines in such surroundings. I am sure I appear just as odd to passersby.

The rest area is hidden in a stand of trees that I have been watching grow from a low dark green line on the horizon for the last several hours. It has restrooms with hot and cold water, freshly mown grass, and shaded tables. I am cooking my dinner on my gas stove when a man in a little sports car pulls into a parking spot near me. He is young and casually dressed, with longish blond hair. I do not know if he is heading to Idaho Falls, but right away the possibility of asking him to carry some water for me pops into my head. He steps out of his car and weaves over toward my table.

"Hey, you wanna party?" His voice slurs.

"What's a beautiful black man like you doin' here? Come on with me. Let's go party." It is apparent to me that neither my water nor I will be going anywhere with this fellow. He shakes my hand but does not want to let it go. I simply smile and continue to smile as he asks me again to go off with him. When I do not answer except to shake my head no, he asks another question.

"Say what?" He waits for my response, which is a gentle pulling of my hand until it falls free of his, and then he asks again, "Say what?" He steps back into his car mumbling something I cannot hear, then starts it up and drives away. "Okay, screw you!"

The silence returns. I roll out my bag on a tabletop to sleep, but before I doze off another car pulls up. To my surprise, the man inside is a sign language interpreter from Pennsylvania. He's on his way east and agrees to drop off a bottle of water for me at the next 20-mile marker. That is a gallon of water I will not have to carry. I go to sleep feeling pleased.

In the night, coyotes scream and a helicopter on patrol hovers low above where I sleep. The searchlights stab into the darkness, and for a moment I am afraid that they will find me.

Special response teams from the INEL man the helicopter for routine perimeter surveillance flights as part of an airborne security program that began in 1984, to raise the level of security of America's "special nuclear materials." The 894-square-mile site has little farming around it, but after a bomb killed more than 240 U.S. Marines in Lebanon in October 1983, INEL trained a special response team in counterterrorism to overlay the more traditional security measures.

In 1985, while flying a random pattern over the INEL, one of these surveillance flights discovered a cave used hundreds of years ago by the Shoshone and Bannock people. Their ancestral home extended across the entire length of the Snake River Plain, across the INEL, and into the north beyond the rugged Bitterroot Mountains. To the southeast they lived on the northern fringe of the Great Basin and in the bison country of Wyoming and Montana.

Traveling in family groups from winter and summer villages, these ancient peoples followed paths across the INEL site toward the Big Lost River, one of the waterways that reliably flowed in the spring. The cave contained many items that provided archeologists with insight into how these early travelers lived, including well-preserved perishables such as rush mats, hides, rabbit fur, and robes. As I prepare to cross the desert, I ask the spirit of the native people to guide me.

Beside the road, death
Empty eyes stare at blue sky
Spirits fly at night

August 5, 1986
Arco Desert, Idaho

Morning starts before sunrise with a maintenance woman banging trash can lids in the desert stillness. A long dark cigarette hangs from her mouth. She curses and swats at a moth.

"Damn those millers." She disappears into the men's bathroom, leaving a sign at the door saying it is closed for cleaning. After a few minutes she emerges, still wearing dirty yellow rubber gloves. The cigarette, now a long gray ash, breaks off and falls to the ground.

When I get up she comes over with a dented green thermos of coffee and offers me her green plastic cup.

"Hi, how ya doin', honey? What're you doin' out here? You the walker?"

I nod yes.

"I thought so, 'cause yesterday I seen you in town."

I try explaining to her my plan about the water. I even show her a note I have written and point to different locations on the map, but I do not think she understands.

Another woman pulls in on her way to work somewhere on "the site," what locals call INEL. She looks at my note and map, but I guess it is too early in the morning for me to make any sense to anyone.

"Hey, I can fill those water jugs up if ya want," says the maintenance woman, picking up the two extra jugs sitting on the picnic table.

I thank her in sign language, pulling my hand down from my mouth almost as if I were blowing a kiss. No spigots are visible outside, and the bathroom washbasins are too small to get a jug under the stream of water.

"I'll get 'em to ya before ya go," she says.

During breakfast I look over my map. I see that 10 miles east of the rest area is a turnoff from Route 20 to Route 26, heading southeast through Atomic City and on to Blackfoot. I look at it again, and then once more, and only then realize that the jug of water I gave the man last night to put by the next 20-mile marker may end up on Route 20. I will have to assume the water has gone that way.

I am angry with myself for not being more careful. The anger comes from fear. I have never crossed a desert before, and in this new environment, water and dehydration have become major issues

I am angry with myself for not being more careful. The anger comes from fear.

of survival. I have been procrastinating all morning. I am not sure that I am prepared to face this desert. I look at the map again. It is about 50 miles to Idaho Falls. Walking 25 miles for two days would do it but that means I will have to spend at least one night on INEL property. I have been told that you are not allowed to stop or camp. I have already experienced that helicopter last night. Then I see it. About midway between the rest area and Idaho Falls, the map shows what looks like a small lake. My spirits rise a little and I start across the desert with the extra weight of three gallons of water. The weight makes me cranky and, given the heat, I am not even sure three gallons will be enough. Still, I walk on.

I have not gone two miles when a red four-wheel-drive pickup with a kayak on top and New Mexico plates passes me, then turns around, comes back, and stops. The woman inside is tanned from the sun, with steel gray eyes that show surprise and curiosity.

"I didn't expect to see anyone walking along this road," she says. "Do you need a ride?"

I hand her the note.

"Oh, that's the problem," she says, smiling.

She parks her truck and steps out to visit.

"What is that you're carrying," she asks, pointing to the banjo sticking out of my pack, "a tennis racquet?"

I mime the answer, and in a few minutes we are sitting beside the road and I am playing "Life's Celebration" on the banjo. The music sounds particularly sweet here in the desert. The morning is still cool, the shadows long and the sky crystalline blue.

Her name is Karuna and she has just finished kayaking 120 miles of the Salmon's middle fork. She is on her way to Jackson, Wyoming, to do some hiking in the Tetons and visit her sister. I am happy that someone has stopped. Karuna agrees to carry water for me and place it every 20 miles, in two drops, at mile marker 290 and mile marker 309. After she leaves I walk a lot lighter, while the INEL buses grumble by, making up the rush hour traffic in the desert.

Roads lead off from either side of the highway to reactor facilities and to ERB-I, the first nuclear reactor to produce electricity, on December 20, 1951. It has been designated a historical site but I am in no mood to visit; seeing the outlines of the buildings in the distance is enough. After ERB-I comes ERB-II, a hot-fuel examination facility, a transient reactor test facility, and a zero-power plutonium reactor. I guess we are all operating on faith, I hoping the water will be there, and the nuclear scientists hoping to find some way to handle waste and make the technology safe.

As I walk through the desert heat and solitude, sun spirits dance on the horizon, and pools of water on the road reflect the sky. There are no clouds and I never reach the water; the pools are illusions of temperature, terrain, and distance. I think about my father, a lineman for the Philadelphia Electric Company. He took me to see the construction of the company's Peach Bottom-I power plant. Peach Bottom was the pioneering commercial nuclear power plant in the United States. Looking over the construction site my father told me how you could fit in your hand all the fuel needed to produce electricity for an entire city. A little exaggerated, perhaps, but I was impressed. In those days, I had no questions; nuclear plants produced clean, inexpensive energy. Thirty years later, a man walking across this desert, I question all my beliefs.

I think about my father, a lineman for the Philadelphia Electric Company. He took me to see the construction of the company's Peach Bottom-I power plant.

As well as being a laboratory for all kinds of nuclear research, INEL has designated its land as an environmental laboratory to study the effects of human activity on the desert ecology. Some unfortunate discoveries are being made. Beside the road lie the desiccated bodies of hundreds of owls and other raptors. They have been killed by night traffic through the desert, the most frequent cause of death for these nocturnal predators. As a scientist, I hypothesize that it has something to do with headlights and the animals' disorientation. Then the sheer number overwhelms me with a sadness that settles in my soul. I stop and stare into their vacant eyes.

I drink from my canteen. The water tastes as hot as the air around me. It quickly finds its way through my body and evaporates. I hardly have time to sweat. Another red truck slows down and stops. The young man inside sticks his head out the window and calls back to me.

"Hey, do you want a ride out of this damn desert?"

I shake my head no as I hurry up to where he has parked, at least to thank him.

"Well, if I can't give you a ride, then how about some water?" he says. "Though it's still frozen." He produces a plastic jug, frozen solid, and offers it to me.

I stare at it as if it is an object from the moon, but once it is in my hands, for one brief moment I am on the shore of a frozen tarn beneath the summit of Mount Shasta.

"Hey, are you all right?" He looks at me worriedly.

By now I have realized that at the turnoff to Highway 26 the mile markers on Highway 20 lose seven miles, so my first water drop is farther than I can travel in a day, especially in this heat. I have at the most three more miles in me, so I write a note asking if he can drive the jug two mile markers up the road.

"Sure," he says.

For the next two miles I fantasize about the water, about where and when I will find it and how it will taste. But when I reach the second mile marker the water is nowhere to be found. At first I think that maybe he decided he did not like my attitude and kept the water for himself. Then I tell myself that I must have made the whole thing up, that it was an illusion, a mirage, a hallucination. I hurry on toward the next marker. There it is, a little farther on, between the second and third markers. He has used his odometer to place the water exactly two miles from our meeting place. A wave of relief washes over me. The ice has begun to melt. I take my first sip of the freezing cold water and my forehead explodes in delicious pain.

I walk a little farther, taking sip after cooling sip of ice-cold water. It is four in the afternoon when I see what looks like a small pond off the north side of the road. I breathe a sigh of relief.

I find a spot close to the water to set up camp. It is a watering hole for cattle, surrounded by hoofprints and cattle manure in various stages of decomposition. The water is not inviting to drink, but I boil some to use for cooking. Tonight I am having beans and rice. The INEL rush hour begins, yellow and silver buses as far as I can see. I have walked 28 miles today. I collapse onto my backpack and watch the stars that begin to twinkle in the velvet darkness, along with stabs of amber headlights rushing through the desert night. In the east, there is a faint glow from the lights of Idaho Falls. I hear the helicopter searching in the sky, back and forth, back and forth. Maybe they are looking for me, but I have no fire. I use only my stove. The night turns cold. I fall asleep listening to the piercing call of the coyotes.

On a desert road
Sunrise takes the longest time
Blooming like a rose

August 6, 1986
Arco Desert, Idaho

I start in the early morning. The road is still quiet before the INEL rush. I walk only a few hundred yards before coming to the water that Karuna left the day before. It is still cool from the desert night. I walk the first five miles and then stop to rest in the shade of a fleece jacket draped between my pack and some sagebrush. I sip the water. It is still early and I am already hiding from the sun.

Walking again, the next five miles, I do not hurry. I seem to be standing on my shadow, unable to project myself out of this desert into a future. I am always in the desert, on the edge of existence. After each step, I am still here, trying to remember something, a question—what is faith?

When a van of INEL employees on their way home pulls up beside me, I stare at them with the vacant eyes of a thousand desiccated owls lying by the side of the road. I smile. They all smile back, and someone hands me a can of beer, and they drive on. The can is cold in my hand. I stop to drink it and roll the cool smoothness across my face. A voice tells me that I should not drink it because the alcohol will dehydrate me, but I do not listen.

In a blur, I walk five more miles, and then five more. At the mile marker there is another bottle of water; this one is frozen. It is not one that I had asked to be left, but I take it just the same and carry it melting all the way to Idaho Falls, delirious at my good fortune, the desert behind me but now always with me.

As I walk into the city I cannot help thinking of Peace Pilgrim and her journey. Did she ever cross the desert? For my thesis at the University of Montana, I had written about my journey and the events that have brought me to the place in life where I am now, but just as important was my looking at the journey and life of Peace Pilgrim as a way to understand my own.

In 1908, Peace Pilgrim Mildred Norman was born into a poor farming family living on the outskirts of a small northeastern town. Despite the poverty, she saw wealth in the natural surroundings of fields, woods, and creeks. "There was room to grow," she writes, calling this her "very favorable beginnings."

In contrast to the tolerant and humble person of later years, Norman was the captain of her high school debating team and cultivated a commanding presence that demanded others take notice. Makeup and expensive clothes became her trademark, and she often made special trips to Atlantic City to get her shoes dyed to match her other fashion accessories. Surprisingly, she was not a tolerant person, especially of other races, and disapproved of her sister's friends, whom she felt were not of her class.

Ultimately, the realization that money and things would not bring happiness got Peace Pilgrim started on the preparation for her pilgrimage. "Finally I had to find another way," she writes. "The turning point came when in desperation and out of a very deep seeking for a meaningful way of life, I walked all one night through the woods. I came to a moonlit glade and prayed."

After her death, two longtime friends, John and Ann Rush, speculated that the combined unhappiness stemming from an unsuccessful marriage and the death of her father in an automobile accident two years prior prompted Norman to walk in the woods that night, which led to the vision of her pilgrimage.

Inner peace was the key to Peace Pilgrim's pilgrimage; without it, she writes, no other peace can be attained, and she defines four steps, besides adopting a humble stature, that she took in preparation. The first was "a right attitude toward life. Being willing to face life squarely and get down beneath the surface of life where the verities and realities are found."

The second step had to do with living a harmonious life. Reminiscent of the earliest theories of ecology, Peace Pilgrim professed that certain laws govern the created worlds and beings, not the "eye for an eye" laws of the Old Testament, but principles more in keeping with Barry Commoner's "Laws of Ecology" dealing with the interrelatedness of the natural environment. The further we move from adhering to these principles, the more difficulty we create for ourselves. "We are our own worst enemies," writes Peace. "So I got busy on a very interesting project. This was to live all the good things I believed in."

The third step was finding a special place in life's pattern.

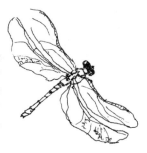

"No two people have exactly the same part to play in God's plan. There is a guidance which comes from within to all who listen." She suggests that people try seeking that guidance in a receptive silence. From her own silence, she received "wonderful insights," and at first she helped people in simple ways with errands, gardening projects, and reading to them. She later worked with "troubled teenagers, the psychologically disturbed, and the physically and mentally handicapped." She writes, "My motives were pure and much of my work did have a positive and good effect."

This was a startling statement even for Peace Pilgrim, in a historical period given over to skepticism. I think her statement is misleading inasmuch as it suggests that we should act only when we have determined that our motives are pure. Such a prerequisite might preclude any action, no mater how ingenuous, that can effect change in our world.

Peace Pilgrim comes closest to touching on this idea when she states, "We begin to prepare for the work that we have to do and customarily we have no idea what we are preparing for."

In January 1953, the same year Peace Pilgrim began her pilgrimage, Henry G. Bugbee published his paper "The Moment of Obligation in Experience" (*Jounal of Religion*, January 1953), in which he explores the difficulty of determining the ultimate justification for any action, whether our motives be pure or not. However, he suggests that the effects of our actions, regardless of their motives, can be for the good: "That spirit out of which men may benefit each other most profoundly seems to bear on their actions, however complex and planned, with simplicity and directness. Perhaps even an intention of benefiting others is irrelevant to our capacity to do so."

Through insight into the nature of the creative process we can transcend this fascination with purity of motive. Granted, motives are an important consideration because they move us through the process of change, development, and evolution in the organization of our subjective life. Peace Pilgrim comes closest to touching on this idea when she states, "We begin to prepare for the work that we have to do and customarily we have no idea what we are preparing for." This creative state is similar to the liminal phases in van Gennep's study of rites of passage, when the pilgrim is connected neither to where she has been nor where she is going. In the words of Brewster Ghiselin in *The Creative Process* (University of California Press, 1985), "Yet, it is only as the work is done that the meaning of the creative effort can appear and that the development of the artist brought about by it is attained."

The fourth and final step of Peace Pilgrim's preparation was "the simplification of life." "Just after dedicating myself to service," she writes, "I felt that I could no longer accept more than I need while others in the world have less then they need. This moved me to bring my life down to a need level. I thought it would be difficult. I thought it would entail a great many hardships, but I was quite wrong. There is a great freedom in simplicity of living, and after I began to feel this, I found harmony in my life between inner and outer well-being."

No special order is necessary in the steps of preparation to inner peace. Peace Pilgrim even suggests that they could be condensed or expanded. "The first step for one may be the last step for another," she acknowledges. "So just take whatever steps seem easiest for you, and as you take a few steps, it will become easier for you to take a few more."

This articulation of Peace Pilgrim's inner pilgrimage touches me deeply. For me her spirit serves as a guide and her words as a crude map, as I realize that I have embarked on the invisible journey. We all have. As Thomas Merton says: "The geographical pilgrimage is the symbolic acting out of an inner journey. The inner journey is the extrapolation of the meaning and signs of the outer pilgrimage, one can not have one without the other. It is best to have both."

On New Year's Day, 1953, Mildred Norman left behind all claims to her name, property, and personal history. She took the name Peace Pilgrim, and with the Pasadena Tournament of Roses Parade as a backdrop, she began her pilgrimage. In 1981, after walking for 28 years, Peace Pilgrim made what she called her "glorious transition to a freer life" when she was killed in an automobile accident near Knox, Indiana.

Find ways to create community as you make your Planetwalk. Writing letters to new and old friends connects them. Mahatma Gandhi believed that by publishing his journals he created community, and at the same time provided community service by writing on difficult issues that demanded the community's attention. Consider stopping to offer your services as a volunteer in a new town or neighborhood that you are passing through.

Unlike the millenarian pilgrims of the past, who interpreted vague signs alluding to the world's imminent destruction, today's peace pilgrims, and perhaps the world at large, recognize the eschatological threat of not only nuclear annihilation but also climate change and social disruption. What makes this apocalyptic vision more real and therefore more demanding of our action is our realization that it is of our own creation and not the product of any particular religious doctrine or superstitious interpretation of the vagaries of nature. The motivations and goals of the new pilgrim incorporate that which is intensely personal with universal concerns for peace and the environment shared by all.

The importance of Peace Pilgrim is not her apparent saintliness or purity of motive, but her humanness and the sincerity of her actions. For in her sincerity, she is humble and ordinary, a person who has accepted the obligation of extraordinary action, as does Kurosawa's hero in *Ikiru* who uses the last year of his life in the action of service, and like other pilgrims on the path of peace, with people and nature. In "The Moment of Obligation in Experience," Henry Bugbee writes:

"We may find ourselves acting under difficulty; our resources may be taxed to the limit; we may be faced with the most uncertain future; and the failure of enterprises on which we have set our hearts may stare us in the face; yet under genuine obligation, we may stand and stand firm, we may act decisively."

The gas station attendant calls my friends John and Patsy Shipley. I had met John and his ten-year-old son parked in a tractor-trailer admiring the view on a mountain pass in Montana. I promised to visit them when I reached Idaho Falls. While we wait for John, the attendant and I talk.

"I seen you on the highway yesterday," he says. He reads my little handout and then we trace my route from California on a map hanging on the wall.

"I am really pleased to meet you," he says.

He is young, perhaps in his early twenties.

"I am really pleased to meet you," he repeats. This time we

shake hands. When John arrives, he takes my pack in his pickup, but does not understand why I follow him to his home on foot, playing my banjo the whole way. It is a nice reunion and a good visit. Later, a local church gives me a room at Nelson's, a men-only hotel above a downtown bar. There a sign reads, under new management, absolutely no girls allowed, and no ladies of the night, the girls are out of business.

I dream of coyotes, hawks, and the desert.

"When a man walks in the fear of God, he knows no fear, even if he were to be surrounded by wicked men. He has the fear of God within him and wears the invincible armor of faith. This makes him strong and able to take on anything, even things which seem difficult or impossible to most people."

—St. Symeon the New Theologian
Sayings of the Desert Fathers:
The Practical and Theological

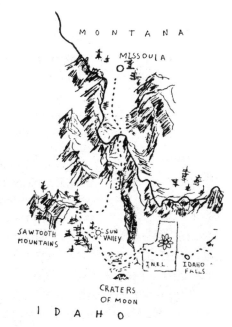

CHAPTER 14

Yellowstone and the Plains: Bears and Missiles

Waking in the grass
Sunrise wet with morning dew
Waking by the road

August 13, 1986
Jackson Hole, Wyoming

I come down the back way from Teton Pass, along the old road closed to motorized vehicles that switchbacks down the mountain to the valley. It has been a long time since I have been in a town so busy with tourist traffic. Cars jam the streets, their exhaust yellowing the air and adding to the discomfort of the summer heat. I want to hurry through and find a quiet place to camp. In the morning I can walk the ten miles or so to meet my friends in Kelly. These are the people I was on my way to spend the winter with before I decided to stop in Missoula and enroll in the environmental studies program at the University of Montana.

"Hey, do you need a place to sleep?" I look up and meet the eyes of a man who had stopped to offer me a ride a few days earlier as I labored over the pass. His name is Larry.

"Did you eat yet?"

I smile, nod my head, and then shake his hand. He takes me under his wing, leads me down a side street, and deposits me in front of the Good Samaritan Mission. The entrance is in the alleyway. The double doors open into a kitchen and dining area. Beyond the kitchen is a second-hand store. A short, round-bellied man dressed in brown Western-cut slacks and a printed shirt sitting by the door introduces himself as Ron.

"You're almost too late for supper," he says, sounding a little angry. "Let's see if we can find you something to eat." As he leads me through the doors Larry waves and retreats into the street.

It is a hearty meal with barbecued beef, potatoes, fresh vegetables, milk, and coffee, all donated by local merchants. I discover that Ron is not actually angry—he just talks that way. His voice is deep and with his rotund figure, he has the air of Friar Tuck in Sherwood Forest. When I finish my meal, he sends me upstairs to see Orville.

Orville is the mission's chief Good Samaritan. He is sitting at a cluttered desk when I enter his office. With his head bowed as if in prayer, he explains that he is a Christian and that I can stay for seven days. Shyly I raise one finger. His demeanor is solemn and he looks at me through tired eyes. The folds above them droop. After he takes my name and the address from the Planetwalk introduction, he asks me a few questions about my pilgrimage. They are the questions of someone trying to understand how what I am doing fits into his own life. I return downstairs, not sure if I am going to stay.

The sleeping room is in the basement. Nine bunks with mismatched bedding press against the walls. A wagon-wheel chandelier hangs from the freshly painted ceiling. In the center of the room is a Formica table, some chairs, and a jumble of green and yellowed brown couches. The cushions are piled on the floor. Box springs and mattresses are stacked in the spaces between the bunks, ready for a crowded night. In the far corner of a natural rock masonry wall sits a large wood-burning stove. Above it on a clothesline hang a stiff pair of jeans and a dozen or so empty clothespins. A hole in the stone wall lets in the only outside light. A claustrophobic atmosphere pervades the place, yet I decide to stay.

About eight other men are spending the night. Bunks are available but I opt for the firmness of a couch without cushions. I make my choice, and then go over to the park with my banjo to play away the last of the daylight hours. I return just before ten

o'clock, when the lights are shut off and the mission doors are locked. Some sort of argument is going on, escalating. Someone has been drinking. That is against the rules and he is sent away. In the darkness, the dull green exit light gives the appearance of an eternal false dawn. The night talking begins, mixed with sounds of soft snoring.

"I've gotta stay another day." It is a voice I don't recognize, but I listen to the story of how he found a job and is now just getting to the place where he will be able to support himself. "If only I can stay a few more days." In the darkness someone tells him that eight or nine days seems to be the maximum that anyone can stay.

"I'll have to talk to Orville," he says. "I've already been here over a week."

The darkness creates anonymity and a certain closeness, as if the voices are one's own. Then George begins talking in his sleep, moaning until one of the two brothers from Eureka, California, tells him to shut up.

"That's enough, George." George is in his early twenties. He sleeps with a plastic model of an attack helicopter and a picture from the movie *Top Gun* of actor Tom Cruise sitting in the cockpit of a navy jet. He plays war games during the day. I do not sleep very well. Someone's watch beeps every hour. Beep-beep . . . beep-beep . . . beep-beep . . .

In the morning, I leave Orville's mission to sit and write in the coolness of the city park before I start out for Kelly to find my friends at the yurt village.

In the morning I leave Orville's mission to sit and write in the coolness of the city park before I start out for Kelly to find my friends at the yurt village. A serendipitous meeting with Lyn Dalebout in a bookstore just off the square presents me with the option of carrying my pack or having her drive it the 15 miles to Kelly. Driving it there would make her feel a lot better about my not accepting a ride, she tells me.

It takes me all of breakfast to ponder the ethical question, "If I don't use motorized vehicles, why would I allow some of my stuff to be transported in a car?" As I down the last cup of coffee, I remember that I have been in this situation before, and that many times I have declined such offers of assistance, but not for the sake of ethical purity. How, I ask myself, could I justify sending a letter by mail if I knew that it would be put into trucks and planes to get where it is going? How could I in good conscience eat food delivered by oil-guzzling big rigs crisscrossing the country—not to mention all the petrochemicals going into growing the food? Like those other times, in the end I decide that I am not that pure, and leave town carrying only my daypack and banjo. My friend can follow and feel a little better.

Lyn lives in Kelly, and we have been corresponding faithfully for about three years. While we have never met before, this feels like a great reunion and nothing short of a minor miracle. Without my heavy pack, the 12-mile walk is a delight filled with music and casual meetings along the road.

For centuries the nomadic people of western China have lived in traditional yurts—rugged, portable structures that are warm in winter and cool in summer, able to withstand the most extreme conditions. Some of the comforts of modern technology have been added to the Kelly yurts without sacrificing the qualities that make them a unique living experience.

The yurt village nestled in the shadow of the Tetons was a recreation park catering to trailer and motorhome camping until Dick Simmon, a modern yurt builder, leased the land. He had a vision of establishing simple community living within the influence of the mountains he felt were sacred. After a long struggle, the county made a landmark ruling classifying the yurts as permanent structures. Eleven yurts are now allowed on the 16-acre parcel.

It is a sensible ruling. After a flood whipped through the town in 1926, it was determined that the community had been built on a flood plain and that floods and slides would be a natural occurrence. Before that, Kelly had been bigger than Jackson Hole, but the prospect of rebuilding and being wiped out again effectively quashed any major development. Rebuilding would be too expensive, unless you lived in something like a yurt.

Bordering the National Elk Refuge, which harbors the largest herd in the country, Kelly is off the main road and stays quiet even during the busiest part of the tourist season. I stay almost a week. When I leave I follow a trail of lingering goodbyes out to the road. Dick and his son, Live, walk with me a while across a meadow and along a dirt road. Dick carries my pack much of the way.

It begins raining. Alone again, I walk the road of smooth asphalt into the national park, facing the oncoming traffic, sometimes waving at the people inside their cars, who seem disappointed that I am not a moose or a bear. They snap their cameras just the same. It is early evening when I find the climbers' ranch, a collection of log

The yurt village nestled in the shadow of the Tetons was a recreation park catering to trailer and motorhome camping until Dick Simmon, a modern yurt builder, leased the land.

cabins and newly constructed bathhouses next to the mountain. The charred trees, someone tells me, are from last year's fire. I check into a cabin.

In the bunk next to mine is Mary Beth Moore, a naval intelligence officer on her way to Hawaii. Her job is to interpret for her squadron the military threat of any Soviet encounter at sea. She likes her job and sees it as her way of contributing to keeping the peace. We talk very little about the military. We talk more about bears—she is reading a book on the dangers of bears attacking humans. Fear of being the victim of a bear attack has changed her vacation plans. This is how she is dealing with the fear, she tells me. Climbing frightens her too, but just the same, she is scheduled for an intermediate climb with a class and instructor in the morning.

A little later, Steve and Mary Pat arrive from Missoula. It is a fine reunion.

Mountain clouds gather
Ravens fly tossed by the wind
And then the rain falls

August 19, 1986
Teton National Park, Wyoming

In the morning after breakfast, Steve and I sit down to play some music. He has brought his banjo and is eager for another lesson. I find great satisfaction in the deep communication of transmitting a tune or a technique and then hearing it played back by someone else in his or her own style.

The persistent pain in my ankle convinces me not to attempt climbing with Steve and Mary Pat as we had planned. Instead I decide to continue north through the park to Yellowstone with Cinda Spencer, a friend from my stay in Kelly. Cinda is an Outward Bound instructor visiting the yurt village while taking a climbing break. She suggests that I take the cross-country route around Jackson Lake, in the middle of the park. I had all but resigned myself to walking the busy road, so I welcome the company and we make plans to rejoin Steve and Mary Pat at a hot spring just outside of Yellowstone in three days.

We walk through the meadow that parallels the highway to the main ranger station at Jenny Lake to get our backcountry passes. The place is packed with cars, campers, and tour buses. The Trans-American Asian tour guide herds a group of young and older Korean tourists from their bus to the gift shop and restrooms. They speak softly and dutifully snap pictures of each other and everything else. They remind me that my own camera is nearly out of film.

We leave the crowd and follow the last bit of trail to Jackson Lake. Thunder and the blue sky turning gray, moose grazing, and elk running to hide are signs before the rain. It starts in the night and lasts until past dawn, making it difficult to get an early start. We stay squeezed together in the two-person tent that is really just big enough for one. After breakfast, it rains some more and we see sporadic flashes of blue sky.

Cinda walks ahead of me most of the time at an incredible pace, a carryover, she confesses, from her Outward Bound training. She has me struggling to keep up, something I am not used to doing. She uses two walking sticks like the poles of a cross-country skier, which for a while is a source of great amusement to me, until I realize the benefit of balance.

We enjoy each other's company. Our moods and feelings change from joy to discontent inside cold exhaustion and back again as we move in and out of sun and rain, over the uncomfortable terrain of variegated lakeshore stone, rock, and boulders of deep rose quartz, then sink into soft mud. The wildlife crowds close between the mountain and the lake. Frolicking otters stop to stare from dark hooded eyes; moose and osprey, seagulls and geese are woven into a tapestry, the texture of which is wet, full, and charged with the yellow-green electricity of eternal spring.

None of us has much to say when we hook up with Mary Pat and Steve. As we soak together in the steamy waters of a shallow hot spring beside a little river, we are simply glad we have come to be here. There are no great revelations. In the end we say goodbye, each taking a little of the others along with the mountain and flashes of yellow-green.

Blue-red dragonflies
Hover above steamy springs
Summer turns to fall

August 1986
Yellowstone National Park, Wyoming

I enter Yellowstone from the south and check in at the ranger station. The woman behind the counter is interested in the idea of walking through the park, but it soon becomes apparent that I will not be able to make a designated campsite each night. Camping in developed sites is mandatory. She refers me to an older ranger who tells me to just camp well off the road, tie my food up in a tree, and not build any fires. It is already late in the afternoon and the next camp area is ten miles away.

When I ask about trails and old service roads, the talk turns to bears. It is clear that the rangers prefer keeping me near the main road where I can be seen by the patrol. I do not mind, though the idea of a quiet forest trail is more appealing. The heaviest automobile traffic is during the summer months from 10 a.m. to 1 p.m. I have grown somewhat accustomed to walking highways and tend to tune out the intrusion of traffic.

My first campsite is in view of the road and my sack of food hangs between two pine trees 100 feet away from me, 15 feet in the air. I am still nervous about the bears, especially after hearing the stories of attacks. During the night I jump at the sound of a mouse scratching in the leaves.

In the morning a steady rain is falling. I stand beneath the lodge pole pines when it falls too hard for me to go on. The clouds hang low and the air is charged with lightning. Claps of thunder shake the ground as I cross the continental divide (7,988 feet in elevation) before dropping down to Grant Village on Yellowstone Lake.

Flowers beside the road, cars passing making spray, windshield wipers swaying, my arms swinging and my feet keeping rhythm with my breathing, in . . . out . . . in . . . out . . . slowly making morning steam like the smoky gray geyser basin. Despite the signs motorists stop and venture beyond the barriers. Rangers

Be conscious of your feelings. Examine your fears as well as your joys. On the road, fear can be a sign that your inner journey requires attention. Do not let your fear possess you. Look at it honestly, gather your courage, and listen to the lesson that is hidden in the trembling of your heart. Let go and take the next step.

follow to scold them before they can be scalded by the hot springs. I hear stories of people breaking through the crust and falling in.

It is in this wilderness that I feel the elemental truth of walking, something important and vital not only to me but to all life, to human growth, even as we reach out toward the stars. Sensing our environment in the most elementary manner, with its wildness and diversity, is necessary for our survival. I become thankful for the park and understand better why we must continue to preserve wilderness. It is an understanding best experienced.

Inside the river
Three fish swim against the stream
We watch from above

August 1986
Fishing Bridge
Yellowstone National Park, Wyoming

I spend an evening at the Bridge Bay campfire gathering, listening to Barb, a seasonal ranger from Vermont, talk about the history of the park, the buffalo, and some of the other wildlife. She gives the usual warnings about not getting close to the buffalo or the bears, but inevitably some people do not pay attention. A Park Service sign claims that 12 people were gored the previous summer. In bear country I am always careful to keep my distance and hang my food in a tree away from where I sleep.

Controversy has broken out over the killing of buffalo and elk that wander outside the park boundaries. Part of the problem is overcrowding, and the fact that when the boundaries were established, little or no attention was paid to the migratory patterns of the animals. To the horror of many of the ranchers in the area, there is also talk about bringing back wolves, exterminated in the 1930s. A University of Montana study has shown that a majority of park visitors are in favor of reintroduction. I am happy to hear that. The recovery of the northern Rocky Mountain wolf would mean a more balanced and diverse ecosystem. However, I understand the problem of economics that the ranchers need to overcome.

It takes four days to cover the nearly 70 miles around Yellowstone Lake. Outside the park's western gate a half dozen bears make their presence known around the campground where I am staying. When the people at nearby Pahaska Lodge learn that I am sleeping out in a tent, they insist that I stay in one of their cabins.

Cows in an oilfield
Stand around eating green grass
Seeming not to care

September 9, 1986
Powell, Wyoming

Sheridan County was established in 1888 and was originally inhabited by the Crow, Cheyenne, and Sioux, but despite the treaties signed by the settlers to stay away, the Indians were eventually driven out.

I stop again when I reach Powell, about 75 miles east of Yellowstone. I stay at the home of Dave and Diane Bonner, publishers of the local newspaper, who are expecting me. Our mutual friends, Jim and Sharon Willse, arranged my visit in advance. I am welcomed into their home as another member of the family.

During two of the four days I spend in Powell, I visit several classes at Northwest Community College. I enjoy the title of "guest lecturer," though in the end I feel that I have learned much more than I could possibly have taught. I appreciate the level of communication in the classrooms. For the most part the students are there because they want to be. They, as well as the teachers, are interested in new approaches to social problems and innovations in education. I enjoy it so much that when I am asked if I would consider staying to be an instructor for a semester or two, I actually give it some thought.

The highway that leads over the Big Horn Mountains, a road engineer tells me, is the steepest grade in Wyoming, maybe even in the country. I do not question him but marvel at how it clings to the sheer walls of rock as I make my way to the summit. At the least it is a feat of engineering.

It takes a week to cross the mountain range, with elk hunters and a cold blanket of snow close behind me. The snow turns to rain as I come down into Sheridan. Sheridan County was established in 1888 and was originally inhabited by the Crow, Cheyenne, and Sioux, but despite the treaties signed by the settlers to stay away, the Indians were eventually driven out. The area is steeped in the history of Indian wars and skirmishes. Not too far to the north, in Montana, is where Sitting Bull and Crazy Horse defeated Custer at the Battle of the Little Big Horn. I stop to read each historical marker as I make my way into town. It adds to the sense of place that I carry with me.

Aspens turn from green
To red and golden yellow
Clouds are silver gray

September 19, 1986
Sheridan, Wyoming

I am lecturing at Sheridan College when Kathleen Phalen, a CBS television producer, catches up with me. She wants to make a Planetwalk segment for *West 57th,* a newsmagazine to be aired in the winter. Even after I agree and the first few days of shooting are complete, I learn that the idea still has to be sold to the executive producer back in New York. Walking and not talking, for any reason, is viewed as just a bit strange and maybe not the sort of thing that should be put out over the network. But, if they decide to go with the story, Kathleen and her crew will hook up with me again somewhere else along the way.

We say our goodbyes and I head south on the road to Buffalo, a town of about 4,000 that supposedly took its name from its sister city in New York. Word has gone ahead of me, and I am expected to speak at the high school when I arrive.

It is near sunset when I knock on a door and ask for water, presenting my empty water bottle.

"Oh, I know you," says the man who comes to the door. His voice is friendly. "I read about you in the paper a while ago." He disappears into the kitchen. When he returns my plastic bottle is full. I thank him. "Well, have a good trip."

I stop a short way down the road, leaving behind the family in their neat white house. The light is waning when a patrol car pulls up through the tall grass with its spotlight aimed at me. I prepare myself for the encounter. I wince at the light.

"What's going on?" asks the officer, stepping from behind the mounted light with an equally bright flashlight. I almost laugh aloud as several funny answers pop into my mind. Instead, I thank myself for the silence and show him my half-eaten dinner, point over to my sleeping bag, and pantomime sleep. He does not get it and asks again. This time I go for the newspaper with slow and deliberate moves.

"What, you can't hear?"

I nod that I can.

"People are mighty upset about you walking through, pilfering food and water from them."

His words remind me of a time on a lonely road in California. At the same time I look incredulous, miming that I had only asked for some water.

I marvel at how well he has just understood my recent contortions, and hand him my introduction.

"Well, they're upset anyway. Get your things together and I'll take you to the county line."

I point to the part of the introduction that says I have given up using motorized vehicles. He looks at it again and scratches the side of his face thoughtfully.

"Okay, you can stay here tonight, but no begging." he says. "You are a stranger, and you can understand that people are just a bit skittish and curious about you in the area. You sure you don't want me to give you a ride?"

I shake my head no and he leaves. I think that he was probably speaking from his own fears and not really representing the concerns of others. I sleep uneasily just the same. A mile up the road in Banner, a town with a population of about 40, I walk into the general store. Like many of the other small towns I pass through in this part of Wyoming, the general store doubles as a post office. Mae Johnson is the postmaster.

"Is this all the farther you got?" she teases me.

I smile and nod. She insists on feeding me, first giving me half of her vanilla milk shake and then a piece of home-baked cherry pie. Mae used to own the store. Inside there is a small café and she gets the new owner to prepare a snack and lunch to take with me when I leave. In the middle of this exchange, in walks the officer from the night before. He is not happy to see me.

"Hey, Deputy, look who we have visiting us here," says Mae, her voice full of excitement. She puts her arm around my shoulder. "He walked all the way from California."

"Yeah, I know, I got a call about him last night," he says. "I offered him a ride to the county line but he turned it down."

"Well, Lloyd, didn't you know that he doesn't ride in cars?" she asks. "It says right here in the Montana paper that he don't talk neither, and he just earned a master's degree in environmental studies in Missoula. He's walking across the United States." She gives me a big wink as she hands the newspaper clipping to the deputy. He scans it, more out of politeness than anything else, and hands it back.

"I got to go on patrol," he says, picking up a paper cup of coffee and stomping out the door.

"Some people are just like that," says Mae.

I have the feeling that more people are like Mae. I leave after a few hours of playing music, sharing stories from my watercolor journal, and laughing with the customers who come in.

The weather is turning cooler as I start across the Powder River Basin, 70 miles of sandstone colors and faraway ranches dotted with antelope, and mile-long coal trains smoking slowly across the landscape. The freight trains remind me of the time I lived in Chicago during the late 1960s, working as a brakeman on the C&O/B&O. It is a world away now, connected only by a ribbon of steel.

I am speaking to a Sunday school class in Gillette when Kathleen Phalen contacts me through the local newspaper. She and a correspondent, Meredith Viera, will meet me with a camera crew in Sundance, near the South Dakota border.

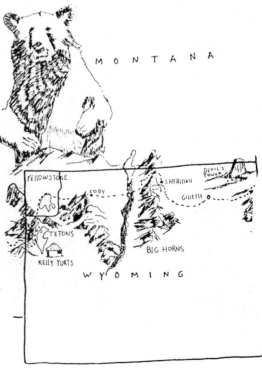

I stop at the high school to visit classes before I leave. On the radio, the newscaster reports on the number of oil wells being shut down and the number still in operation. The price of oil has dropped and Gillette's energy-based boom has gone bust.

Kathleen meets me on the road just as the Black Hills begin to rise. To the north is Devil's Tower (named Mateo Tepee by the Indians, meaning bear lodge). Its stump shape rises 1,280 feet above the valley floor. A little to the east is South Dakota.

CHAPTER 15

Snowstorm: Winter in South Dakota

Beneath the red buttes
Missiles with atomic heads
Wait by grazing cows

October 1986
South Dakota

It showers during the night so I sleep beneath a low railroad bridge. In the morning the highway is still wet as I walk the few miles to the state line and cross from Wyoming to South Dakota. At each footfall, grasshoppers rise on translucent wings into the autumn coolness. I make my way to the rest stop and the travelers' information center. I need a new map.

Beneath rusty-red buttes a herd of cows, patched black and white, graze lazily on tender shoots of new grass growing beside a cyclone fence enclosure. I introduce myself and hand a scribbled note to the two women behind the information counter.

"Is that a missile silo?" I ask by pointing in the direction of the butte, arching my hand like the flight of an ICBM, and ending in a silent mushroom-cloud explosion.

"Oh, yes," they reply matter-of-factly. It is the first silo I have ever seen. There are 150 Minuteman II missile silos with launch control facilities in western South Dakota. I have to tell myself that they will never be used, to stand sanely at the edge of death, and that Mutually Assured Destruction, MAD, really works. I have just studied MAD in the War in the Environment class back at the

University of Montana. Still, I am impressed that just a stone's throw away is a missile capable of reaching the Soviet Union in a matter of minutes with a payload of . . . *Click.* A flash brings me back from my daydream.

"You don't mind if we take your picture?" one of the women asks, just before snapping another photo. "We don't get many people who are walking through this part of the country like you."

I stay a few days in Spearfish, on the northern outskirts of the Black Hills National Forest. There is a lot to see in this part of the state, including the hills themselves, the Homestake mine, the largest gold mine in the hemisphere, and Mount Rushmore. But the seasons are changing and I want to be settled before the snow. I have given up the idea of reaching Madison, Wisconsin, before winter. Minneapolis seems like a more reasonable goal. So I stay in Spearfish, at the home of Kathy Thornes, who has been expecting me since I left Gillette, Wyoming. I am supposed to look into visiting the state college near Kathy's house, but it is "Swarm Week" (homecoming). No one is ready for a lecturer who doesn't speak. It is just as well—I am anxious to get back on the road. I head toward the geographical center of the United States., about 25 miles directly north, but I do not get that far.

Lifting from a pole
Red hawk slides into blue sky
Meadowlark follows

October 9, 1986
Road to Newell, South Dakota

I get as far as Belle Fourche, 11 miles north of Spearfish, and spend the night in a motel as the guest of the county. A newspaper reporter has called the county commissioner, Frank Walton, and arranged it. A strong wind is beginning to blow across the plains; I am grateful for the shelter. On the wall hangs a calendar with a picture of the town's police force and the words, "Remember to stop drug abuse." The date and the muffled sound of the passing storm remind me that the weather is due to turn. With the television on, I fade in and out of sleep, a small boat in a rolling sea.

In the morning, I awake to the traffic sounds and rustling of leaves outside the motel door. I leave town loaded with day-old sweet rolls given to me by a friendly baker. I wave to the people inside the passing cars. The road turns east and heads into the country; I follow. There is a chill in the air. The smell of winter makes me think of snow.

In the night it rains and I sleep in my waterproof bivy sack under a concrete bridge. The sack is small and light, and I can just barely fit, but it keeps me dry in heavy downpours. When I get up, I am impatient with myself over how messy and disorganized I am at packing and getting back to the road.

Efficient packing is a skill that comes and goes with the seasons. If it were still raining, everything would be soaked. I have also missed a dirt road turnoff and have to walk all the way to Belle Fourche reservoir dam, several miles in the wrong direction. I shake my head and wander a few more circuitous miles until I find the road to Newell. A straight road, it cuts through fields of low red-green sorghum. Beside the road and on the distant horizon sit the occasional farmhouse, including barns and collections of silos, not the kind for missiles.

I sleep behind a gas station. When I get up I begin preparing myself for the rain which I know is coming.

I sleep behind a gas station. When I get up I begin preparing myself for the rain which I know is coming. In my silence a mariner's rhyme comes to mind: "Red sky in the morning, sailors take warning. Red sky in the night, sailor's delight." I am not sure I remember it correctly, thinking it over and over, and each time differently. I am far away from any sea but the sunrise is magnificent.

I stop by a church. A half dozen people are there for morning service. Outside on the steps some older women and men ask me where I am going, and at my silent answer respond with a prayer, right there, putting our hands together like a basketball team in a huddle. In my mind, I see us all giving each other the "high five" and running back out onto the court to play ball. I laugh at myself as we walk away.

The sign outside the café reads, open 24 hours, welcome hunters. It makes me nervous to think about walking during hunting season but I try to put it out of my mind. Inside, most men are dressed in chaps and spurs, caps and Western-style hats pulled down, catching the rising steam of hot cups of coffee, their faces lined with wind and hard times. The talk is about looking for cattle. Fresh marigolds are on each windowsill, and I remember spring in Montana and the sweet green smell of cut hay and the hot summer

dream that is Idaho, crossing the Arco Desert. Outside gray clouds gather and cold rain falls. The coffee fills me with jittery warmth.

Hawks fly in gray sky
Snow blowing across the road
Cold chills to the bone

October 11, 1986
Mud Butte, South Dakota

Clouds of geese in ragged *V*s head south. Two cars stop for me but I walk on, past a missile silo and drivers' vacant stares. I am thankful that my winter coat has arrived from Montana by mail in Newell the day before. I have sent my light rain gear and summer tent some 100 miles ahead to Eagle Butte on the Cheyenne River Indian Reservation, where I plan to make another stop.

Highway 212 is the two-lane blacktop road to Eagle Butte. It is one of the more lonely stretches beyond a day's walk. In the western part of the state many towns are just a few houses sitting off the road. If I had taken Route 90, on the other hand, I would be on a big four- or six-lane highway attended by all the well-stocked little towns, restaurants, motels, and service stations that a traveler might want. Many people along the way question my route, calling it desolate, but I do not mind the solitude that comes with walking through the empty plains. Are they empty? I am looking forward to spending time on the reservation.

Mares' tails in the sky
Across the prairie grass bends
Walking with the wind

October 14, 1986
Faith, South Dakota

During the night the temperature drops into the 20s. Coyotes yip as they run across the moonlit prairie. Sometimes they come close, and in chorus with the hooting owls, wake me from my sleep. On the cold days I can hardly write or paint. It is all I can do just to keep going, prepare a hot evening meal, put up and take down the tent.

Today morning sun warms the tent. Walking, I pass another missile silo, and wave at the guards driving by, M-16s beside them. They are dressed in military green with colorful silk scarves puffing out at the open neck of their shirts. Some nod and wave; others stare vacantly ahead. On my little radio I hear that President Reagan and President Gorbachev are making progress in Iceland on their nuclear arms-reduction talks. I smile at the irony and almost unconsciously let the weight of my pack shift to a more comfortable position.

Along the road that rises and falls gradually over rolling hills, I encounter the dead, the roadkills that stare with vacant eyes—coyotes, pheasants, foxes, field mice, snakes, prong-horned antelope, and deer. Two years ago, there was an antelope slaughter after farmers' complaints of too many antelope reached the Department of Fish and Game. In response, Fish and Game issued an inordinate number of hunting permits. Now antelope in the area are scarce, and it is a sensitive issue, especially now that it is hunting season.

Walking all day, I make only the 11 miles to Faith, a small town on the edge of Indian country. The land is flat and an angry wind sweeps across it unchallenged. A reporter for the *Faith Independent* speaks with me about my journey, her manner like that of a housewife comedian. I leave her office laughing all the way to the motel where I take a room. I am tired of sleeping out in the cold.

Hunter's moon rises
Over the stubble hayfields
Making dreams silver

October 16, 1986
Cheyenne River Indian Reservation
South Dakota

The weather is clear and warm as I prepare to leave the town of Faith, just west of the reservation. I roll my winter coat into a tight coil and strap it to my pack. A few days earlier, I used my portable radio to insulate me from the cold, wind, and loneliness that sometimes slip inside. But in the mildness of this day, traffic is light and the only sounds are the whispering of a gentle breeze mingled with the snap of dry twigs and the crunch of gravel beneath my feet. The hills roll out in front of me . . . endlessly.

In the evening I stop and scoot under a barbed-wire fence,

into the tall grass to find sleep. The moon is bright; only the quiet buzz of an occasional passing vehicle and the yapping of dogs from a nearby ranch house break the silence. I give in to sleep.

The night lets go of darkness and the long red line across the eastern horizon finally gives up the sun. I rise with it and continue walking into the first reservation town of Dupree. My map shows it as the county seat, but the wide main street seems deserted and storefronts are boarded up. For breakfast, I find an open café in what looks like a converted mobile home. An attached wooden structure appears to serve as a community center. Inside, the spirit of the community flickers in the eyes of the half dozen old women drinking coffee around a yellow Formica table. They are talking in whispers, loud enough for me to hear.

"He's walking around the world for peace, ya know."

They exchange flirtatious looks and then a peal of laughter rises with great puffs of cigarette smoke.

"What's he gonna do when he gets to the ocean?" one woman asks.

"I dunno," a voice answers.

"Maybe he's gonna swim, hey."

"Well," says another woman after drawing deeply on her cigarette, "I know of only one person who could walk on water."

"That don't look like him," another says. They all look over toward me and laughter fills the small room. I hand one of them my little introduction, which they pass around, if not to read, then to touch and smile at the picture of me walking and playing the banjo.

As they leave the oldest woman stops to shake my hand. She smiles and looks at me for a long time until the smile comes through her eyes and reminds me of the home I have left and the community I am part of and carry with me. The next day I reach Eagle Butte, in the heart of the reservation. Lucy Gange comes out to meet me and welcome me into her home.

The moon rising red
Over South Dakota Hills
Quiet steps at night

October 20, 1986
Cheyenne River Indian Reservation
South Dakota

Lucy lives in a large rented house in town with her four children. During the day she works in the print shop below the tribal telephone company. I arrive on a weekend and am included in whatever activities are planned. I go to the family picnic with a barbecue and volleyball at the end of a 20-minute bike ride just out of town, and on Sunday we go to a church service. Eagle Butte seems less depressed than the other reservation towns I have walked through. The Bureau of Indian Affairs has a large office building in town and there is a community college nearby. I spend three sun-splashed days considering whether to stop here for the season. But the weather is too nice to sit still, so I leave in the morning after breakfast with Lucy and the kids. Saying goodbye, Amber, the youngest daughter, begins crying after the second hug. The family gives me a beaded medallion as a parting gift, which I wear around my neck.

I stop for water at the next small town, Parade, which is only a little store that is someone's home and the local post office. Outside the weathered wood structure sits an old gas pump, red and rusted white. No sale is written on the pump in black block letters. I walk all day and 20 miles into the night, then turn up the dirt road to Donna and Jim's ranch, where Lucy has arranged for me to spend the night.

We talk about cows, cattle, and pigs. The calves are due any day. The pigs stay in little A-frame structures about the size of a three-person tent. Last year they lost nearly 50 calves, worth about $14,000, Donna tells me, as she works over the stove fixing something for me to eat.

We spend the evening trying to put into words how people of the prairie are different from those living in the mountains or by the sea. There does seem to be some difference. Perhaps they are more exposed, naked to the sky, seeing the distant horizon day after day, and feeling the ever-present wind. If you know the land, then you know something of the people.

The phone rings and I end up playing the banjo into the receiver so that Donna's mother can hear. "O-u-spa!" she exclaims. Donna tells me it means "You better hold on to him." I laugh. There are more phone calls to arrange lodging ahead, and a call to Donna and Jim's son's teacher. I learn I will be the show-and-tell at Luke's school in the morning. It is a two-room schoolhouse with only nine students in grades one through three. Two teachers take turns coming to class.

In a muddy sky
Honkers over highway twelve
Fly in ragged lines

October 22, 1986
Cheyenne River Reservation
South Dakota

Ed, who works on the problem of chemical abuse on the reservations, wants to walk with me across the remaining stretch of reservation.

It looks like rain when Ed Parcell, a minister I met at Lucy's church, catches up with me on the road west of La Plant. There has been a shooting in the little town only a short while before. I heard about it on the news as I listened for the weather over breakfast. A service for the victim will be held sometime during the week. Ed, who works on the problem of chemical abuse on the reservations, wants to walk with me across the remaining stretch of reservation. He and the council head are disappointed that they don't have enough time to organize a powwow and sobriety walk to accompany me.

"I will have to do," says Ed. He is a small, compact man with wavy black hair. He unloads his car while his wife waits behind the wheel. First comes a jacket, then a water bottle, then he fills his pockets with dried meat snacks, sunflower seeds—and, almost as an afterthought, a small chrome-plated automatic pistol.

"Things can get pretty wild out here," he tells me. I nod silently as he tucks the gun out of sight. Alcoholism and chemical abuse are the big problems on the "rez," as Ed calls the reservation.

As we walk, Ed talks. "My mother was Indian and my father was a white serviceman from Ellsworth Airbase. Trying to live in two worlds has not been an easy life, but I feel more at home here."

He is not complaining, but just then, a gunshot rings out and we hear a dog barking. Looking back in the distance, we can see someone standing in the doorway of a shack shouting and holding what looks like a rifle. Nervously, Ed urges me to keep walking.

In the evening Ed's wife catches up with us on the road with a light dinner. It is raining. Ed stays with me until my tent is up just off the side of the road. Then he returns to Eagle Butte with his family. He comes back in the morning. I am packed and waiting for him when he drives up.

At lunchtime, Ed's wife appears again with a picnic basket filled with fried chicken, potato salad, and sweet desserts. We have our lunch on the other side of the road, and then it begins to rain. Dressed in rain gear we walk on, with the wind blowing in our faces, past a lone buffalo standing behind a tall game fence. A coyote, almost invisible, runs through waving brown grass. Ed finds a dead skunk, lifts it from the middle of the road, and puts it in the tall green sweetgrass on the road's shoulder.

"*Desapa.*" He whispers the Sioux word as a prayer. We walk on to the swollen Missouri River. Once across the river, we have dinner at a resort with Ed's family. "You'll find it different on this side of the river," he says. It is a view I heard many times as I walked through western South Dakota, not only on the reservation. I wonder if it will be true. We shake hands in a silent goodbye and I go to sleep under the bridge.

> *Meadowlarks fly by*
> *Low across the furrowed ground*
> *Dew gleams on the grass*

October 26, 1986
Seneca, South Dakota

I have not seen the grasshoppers for days. Usually they gather, then scatter, at my feet as I walk along the roadside. Today I have seen only the crickets, crawling and hopping, black against the asphalt. I hear them at night, and in the evening before I stop walking. The temperature dips below freezing and the dew clings frozen to my tent.

I find the cafés as I pass from one town to the next. The Seneca Café looks like someone's house on the outside, and inside it feels like Aunt Ophelia's kitchen in Philadelphia, mustiness mingling with the smell of something good to eat. The harvest-pattern wallpaper comes down from the ceiling halfway to meet the dark, grooved wood panels. Eight chrome stools with green plastic-covered seats line the counter. About a dozen older folks sit in Naugahyde booths and at tables, talking about the dance the night before at the Legion Hall. I can hear them whispering about people they know who walked from one place or another, and lonely roads that scare them, as if I cannot hear.

"It's about the environment," someone says. "I saw him yesterday."

"Where did he sleep?"

When I get my bill and am preparing to pay, a woman comes up from around the other side of the counter and writes on it "Paid."

"You're on quite a mission," she says.

Outside, frogs dot the road, quietly waiting for crickets to come too near. Snakes sun themselves and wait for fat frogs. In the evening I set up my tent while dinner cooks on the simmering camp stove. Mars and Jupiter appear in the night sky, closer to each other than the night before. The ground is soft with tall grass leaning over. There is a rabbit run nearby. I hear them thumping during the night, after moonrise. Slugs leave silver traces on the netting of the tent, and in the morning, pheasants lift into the sky and fly just overhead as traffic begins to pass. The sun is in my eyes as I walk east into the next town and on to the next café, where the talk is about the weather and irrigation, John Wayne, and Halloween treats for the kids.

Sometimes I leave the highway for the back roads and a silent autumn walk. When the wind comes up in violent gusts I hide behind haystacks the size of small houses. I have been watching the farmers move them, piled on trailers pulled by tractors, swaying down narrow country roads. Motioning with their hands the farmers sometimes ask if I want a ride. I always smile and shake my head, and as they pass, I wave . . . hello, goodbye.

Leaden sky hangs cold
Above the winter landscape
First snow approaches

November 6, 1986
Watertown, South Dakota

When I arrive in Watertown, a city of about 30,000 on the eastern edge of the state, it is early November. I find an inexpensive motel and prepare myself for the walk to Minneapolis. The nights are cold now, always below freezing, which makes it hard to get started in the mornings when sleeping out. Because of the cold, I change from painting watercolors to making quick pen-and-ink sketches. But my mind still resonates with the subdued pastel colors of the cool autumn days that begin with fog rising above the land, making the landscape soft. Perhaps that is the difference between the east and west sides of the river. The east side is softer, as if the edges have been rounded, with more farms and cultivated land, and the towns are closer together. The west side is harsher and more isolated. The towns are separated by herds of rangy cattle, sprawling ranches, and more hills, all at risk of being ripped away by a wild wind.

On the motel television the weatherman is going on about the winter storm approaching, and how a person should be careful.

"This storm could be a real killer," he cautions. A part of me is listening and saying I should wait and see. The part that wins out convinces me I can see it just as well from the road. I make it to the next small town, Krantzburg, ten miles down the road, and spend the night in the church confessional. In the morning I meet the priest, Father Krantz, who is not related to the founders of Krantzburg. He is 44, from Howard, South Dakota, about a hundred miles southwest. A special mass is being held over at the elementary school for the children and the community. Afterward, Father Bob (as his parishioners call him) fixes breakfast for me. We talk a bit and then I leave. A cold wind from the east blows drizzle in my face.

At a coffee shop ten miles farther on, I overhear a customer say that behind me snow is falling. When I hear this news my gut begins turning and wringing itself into a knot. I think that it could be the coffee, but I cannot mask my disappointment and fear. The disappointment is that with the arrival of snow, I know that I will not reach Madison, and now I do not know if I will be able to reach Minneapolis. The fear, though, is more powerful: Can I survive in these conditions? Even with my winter gear, I am not prepared for this cold, for this storm. I stay at the café until nearly closing time. I have been uncharacteristically still, and not my usual animated self. It is night when I step back out into the cold. I make my way across a field strewn with rolls of hay. I can feel the proprietor's and the few customers' eyes on me as I disappear into the darkness.

I hunker down beside a hay roll and begin the laborious process of putting up my tent in the windy darkness. Once inside I climb into my sleeping bag and stare at the flickering candle in my

lamp. The words of the weatherman are ringing inside my head: "This storm is a killer. This storm is a killer."

I am asleep when the full force of the storm finally hits. The sound of the wind slapping at my tent and the plummeting temperature wake me up. I reach lethargically for every bit of clothing I have, and for a moment curse myself for not carrying the plastic food wrap that Kathleen Phalen of CBS gave me for just such occasions. Wrapping yourself with a thin film of the stuff will cut down on your heat loss, she told me, and could save your life. I think of the warmth and light of the café and wonder why I ever left.

The cold wind stings and bites my face. It seems to take forever to get back to the Turnerville Café.

Now sleep is the enemy. If I fall asleep, I imagine that I will not wake again. All I can do is wait through the cold and cacophony until dawn. When dawn comes my hands are frozen, my gut is still in a knot.

The winds are blowing at about 40 miles an hour, and the temperature has fallen well below zero. For a moment I think of running to the café, leaving behind anything I would have to carry, dashing through the doors into the nourishing warmth and good smells, throwing myself onto the floor, and asking to be saved. But in the cold, I can only think slowly and move slower. It takes me until three in the afternoon to break my little camp.

With my pack slung over my shoulders, I trudge across the field through knee-deep snow. It squeaks with the compression of each step. The cold wind stings and bites my face. It seems to take forever to get back to the Turnerville Café. Inside, I soak up the warmth, and after having something to eat the knot in my stomach loosens. The fear is gone. I decide that I will not die frozen on the road, but I am not sure what to do and feel discouraged. Only eight miles from the Minnesota border, I want to go on. I stay all day inside the café, writing in my journal, studying my road map, and sampling orders of fries and cups of coffee. It is evening when I write the note.

"Help," the note begins, "I need help."

"We were wondering when you were going to say something," says Barb. She hands the note to Terry, who reads it and hands it back to Barb.

"We weren't going to let you go back out in this storm."

Tears well up in the corners of my eyes, as the snow continues to fall outside. I want so much to reach Madison or Minneapolis that I forget to be where I am.

"Hey, John, it's all right," Terry says. "You can stay in our garage tonight." I accept. In the garage Terry burns tires in the furnace, sending black smoke into the night air. I sleep in the carpeted truck bed. I am ending my walk for the season before I had anticipated. In the morning I will return to Watertown to spend the winter, the wind at my back.

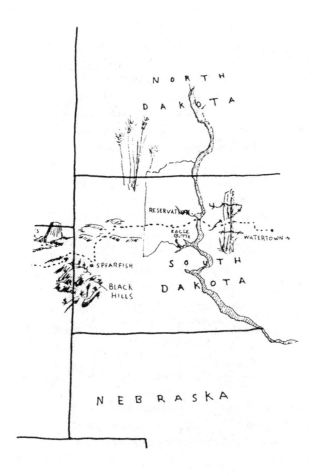

CHAPTER 16

Powwow: Broken Arrow

Footprints in the snow
Blue cold, white squeaky softness
Along the highway

November 10, 1986
Watertown, South Dakota

It takes two days to reach Watertown after being turned back by the storm. The wind from Canada keeps the temperature below zero as it blows across the South Dakota plain and through the Watertown streets. Lillian, the manager at Scott's Motel, is not surprised to see me struggle through her door. She gives me a special rate while I spend the next week looking for an apartment, to wait out the winter that has put a stop to my walk.

I find a second-floor one-bedroom apartment in the corner of an old two-and-a-half-story Victorian on the northwest side of town. It is on a quiet residential street lined with tall old trees, houses with lawns and large backyards. The apartment is furnished, with a dirty brown sofa and matching easy chair that face each other from opposite walls papered in a yellowish-green floral pattern. Beside the sofa is an end table and beside the chair an empty magazine rack. Against another wall with wallpaper depicting scenes from a colonial kitchen is squeezed a small yellow Formica table fitted with two plastic-covered chrome dinette chairs from the 1950s. The floor is covered with a green rug, freshly shampooed. It smells of pine. On the table is a single lamp with golden metal swirls and curves on the base. A doorway leads through a narrow galley kitchen into the bedroom containing a mirrored dresser and

a double bed. The bed is too small for me unless I sleep at an angle, but I decide it will do. Besides, the bathroom has a full-size tub, which I can fit into.

For the first few days I stare out the window at the snow that continues to fall and listen to the rattle of the hot-water radiators. It is difficult for me to comprehend that I have been walking all summer. It is difficult for me to grasp that winter is here . . . that I am here. I thumb through the pages of the paintings in my book and drift back into a watercolor dreamscape. My mind fills with color memories right up to the cold, stark pen-and-ink drawings of winter. But the days, though cold, are filled with sun and an icy blue sky.

Squirrels across the street
Feeding with a flock of birds
They live in the trees

November 17, 1986
Watertown, South Dakota

It is difficult for me to grasp that winter is here . . . that I am here. I thumb through the pages of the paintings in my book and drift back into a watercolor dreamscape.

The South Dakota Peace and Justice Center is located above a hardware store in a brick building near the middle of town. I climb the musty stairway and introduce myself to Jeanne Koster, who along with the director, Tim Langley, manages and coordinates the center's projects. One of the projects involves assisting residents of nearby Clear Lake to set up a fact-finding committee and a dialogue with a munitions company that wants to establish a plant in the community.

People have the usual concerns about safety and pollution of the groundwater. But they are also motivated by the moral consideration of using land that is predominantly agricultural for the production of bombs and grenades. Many in town feel the economic benefits outweigh any other consideration. And because there have been many farm foreclosures, the economy is a powerful consideration.

The Peace and Justice Center shares the building with the Water and Natural Resources Department, whose job is to investigate water pollution. They have their hands full with a recent gasoline leak, which threatens Watertown's water supplies. The news covers the reaction of local citizens to the air force's proposed installation of a new over-the-horizon radar system. Ninety-eight percent of the people polled oppose it. I am amazed that so much is going on in such a sparsely populated state.

When I meet Tim, I offer my services as a volunteer, and I actually do some preparatory work for writing a grant to get the center a computer. But in the end it is the center that provides me with the more important feeling of home, continuity, and community. As time goes on, Watertown gives me that feeling as well.

Around the corner from the Justice Center, I stop in at Print'em Now, a print shop I had visited to make some copies as I passed through Watertown the first time. This time I want to find out about printing the next edition of *Planetwalker*.

Colleen Thyen, just out of high school, is working behind the counter when I walk in. She tries hiding the braces on her teeth with a friendly closed-mouth smile. She is unable to hide her surprise and excitement at seeing me. It slips out from behind her eyes and in her manner.

"It's just that Father Bob talked about you in his sermon last Sunday," she explains, "and I thought how much I would like to meet you, and here you are!" I smile sheepishly and explain about wanting to print *Planetwalker*.

The shop is a family-owned business. I am introduced to Mike and Kathy Linder, who manage the operation. Dale, Mike's brother, is the chief printer in the basement, and their sister, Loriann, works on layout and design upstairs. The several other employees seem to be welcomed into the family. We agree on a trade of labor for printing. My labor will consist principally of helping in the print shop bindery for a few weeks during the Christmas rush. As it turns out, I learn how to operate a press and a few weeks stretch into a month. I become a regular employee and a member of the family. When it comes time to print *Planetwalker*, for the first time I am able to print it myself.

In the attic squirrels
Scamper across the wood floor
Wake me from my sleep

December 29, 1986
Watertown, South Dakota

It is a cold but sunny winter. For the first several weeks, I wonder if I have done the right thing by staying. Sometimes the weather seems mild enough to continue walking, but the relative warm spells are punctuated by fierce stretches of cold. There is always ice on the sidewalk, a morning rime on the concrete. I walk slowly and throw myself into working the press and getting to know the community, letting the community get to know me.

A lot of information, I discover, can be gleaned by paying attention to what comes through a printing establishment: 10,000 double-sided bingo cards for the Sioux reservation, several hundred tickets for the Christian Women's group, catalogs for a nearby college, sales notices, and a dozen different club announcements and newsletters, including that of the Peace and Justice Center, along with hundreds of flyers, cards, and notices. They all paint a picture of the town.

Some afternoons I have lunch with a new acquaintance, sometimes with a colleague from work or someone that I meet in the shop, on the street, or in church. Father Rogers is a priest at the church I attend. Solidly built with a boyish face, blond hair, and an easy smile, he is deaf. We visit together often, as we both can speak in sign. He is from North Dakota and the youngest of a family of 15. We talk about silence, vocation, and obstacles on his path. We laugh. He sometimes wears a clown costume, which is especially delightful for the children in his parish. There is a gentle sadness in the depths of his clown eyes.

Moon in the evening
Sun below the horizon
Behind the bare trees

January 8, 1987
Watertown, South Dakota

I wake up not being able to remember my dreams, but I get up not feeling as wasted away as I did in Montana. Back then I would wake up still exhausted from the road, with what felt like the weight of the universe on my shoulders, asking myself how I thought I could possibly walk around the planet, or even the United States, when I felt so bedraggled. Looking back, I might attribute the run-down feeling to the brown winter air of Missoula. It was hard to accept that the air quality of the little town was so bad, but because of the surrounding mountains and an atmospheric inversion that traps pollutants close to the ground, Missoula's air quality was rated among the worst in the nation. The winds that sweep across the plains continually scrub the South Dakota air. On my way to work the air is crisp and clean, and more often than not the skies are clear, and the days filled with sun.

We have a new man at the print shop, Amos Spider. He is a Sioux from the Pine Ridge reservation. Before long we strike up a friendship and begin spending a lot of time together. In the evenings we play pool or eat dinner, watch a movie, or share each other's silence. We talk a lot about Native American culture, and how he feels about peace, and how he wishes he could walk with me. Walking, he says, is strong medicine.

I stop to visit Tim at the Peace and Justice Center. He calls the CBS television network and talks to producer Kathleen Phalen about the date for airing the Planetwalk segment. Kathleen tells him about another man walking around the world who will complete his journey in the summer. She wants to profile him and wonders if I know him. I do not usually listen on the phone, but this time I do. Inside I feel heavy, torn between wanting to make a forced march around the globe so that I can get on with my life, and the knowledge that walking and the journey is my life. It will unfold at its own pace.

> *Geese are flying north*
> *Rain sweeps across the prairie*
> *A promise of spring*

March 25, 1987
Watertown, South Dakota

Paper is shredding in my press when Amos tells me he wants to have a powwow, or *wachipi*. Powwows are part of the heritage of the Native American culture; they include singing that celebrates life, dancing, and visiting with old friends. The term originates from a Narragansett word meaning a leader of religious ritual, singing, dancing, and feasting, but over the last few centuries it has come to be accepted as a term for many Native American celebrations, and recently to mean a celebration with singing and dancing. Amos wants this powwow to be in honor of our friendship and Planetwalk. I am deeply touched.

There is always a powwow going on somewhere, especially in the Indian communities and on the reservations. The urban Indian centers in most major cities also frequently sponsor powwows. A large gathering takes place each year at the University of Montana, but there has never been a powwow in Watertown, South Dakota. The lack of precedence worries Amos.

He writes his family and contacts Gary Holy Bull, a spiritual leader. A spiritual leader is someone respected and venerated for his or her knowledge of traditions and religious ritual, experience with visions, and medicinal powers. The vision of the powwow takes on a life of its own, growing from a small community affair of a few dozen to a three-day celebration involving thousands, including meetings with the mayor and the chamber of commerce.

More than a month passes when one day I am at a local TV and video rental business. I am speaking with one of the saleswomen with whom I have become friendly with over the months. She is telling me about her plans to go drag racing during her summer vacation. All winter she has been getting the dragster ready, and in the color snapshot it glistens. Her news is exciting to me; it makes me feel excitement for her as well. When the manager comes up and joins in, the conversation turns to the fact that I am getting ready to resume my walk, and then he asks the question.

"What's a powwow, anyway?"

I show him one of the earlier press releases that Amos printed up when the vision of the powwow was gigantic.

"I have to tell you," he says, "that I do not have a particularly unbiased view of Indians, because many have reneged on rental contracts, leaving without returning their units or running off with them. I guess there's another side to it, though, but for the life of me, I can't see it. I mean, I'm a good Christian and I really want to understand why they can't honor a contract."

In some situations like this, I would just listen and maybe shrug my shoulders, but his desire to understand is sincere. On a scrap of paper, I write,

"Imagine all the Indian treaties broken by the U.S. government."

"I never thought of that." He sighs. "I'm ashamed to say I've never thought of that."

A silence can be heard amid the chattering TVs on the showroom floor. "Anyway, there aren't many blacks around," he says softly. "So I guess you don't experience much prejudice." I smile.

"I'm just talking to you about this because I understand what you're walking for and thought you'd be interested in how I felt." I nod. His words help me understand how Amos feels.

"Maybe I should come to this powwow. Maybe I need it." The voices from the TVs seem to rise. We shake hands goodbye.

The wind in the trees
Sends the blossoms to the ground
And clouds through the air

April 22, 1987
Watertown, South Dakota

My dad arrives for a visit. It has been about ten months since I last saw him in Montana, at my graduation. He enjoys coming to visit wherever I stop, and I enjoy having the time with him. I have not seen my mother since our visit nearly two years earlier in Washington, and the thought of seeing her in the fall, in Philadelphia, fills me with a pleasant anticipation. I am scheduled to begin an appropriate technology development program at the University of Pennsylvania. Just the same, over the winter I begin to inquire at other schools for information on advanced degrees in environmental studies.

In February I received an encouraging letter from Barbara Borns, the academic specialist from the Institute for Environmental Studies at the University of Wisconsin-Madison. I accept her invitation to visit the campus in June on my way east. In the meantime, I am preparing to leave Watertown.

The powwow turns out to be small, almost a family affair, with a community potluck of about 30 friends and a dozen dancers who come from the Flandreau Indian School, representing 12 Indian nations. Amos presents me with a friendship quilt with a golden sunburst design made by his mother. At the conclusion I am given a tobacco pouch, and then I am asked to lead the honor dance around the elementary school auditorium. Everyone joins in the dance after the first time around. The drum beats, feet move, and the singers' voices rise through the ceiling.

May has just begun when I finally walk out of Watertown and head south along Highway 91. It is raining and I stop after only four miles at Jean and Jim Kosters'. I let them convince me that it is terrible weather to begin my walk, and that I'd best start out slowly. I take a long nap in their spare room and leave early the next morning after a leisurely breakfast. Continuing south, rain falls sporadically, gray clouds gather, and the wind blows out of the northeast. Many people wave as they drive by and my feet feel better than they have in a long time. In the afternoon, I turn east toward the little town of Castlewood. Sometimes the force of the wind stops me cold, and I lie down in the tall grass and listen to the leaves rustle and watch the clouds pass. I go on.

A big red Lab with playful yellow eyes appears to walk along with me, and for the next three miles, I am worried about his being lost or hit. When I cross the Big Sioux River he stays behind. I am relieved. On the other side, I take the railroad tracks that slice at the wind to the southeast. The walking is pleasant, and reflecting on the pilgrimage as a whole makes it not so urgent. When I stop for the night I have gone a little more than 15 miles. I tell myself that I will build up to 20 or 25. Already I am settling into the old mental dance of thinking how to lighten the load of my pack. Maybe I could get rid of the television, I muse.

The television is about the size of a deck of cards, with a 2 by 1 1/2-inch black-and-white screen. At 40 dollars, it was the latest battery-operated electronic innovation at a local department store, and I had to have it. I had to have it because I doubt that I will be around a TV set when CBS airs its *West 57th* segment on Planetwalk. I want to see it. No, I will not get rid of the television just yet. The thought of carrying a TV set, however, smacks of the "kitchen sink" and brings a smile to my face.

I have been on the road nearly a week and I am two days north of Sioux Falls when I stop for the night and set my tent up

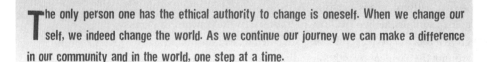

The only person one has the ethical authority to change is oneself. When we change our self, we indeed change the world. As we continue our journey we can make a difference in our community and in the world, one step at a time.

on the other side of a barbed-wire fence. A break of bushes and trees shields me from the road. Around me in the field some cattle graze, barely taking time to lift their heads to notice me. After dinner, I retreat with a cup of hot tea and a chocolate bar to the protection of my netted tent. I enjoy the silence, seasoned with the early evening songs of a few birds, the occasional sounds from the animals in the field, and the passing cars beyond the break.

Then the tent is filled with the blue-white of the television and I watch in amazement as I see myself walk across the land that is Wyoming. My mouth falls open when the voice of my mother and Wyoming dissolve into the image of my childhood home in Philadelphia, with my family sitting on furniture I can remember. My brother, whom I have not seen in 16 years, since he was still a freshman in high school, wears a full beard now, and speaks to the interviewer about following your dreams. Just in view is a framed photograph of his two sons, my nephews whom I have yet to meet. And then there appears Jim Willse, my friend from San Francisco. He is living in New York now with his family. It seems to go on forever, and then it is over. It is too short. I return to the silence and the incongruity around me.

"Excuse me, please . . ." It sounds as if someone is shouting. I am up on my elbows, wondering if I am hearing voices. I listen. "Excuse me. Excuse me, please . . . John Francis . . . Oh, John Francis, oh, it is him!"

I open the flap of my tent and peer out toward the road. I can make out the silhouettes of a woman and a man next to the fence. They have pulled their car onto the grassy shoulder and are now waving at me. I wave back, climb out of my tent, and start toward them.

"It's him; I'm sure it's him!" she says to her companion. As I approach, another car pulls up and the young man who is driving asks if there is a problem. At first I think I am going to be told that I cannot sleep in the field, and then I am sure it is a case of mistaken identity.

"You walked past our house and then we saw you on TV. We just had to find you. We could hardly believe it was you!"

We talk for a few moments. I give them my printed introduction and an extra newsletter before they drive off and I fall asleep in the quiet of my tent. I leave early the next morning with the wind at my back.

My mouth falls open when the voice of my mother and Wyoming dissolve into the image of my childhood home in Philadelphia, with my family sitting on furniture I can remember.

Hawks above the field
Flutter in the northern breeze
Following the plow

May 7, 1987
Sioux Falls, South Dakota

When I reach Sioux Falls, I am greeted by several girls from Bishop O'Gorman High School who have come out to the edge of town to find me. I met them and other students at a Christian retreat for teens in Watertown during the winter. I promised one of their teachers, Sister Maris, that I would try to visit the school when I passed through. She arrives with a ten-speed bike and directions to the high school. For the next week and a half, Sister Maris has me on a full schedule. First I address the entire high school at a special assembly and then visit individual classes. I visit elementary schools, the nursing home, and a home for disabled children. On Sunday, I play the banjo and give the homily in sign language at all three morning masses at the Little Flower church. Sister Merita, a deaf nun who knows sign language, translates for me, as she did in the high school auditorium a few days earlier. Later she takes me to visit a deaf school, where we have a large gathering in the boys' dorm. I am amazed that I can speak in sign and be understood by so many so easily. I speak about the possibilities within us.

I spend the last day saying goodbye, remembering the children from the elementary school who gathered close and whispered good words in my ear. Three red-winged blackbirds hover beside the freeway as I walk out of town. There are still a few hours of light left when I see the sign, welcome to Minnesota.

CHAPTER 17

Five Lakes: Minnesota and Wisconsin

Three red-winged blackbirds
Hover in a pale blue sky
Beside the highway

May 5, 1987
Southwestern Minnesota Border

I walk 25 miles along the back roads without much strain. On either side, the fields of spring corn and wheat begin as soft green shoots, green corduroy rows set in rich black dirt. For a moment the rain stops and the sweet smell of the earth is intoxicating.

All day the storms roll across the sky in a vernal rhythm. Toward evening, I can see the next one coming. It is racing out of the south, angry gray, kicking up dust as it moves from farm to farm, across the tree line to the asphalt road. Suddenly it enfolds me in stinging wet arms. The wind tears at my unzipped raincoat. There are no trees close by to give shelter. I gather myself and press on.

Cars appear briefly with muted headlights, splattered windshields with wipers flicking wildly, and then disappear through the curtain of rain. Inside the cars people stare and mouth unheard words. Some smile, and others frown at me as if to disapprove. A few stop to ask if I need a ride. As usual, I thank them but refuse.

Farther on, the rain passes and violent gray turns to a peaceful sunset red. I find a place to camp off the road beside steel tracks. Wet and tired, I begin my evening ritual.

In the morning I start out with wet feet. The memory of last night's rain is still fresh. The weight of wet clothes and gear presses down onto my back. But I am thankful for the wind that pushes me from behind. I will make good time. I pass fields of new corn and faraway houses that look empty.

When I stop to have breakfast the café is filled with farmers talking about corn and the rain that is falling again, and how it missed some farms and drenched others.

"Oh my God, I saw you on TV!" says Mary Weiss, a reporter for the local paper. She is having breakfast in the café. "Will you give me an interview?"

I nod my head and oblige.

Later KWOA radio catches up with me and I unwrap my banjo and play a few tunes with cold hands. The rain continues. I find a motel to dry out.

In Worthington, Chris Fennwald, a reporter for the *Daily Globe,* and Carolyn Beerman of the Church of Christ arrange to put me up in a motel for another night. My ankle is starting to bother me again and the cold and rain dampen my spirits.

The next day I find my picture on the front page of the paper, then I start off down the road. The gray sky is becoming partly cloudy. Before long, I am wearing sunglasses and enjoying the walk along old Highway 16. It passes through more farmland. People wave, and some turn around and stop to talk about their concern for the environment and world peace, and to thank me.

Brad Swanson has been out planting seed when he runs out of chemical fertilizer. I have run out of water, and I ask him for some in sign from across the road by showing him my empty bottle. He answers in kind, nodding his head and jerking his thumb in the direction of the house.

The water pipe is already running when I walk into the yard. Brad is sitting beside it with his uncle Barney, a smiling older man with a face aged by the elements.

"Hey, can you play that thing?" Brad asks when I reach the pair. So I sit down with them and play, watching to see if they will tap their feet. They do.

The land, I learn, has been in their family for generations. No one has lived in the old house for years. Uncle Barney lives in town and Brad on another farm. I am welcome to the water, but they apologize for the taste. They are not sure what the bad taste is from, maybe the nitrates.

I remember listening to reports earlier in the week about nitrate contamination of rural water supplies from septic tanks, barnyards, and heavily fertilized crops. Once ingested, nitrates are converted into toxic nitrites in the human intestines. There they combine with the hemoglobin in the red blood corpuscles and reduce their oxygen-carrying capacity. This problem is being linked to an abnormal number of infant deaths in the area. I am not sure it has been proven, and I cannot remember if other health hazards were mentioned in the news. I tell myself that I will have to check on that later. But for the moment, like many other people in the world, I have no choice. I am thirsty.

I camp behind the hedges of an abandoned service station at a highway intersection. A starling looks at me sideways from a power line stretching overhead. The water smells and tastes terrible, perhaps in part due to old pipes and other contaminants. It seems good enough for cooking hot chocolate and tea. Left overnight, a thick brown mud settles onto the bottom of the cup.

A few days and several miles pass along with severe weather that includes rain, windstorms, and the threat of tornadoes. The landscape here is a contrast to the cultivated and gently rolling hills of southern Minnesota. A light wind blows from the southwest, making the walking easier. Between towns, I pluck out a tune with a rhythm that quickens my pace. The music always leaves me humming.

Sherburn, says a sign erected by the chamber of commerce, is the birthplace of shuttle astronaut Dale A. Gardner. Inside the Cup and Saucer Café, red, white, and blue Dale A. Gardner souvenir hats are on sale for five dollars. Only a few are left, hanging on the potato chip rack next to the milk shake machine.

It is cool inside. A group of women sit talking at a round table while playing a nickel dice game. One of them has just returned home for a visit. She is catching up on the town news: who is buried in what cemetery, or living in what rest home. Someone who is 90 is now blind and still living at home alone.

I finish my lunch and take a few minutes to rub my ankle. More of the lunch crowd comes in, wearing suits and ties. I guess that they are from the bank, or maybe an insurance company. Before I leave, the women's talk grows louder and more boisterous

I remember listening to reports earlier in the week about nitrate contamination of rural water supplies from septic tanks, barnyards, and heavily fertilized crops.

until I realize that once again news of my journey has preceded me. They ask me to play them a tune. I do. It leaves me humming.

As I leave town I pass wild roses growing by a little lake. Their petals are delicate and pale pink. Cottonwood fluff falls from the trees in a winter flurry, but the air is thick and humid. My ankle aches again. I exchange my banjo for the diamond willow cane that is strapped to my pack, and continue.

Two weeks have passed since I crossed into Minnesota. I have traveled a little more than a 110 miles, averaging about eight miles per day. The low daily average frustrates me. For the moment, any patience I might have had is washed away in the persistence of spring rains. Though, as I think about it, moving slower makes for a closer relationship to the land, the people, and the towns I have been passing through.

My slowness reminds me of the two monks I met on their way from Los Angeles to a new monastery in Vancouver, British Columbia. They passed through my California community one spring years ago. At the time I had already given up the use of motorized vehicles and had made two walks to Oregon and back. They were also walking, but one monk would stop after every three steps, kneel, bow his head to the ground, say a prayer, rise, and repeat the process. The other monk followed with a shopping cart of supplies and acted as an assistant. They spent several days in a neighbor's garage recovering from a severe allergic reaction to poison oak, which to them was an unfamiliar plant. They mistook it for something they could use for their toilet.

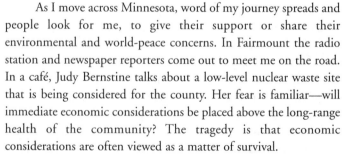

As I move across Minnesota, word of my journey spreads and people look for me, to give their support or share their environmental and world-peace concerns. In Fairmount the radio station and newspaper reporters come out to meet me on the road. In a café, Judy Bernstine talks about a low-level nuclear waste site that is being considered for the county. Her fear is familiar—will immediate economic considerations be placed above the long-range health of the community? The tragedy is that economic considerations are often viewed as a matter of survival.

In Guckeen, economics forced the closure of the post office and the general store. I sit down on a shaded wooden bench in front of the Guckeen Garage, and notice an old single-piston gas engine glinting in the afternoon sun. Its cast-iron parts are freshly painted in bright green, red, and yellow. Cecil Keithson finds me there and sits down to chat. He rebuilds old engines with his dad.

"Things are slow now," he says, looking around at the deserted buildings. "The farm economy, ya know."

I sip on a cold can of soda, enjoying the chance to take off my pack and listen to his story. I enjoy every drop sliding down my throat. My internal memory of the desert remains strong and I notice my appreciation for things cool and wet.

"Use' to be the farmers brought a lot of their implements in for repair. That's about all we use' to do here, ya know. But now the farms are bigger and they have their own tool-repair shops."

Cecil has lived in Guckeen all his life except for a two-year hitch in the army in Germany. He is married now with four kids.

"There isn't much in Guckeen for the kids to do, ya know, except mowing lawns and summer baseball in another town."

When I get to Blue Earth, I find a place in the trees to camp beside the Blue Elm River. The night passes peacefully. In the morning I climb back to the road and begin to cross the bridge. John is waiting. He is a young man who saw me scurrying off the road the evening before as I searched for a place to sleep. He works for a local radio station and wants to take me to his house to meet his family and have breakfast. We made plans to meet at dawn.

In the stillness of the morning, he assaults me with a barrage of questions. Before I can answer one, there is another, and another, and another.

"*Shhhh.*" The sound escapes quietly through the spaces between my teeth. We walk the remaining several blocks in silence, experiencing the sunrise, orange-red through the trees.

I leave John's house to explore Blue Earth and inspect the county building-restoration project. It is a beautiful red brick building atop a hill. Its tower overlooks the town.

The rain starts again by the time I walk, full of coffee and french fries, out of Juba's Super Save, the latest café. As I fiddle with my pack and rain gear, a pickup truck pulls up to the curb. From the corner of my eye I see a man jump out from the truck in soiled coveralls and walk purposefully toward me. One hand is clenched.

I assess the situation quickly and decide that I cannot run away, I can only smile and be ready for what comes next.

"I been looking for you since yesterday," he says, in a perturbed voice. "I read that article about you in the paper." Then he puts a 100-dollar bill in one hand, reaches to shake my other hand, and is gone, leaving me in the street, stunned. Given all the economic hardship in the county I have learned about, I try to understand what he must be feeling to do what he just did, a perfect stranger. But it is typical of the spirit of generosity I have felt in the communities I have been passing through.

A little while later I am taken under the wing of Judy Holland from the chamber of commerce. She is the town's official welcoming committee, and had even come out the evening before to find me on the road, but by then the trees had embraced me down by the river. She makes sure all the local radio and television stations are contacted and that I have a place to stay.

The motel is out by the freeway. Decorated with handcrafted furnishings, it has the feeling of home. Close by are the county fairgrounds and the world's largest statue of the Birds Eye Jolly Green Giant, attesting to the agricultural roots of the community. Blue Earth is located in one of Minnesota's richest agricultural areas. I stay for two days.

Close by are the county fairgrounds and the world's largest statue of the Birds Eye Jolly Green Giant, attesting to the agricultural roots of the community.

White-hot dusty road
Goes on past a lonely house
To meet cool blue sky

May 14, 1987
Elkton, Minnesota

Three days and 50 miles later, I ask a farmer if I can sleep beside his field. His face is caked with the chocolate-brown dirt that his tractor and implements kicked up as he planted seeds and dropped chemicals into the earth.

"I'd rather not," he says, after staring at the slip of paper I give him. His son is helping him load more seed into the bins. He stops and listens.

"There's too much going on in this field right now. Someone down the road will let you."

The tractor engine starts again and they pull back onto the field, racing the setting sun.

A half mile down the road, I am in a ditch hiding from the wind behind my pack. It gets cold before I leave and cross the county line. I follow a dirt road into the middle of a cornfield. The corn is now calf high. A derelict windmill and a rusted water tank lie on their sides in some tall grass. I set up my tent and pass the evening listening to the wind and the creaking of metal. The stars come out. I lie on my back and fall asleep looking at them through the mosquito netting of the tent.

The wind is still blowing from the northwest. It eases me along the road to Austin, the next town. I play the banjo as I walk. Not a cloud is in the sky.

I cross the interstate. Above me in the blue sky, three blackbirds harry a harrier hawk. Lee Bonorden interviews me for the *Austin Herald,* saying it is like meeting Reggie Jackson. I laugh and swing my banjo like a bat. In my mind's eye I see a ball sail out over the second baseman's head and drop just out of the reach of the outfielder, as I lope to first.

"No, really, you're a hero. And the environment needs heroes," he says in a serious tone. I don't see myself as a hero. I shake my head and my face warms.

Lee contacts the Salvation Army, where I can eat and sleep for the night. My shoes need taps. Don, the cobbler, fixes them. He fusses over them like a favorite aunt. A television reporter interviews me in the Hormel Nature Area. The interviewer is the second recent graduate of the University of Wisconsin-Madison that I have met. When he learns that I am on my way to visit the campus, he smiles a knowing smile and assures me that I will want to stay.

I feel out of place walking the main street of the small city with my pack. It is the last day of school and the streets are full, but I feel like exploring.

Harry's Café is a family restaurant that promises home cooking in a working-class neighborhood. It is up the street from Lefty's Bar, squeezed between Charlie's Lounge and Red's. Across the street is a boarded-up Milwaukee Road train depot. The café has an arrangement with the Salvation Army to feed those who are in need. Today I am in need.

The meat packers at the Hormel factory are on strike. The whole town is suffering, and the decline of the farm economy adds to the burden. Signs pointing in the direction of Scab City are common.

I remember seeing the first of these signs as I walked into town. It was in a newly plowed field just off the road. An arrow pointed across the roadless field to the north. I stopped and looked at my map. Of course, I could not find Scab City on it. It was only the sign of a community faced with conflict. Must be a little village, I thought to myself. It took me the rest of the day to realize my mistake.

After dinner, I step out onto the street. At the corner is Bobbie Jo's. A band is playing inside and the bassist taps the plate-glass window and motions me in.

"Hey, can you play that thing?"

> *Rose beside the road*
> *Hidden in the tall green grass*
> *Not yet in full bloom*

May 15, 1987
Stewartville, Minnesota

I get a few miles out of town and set up camp. The sun sets and the moon lifts into a starry sky and a silver light spills over me. The birds begin to chirp at 4 a.m.

In Grand Meadow, I am walking across the newly mowed yard of the nursing home. MEADOW MANOR A NEW ADVENTURE IN LIVING: the letters are in large white block type on the side of a blue van. I am almost to the street when two women dressed in white uniforms come running out of the building. I think that maybe they are escaping. They both start calling to me.

"Young man . . . Young man. Would you wait just a minute?"

A short time later, I am playing to an assembly of residents in walkers, rockers, and wheelchairs. Most clap and smile, a few others stare vacantly across the room. Occasionally one looks my way and expresses some recognition.

Included in the audience are staff and some residents' families who are there for a weekend visit. "They don't have much to be happy about in this world," a visitor says to me when I finish playing, "except for the good care they get here. But of course that comes from the pocketbook, not from the heart."

Perhaps it is a little of both, I mime, by holding my index finger and thumb close together to show "a little." Whatever amount comes from the heart would be immeasurable.

They feed me and reach into their own pocketbooks and hearts to help me on my way.

Before I stopped at the nursing home I had been thinking about peace, what it means and how it comes about. Does it require a sort of tension to exist? I don't know the answer. My mind now turns to ecstasy. I think I feel ecstasy sometimes. It is a fleeting moment of being in touch with all the pleasures and the pain, the vacant stares and touches, the clapping hands, and stars, the music and the rain . . . Tears well up and streak my face.

> *Drumbeats and teepees*
> *Tomahawks hitting the log*
> *Vultures circle high*

May 16, 1987
Forestville State Park, Minnesota

I sit in the grass having lunch beside the road while Merle Dalen, a reporter from Rochester, checks his map for the shortest route to Forestville State Park. There is going to be an old-time rendezvous, he tells me, and I shouldn't miss it.

The road is a thin asphalt carpet that passes over rolling hills of trees and farms, separated by freshly cut hay, steamy wet. Mechanical balers throw heavy green bundles into the air to land in a wagon pulled behind. Some caught by the wind land on the ground. Waves along the way, tall grass in the wind, farmers in their fields. People pass me on their way.

The road that leads down into the park is thick with dust. In a small valley, a thousand people mill among the trees. They follow each other out from the shade into a clearing. I follow them, lost in the anonymity of the crowd. Beside a large red barn stand a dozen tents and teepees. The Indians sitting around the drums beat a familiar rhythm. The singers sing in their native tongue, "He comes from the west to help his friends."

Mark and Suzy Oftendahl, who are camping in a buckskinner's tent as part of the weekend event, immediately take me in. They see to it that I have food to eat and companionship in the crowd. In the evening, I throw my sleeping bag down beside their tent. It is the first time I have seen lightning bugs since leaving the East Coast. They excite childhood memories of summer.

I awake to the sound of a cannon firing just outside the camp. It happens three times a day, at dawn, noon, and sunset, as part of the atmosphere of historic authenticity. Mark starts the morning fire with a piece of flint and tinder and before long the smell of coffee and breakfast cooking on iron grates wafts through the air.

In the afternoon Lt. Governor Marlene Johnson comes to the rendezvous to show the state's support of the weekend's activities, which include music, plays, and craft demonstrations in and around the park's historic buildings. Participants wear authentic costumes dating back to before the Civil War. The drums are beating again, and there is dancing, a snake dance. It takes me back to the farewell powwow two months earlier in South Dakota.

As evening approaches, tents and teepees come down and by sunset, everyone has gone. I am ready to leave also, but decide to spend the night, remembering the importance of going slowly. The Mississippi River and Wisconsin are only five days away. The fireflies lift up from the field of goldenrod as I fall asleep.

Fireflies at night
Stars coming down from the sky
Rising in the trees

May 24, 1987
Esofea, Wisconsin

When I reach the Mississippi, I put my feet in the water to soak away the pain of my ankle. It is not cold, almost warm. A little farther on I come to a bridge said to have been the first to be built across the river. Years ago it was damaged by a boat collision. Abraham Lincoln is reported to have represented one of the sides in the lawsuit. He won.

La Crosse, Wisconsin, is a shock. It has been a while since I experienced a city with 50,000 people, tall buildings, and traffic. It is harder for me to imagine the size of the University of Wisconsin in Madison. It has an enrollment of 45,000 in a city of 350,000, but I am anxious to visit the university's Institute for Environmental Studies (IES). The administrative program manager, Barbara Borns, and I have continued our correspondence and she is keeping track of my progress as I make my way east.

By the time I leave La Crosse, the summer heat turns on to high. I walk more slowly, attempting to keep an efficient pace. Some people recognize me from the newspaper or the TV news. They honk horns and wave. The couple inside one car stops to hand me a soft drink and a plastic bag of ice. I put the bag on my neck, and drink the water from melting ice.

Farther on a family hands me a small vacuum container of water and more ice. The heat and their kindness remind me again of crossing the Arco Desert in Idaho the year before. The sweat drips down my face and the salt stings my eyes, clouding my vision. Kindness, I have discovered, can come from the most unlikely people in the most unlikely circumstances, making it all the more meaningful.

Evening is cooler. I find the quiet of a back road that climbs into the hills. In the twilight, I pass farmhouses with muted lights inside. In the velvet night, the fireflies come out and rest on the trees, looking like the constellations in the sky and cities in the distance viewed from someplace high. They mingle with the stars and confuse me when they swarm in the tree limbs above me. It is the Milky Way.

I feel as if I can walk forever, or at least until the sunrise. Instead, I put up my tent in the dew-wet grass of the county park when I reach Esofea, a few hours later.

In the morning, Lyle, the caretaker, comes by and introduces himself with coffee. A church group is on an outing from Westby. I listen to the afternoon sermon from the shade of a picnic shelter. Afterward the minister comes over. He is about to take issue with my silence, saying it is not using the gift that God gave me. But I write a note about peace being a gift, and how sometimes we have to give something up to find something else, and he is reminded of the words of one of the five missionaries recently killed in Ecuador. When people told the man he was a fool for risking his life, he replied, "A man is not a fool who gives up what he cannot keep to gain what he can never lose."

Walking in moonlight
Laughing silently alone
Then forgetting why

May 26, 1987
Richland Center, Wisconsin

I walk several hours, perhaps ten miles, on a section of the road that is closed for repairs. Yellow bulldozers and cranes on steel-treaded tracks stand idle, waiting for the next workday. I am thankful for being able to walk a while without any traffic.

Before the noise and crowd of civilization creep too close again, I find a roadside spot of neck-high grass to sleep. It waves like the sea, silver in the night, crashing on the shore at each breeze. When I awake I walk into Viroqua and send off a wallet that I found on the road the day before.

At a wayside rest stop, a road crew stops to talk while I stitch a torn pair of shorts. In the next town an older couple wants to wish me well, but they say they do not see much of a chance for peace. I patch a blister on my foot and begin the evening walk. Madison is 76 miles away. I do not hurry.

One morning I leave another roadside camp, this one in a grove of skinny oaks. The cornfields are now thigh high, and Holsteins, heavy with milk, amble in green pastures and watch me as I pass. The two-lane country road gives way to four. The traffic intensifies and the four lanes turn to six.

The next day, just before noon, I climb the stairs to Science Hall. I find the IES office in the basement. Beverly Helms, the graduate secretary, greets me and explains that Barbara Borns has left for a few days of vacation. In the meantime, arrangements have been made for me to stay in the apartment of Gary Ray, who is in the land resources program. Gary is also a friend and colleague from my days at the University of Montana.

It will be good to see him. Suddenly I feel very tired.

CHAPTER 18

Thanksgiving: Seven Years and a Day

On the ragged edge
Water makes a quiet noise
While we walk along

July 16, 1987
Madison, Wisconsin

I have been in Madison nearly a month, and have decided to stay and enroll in the doctoral program in land resources at the Institute for Environmental Studies. I have met with Barbara Borns on a number of occasions to discuss a fellowship. The institute applied to the graduate school for a fellowship on my behalf. So far we have heard nothing on the status of the application.

I walk into Barbara's office in the basement of Science Hall, hoping to hear that the graduate school has made a decision.

"John, there's been no word about your fellowship," Barbara says almost as soon as I walk in. She speaks in a worried tone, looking over the top of her glasses. "This is a long process, but I can't understand why it's taking them so long in your case."

I let out a sigh that travels to the middle of the room and sits there.

"You know what?" Barbara says. "I think you need to go up to the graduate school office and see what the holdup is."

I think she is right, because if I have no fellowship there is no way I can afford graduate school. If I do not go to school in Madison, I should keep walking until I get to Philadelphia, where I

have already been accepted into the appropriate technology program at the University of Pennsylvania.

The graduate school office is located up the hill in Bascom Hall. I make the climb and find the office of the assistant dean. His name is painted in black letters on a rippled translucent window in a wooden door. Inside, a long wooden counter is stacked with piles of program handouts for prospective students and dreamers. On the other side of the counter are some inner offices and desks where secretaries sit typing and talking on the phones. Occasionally a file drawer opens and closes. Then one of the secretaries notices me and walks over to the counter.

"Yes, can I help you?"

I of course say nothing and point to the assistant dean's office. "Pardon me?"

I point again, but this time I make signs for "I want to see," putting two fingers at my eyes and then projecting my hand toward Akbar's office. The secretary looks puzzled for just a moment, and then a light goes on and recognition flashes across her face.

"You must be John Francis, and you want to see Akbar Ally, the assistant dean, about the Advanced Opportunity Fellowship." It all comes out in a rush.

I am puzzled at how she could know so much from so few signs. Just then, Akbar walks in through the door. He is a small man nattily dressed in a cocoa-brown sport jacket with gray slacks and black shoes. His black hair is salted with gray, and he has a neatly trimmed mustache and beard. He looks at the secretary and me with a question in his eyes. The secretary stops him midstride.

"Oh, Akbar, this is John Francis from IES. He wishes to see you."

"Okay, okay, yes, yes. Good to meet you." He shakes my hand. "Give me a minute." He disappears into his office. A moment later he is at the door and the secretary is ushering me into his inner sanctum. Sitting down at his desk, he begins by asking questions. They start out simply.

"So, how did you get here?"

I walk my hands in the air, showing the ocean pounding against the shore, mountains, hills and hot desert, sweat dripping from my head, wind and snow blowing across the plain. He laughs and begins to tell me about the program and the school, and then

in the middle of a sentence he stops and excuses himself. He walks into the outer office, where everything has been strangely quiet for the last few minutes. I hear him talking.

"Yes, I can actually understand him, I can actually understand what he is saying." I hear some commotion and Akbar returns with a big smile across his face.

"We were all curious as to how you would communicate. It is definitely a consideration if you were going to get such a prestigious fellowship." In the next few minutes, he assures me that I am getting the fellowship and that I should look for an apartment.

I find an apartment across from a park that borders Lake Mendota, the largest of the five lakes the capital is built among. It is in a new complex constructed around Nichols Station, an old pumping house that had been used to take water from the lake for city use. I furnish it with a mix of new and used items, given by friends and former IES students or purchased at the university's surplus store at minimal cost.

Summer gives way to fall, and fall slips quietly into the Wisconsin winter. The first ice fishers gather on Lake Mendota.

Summer gives way to fall, and fall slips quietly into the Wisconsin winter. The first ice fishers gather on Lake Mendota. Exposed, they crowd around the crusted holes, waiting for fish to bite. Further into the season tiny shacks appear, sheltering anglers from the bitter cold of winter storms. Ice boats with brilliantly colored sails race across the frozen landscape.

As a degree candidate at the Institute for Environmental Studies, I apply myself once again to the formal study of environmental issues and problems. The land resources program allows an integrated approach to environmental studies. My course work includes remote sensing, policy analysis, political theory, development, and environmental economics. The eclectic nature of the program takes into consideration the complexity and interrelatedness of environmental problems and reflects the belief that solutions to many of these problems transcend the boundaries of any one discipline.

One seminar takes a global perspective. We attempt to look at all the environmental impacts caused by world social and economic development, from plantation farming in developing countries that takes the place of indigenous food crops to the large agribusiness farms that are replacing small family farms in the

United States. We look at these activities, and many others, through the eyes of social and physical scientists.

That seminar helps me put into perspective the environmental biology class that follows, which deals with population. Population and high birth rates have been recognized as major components of problems facing many Third World or developing countries.

For a semester project I look at Indonesia, which in its bid for social and economic development has tried several approaches to alleviate its population problems, including transmigration, mass movements of people from heavily populated areas to unpopulated and underdeveloped areas, and colonization. While substantial progress has been made in reducing the birth rate, some of the solutions—transmigration in particular—have inadvertently led to economic inequity, social tensions, increased deforestation, and soil erosion.

Closer to home, our soil science class dealing with pollution looks at chemical, biological, economic, and social implications of waste disposal. One topic we explore is vermicomposting—a relatively new idea of using earthworms to process sewage sludge, a major product of sewage treatment plants. I found that sewage sludge disposal restrictions are a problem facing many of the rural communities I passed through as I walked across the country.

In the remote sensing lab housed at the university's space science facility we learn how to use aerial photographs, satellite data, and computers to survey and analyze natural resources in the environment.

As the seasons change, other classes, meetings, seminars, and conversations contribute to my understanding of environmental issues and strengthen my commitment to the pilgrimage I have undertaken.

Spring brings the melting of the frozen lake. Ice fishers retreat to the shore and sailboats strain at newly placed moorings. Around the city, farmers begin setting up stalls with early crops of flowers and greens. I join the Hoofers, a university outdoor club, which offers one of the largest sailing programs in the country. When I reach the East Coast, I hope to cross the ocean by sail.

In the middle of the spring my father visits. He is

dumbfounded that I am able to attend a university in a Ph.D. program.

"Your aunt Lucy says I should leave you alone, because you seem to be doing best when you're not talking," he says. But before he leaves he asks, "What are you going to do with a Ph.D.? They're a dime a dozen."

It takes me two years to complete the coursework and preliminary examinations that fulfill the partial requirements for a doctoral degree in land resources. Now I am prepared to research, write, and defend a dissertation. My research topic is an assessment of the costs and legal conventions of managing oil spills from ships in the United States and the Caribbean. It feels like the perfect subject for me, but some of my colleagues frown on it and ask me how I expect to make any money off such a study. But after the *Exxon Valdez* spill in March of 1989 my dissertation takes on a new dimension.

When reporters call IES to speak to "an expert" about the environmental catastrophe in Alaska, they learn about my research, and that I will not answer the phone. Fortunately for all of us, my major professor, John Steinhart, does answer the phone, leaving me the luxury of concentrating on my work. I am lucky to find John at the university, because he has studied and published a book on the 1969 oil well blowout in Santa Barbara, California. In fact, when the committee met prior to my acceptance to the graduate program they decided that if I could not find five professors at the University of Wisconsin who would work with me and serve on my committee, I would not find them anywhere. As fate would have it, I did not have to look elsewhere to see if that was true.

> *Waiting until dawn*
> *Sleep pressing against my eyes*
> *Just before I leave*
>
> September 30, 1989
> Madison, Wisconsin

There is a going-away party for me at the art center complete with African drumming and international foods on the table. The music and dancing go on long into the night. It is hard to say goodbye.

My last day in Madison is hectic. Friends arrive at my apartment to say goodbye and immediately are enlisted into helping me clean. Across the street in the park, more music blares from the annual pot legalization demonstration. In the cacophony that comes through the windows, I wonder how I can possibly be ready to leave in the morning. I feel like I am being born, propelled out onto the road with nothing. If I could stay just one more day . . . But I know that I cannot. Besides having told all my friends that I am leaving the next day, I can smell the weather changing from the warm sweetness of summer to the acrid coolness of autumn. I want to reach the East Coast before winter's onslaught.

On a warm Sunday morning, ten of us gather on the steps of Science Hall to say goodbye. Two friends walk beside me, one rolling his bike for the trip back to town. We stop near the city limits and they hug me, attempting to wrap their arms around my backpack and me. They say something about sandhill cranes and how we are going to have a mild winter. After stopping for breakfast my friends turn back and head north across the freeway. I turn south.

More people wave than I would have thought, some sign "I love you," applaud, and encourage me from their cars. A little farther on I succumb to numbing fatigue and fall asleep while painting beside the road.

Gray sky turns to blue
Fields of corn turn to amber
Geese pass overhead

October 2, 1989
Oregon, Wisconsin

In Oregon, Wisconsin, I stop in front of the Richelieu Banjo showroom and factory. Through the showroom window I can see an older man kneeling on the floor. His large bald head and smiling face remind me of Little Orphan Annie's Daddy Warbucks. He is putting the final touches on a banjo head. When our eyes meet through the glass his smile broadens and he motions me around to the door.

"Let's see what you have cradled in your arms," he says as he unlocks the door. I turn my instrument so he can see the writing on the back.

"Ahhh, it's a little Stewart. What a sweet banjo. I suppose you can play it if you're going to the trouble of carrying it around."

We introduce ourselves. He is C. C. Richelieu, 80 years old, the proprietor of the shop. We spend a few hours visiting and playing banjo music together. To help me on my journey he offers me a few sets of strings and one of his special banjo heads.

"You know, your banjo head is an odd size," he explains.

I nod and thank him. I walk a little farther on and find a place in the grass beside some tracks. The temperature is mild and the sky is clear. A million stars sparkle. I let my body melt into the ground, drifting in and out of a deep sleep, crying silently off and on through the night. Tears . . . How can this be?

A wind comes up in the night and the temperature drops suddenly. I put on my long underwear and go back to sleep. A train rolls by, whistle blowing. I wake up again with a start, trying to remember if I had fallen asleep on the tracks. The cold morning numbs the tips of my fingers. In the distance, the traffic noise grows louder.

I stop for breakfast at a small café. Farther on I meet Scott, a construction worker in his late twenties who moved up from the south to work in Wisconsin. He saw me on a TV show. We share some coffee on the hood of his car.

"I've been wondering about the environment," he says, "and all the dead farms. How could America change so much so fast?"

I shake my head, and take another sip of coffee.

"My wife and I live in an old farmhouse that we thought must have been some farm in its day." He stops and stares into the sky. "You know, I've a dream of having a horse and wagon that I could take to construction sites, sort of like the Amish of Evansville," he says, citing an example of how it could work.

My expression agrees with him, that it is possible.

"I haven't told anyone else about my dream," he explains. "Other people would think I'm crazy. I'm not sure you won't, I just have a feeling like I can tell you."

He asks if I want to work a few days on a house he is building. But the geese are heading south and a chill in the air urges me on to Illinois.

He asks if I want to work a few days on a house he is building. But the geese are heading south and a chill in the air urges me on to Illinois.

Grass turning to brown
Feeling like caterpillars
At the end of stems

October 9, 1989
Kankakee, Illinois

There is frost in the night and the traffic noise does not let up. It is not until morning that I realize I have camped next to a major highway and not the less traveled Route 113. Luckily I find a quiet dirt road that heads toward the river. It stretches off into the distance, brown corn on either side with a line of trees on the horizon. I set my pack down at an intersection. A man comes out of the corner house and asks me if I am lost.

He had seen me looking at the signs and up and down the road as if I was trying to figure out which way to go. After assuring him that I am not lost, I give him one of my introduction cards. He reaches for his glasses and pores over the writing as if it is his favorite meal.

"Well, rest yourself as long as you like," he says, and disappears into the weathered house. A few minutes later I am in the kitchen having breakfast prepared by his wife, June. Johnny is 57 and works in the aluminum sheet mill in Morris, just across the river.

The electric company bought Johnny's property and that of his only close friend, who lives across the river now, so he does not get to see much of him anymore. He has worked 13 years for the same company and has eight more to go before retiring. Then he and June plan to move south. Maybe their son Don, now 19, will move with them. Changing economics make the area not the promised land they had once hoped for.

A few miles down the road I meet Robert Sherman, 16. He comes running out of the tavern operated by his mom.

"I never met anyone like you," he says. "I just want you to know that when I think about you I get this feeling, and I think that anything is possible." He touches his heart softly with a closed fist. He follows me the next few miles on his bike.

The sheriff's K-9 patrol officer wants to give me a ride. I thank him but continue to walk.

I squeeze across the bridge over the Illinois River along with the Sunday traffic and make my way slowly through the next

Illinois towns. I rearrange my morning clothing as the temperature climbs toward 60 degrees.

The traffic mellows a bit and then at the Route 113 turnoff it quiets down a bit more. The shoulder is under construction and I hope it will not be hard to walk. Already the people of Illinois have made the first weeks of my journey meaningful.

> *The moon grew silver*
> *Rising into the night sky*
> *Above the steel tracks*

October 12, 1989
Kentland, Indiana

I walk between the tracks, silver ribbons on either side of my steps. I walk into the night and find a place where the deer have slept. I saw the does earlier, with large white tails, bounding over a harvested field.

In the morning I walk into Donovan (population 300) and have breakfast. Four miles later, in the town of Iroquois, Jack Hutchison of the Iroquois State Farmers Bank treats me to lunch. He saw me walking through the streets and thought I could use a meal. Iroquois is smaller than the last town, and at the café Planetwalk becomes the talk of the day.

The sign says that the post office in the sleepy town of Sheldon is closed until 1:30 in the afternoon. I wait beneath the pavilion in the park across the street. I watch the men work on the tracks. The sickly-sweet smell of creosote drifts up from a pile of new railroad ties sitting black against the green of newly cut grass. Their odors mingle. I try not to breathe much in, but I am not very successful.

I pick up a package from a friend in Madison at the post office. It contains some trail mix for the road and forwarded letters. As I sit writing on a street corner in Kentland, Indiana, I smell the familiar fall odor of burning leaves. I have walked all day, playing music most of the way. I am still filled with the sounds and feeling of the music, and wonder how this state will be different. Again I find a grassy spot near the tracks, just east of Goodland, and fall asleep.

On the road, the paved shoulder ends and gives way to a gravel slope. I stay between the rails. A dog barks as I walk up the

tracks. The air is chilly and the stone ballast between the ties is large, making it tiring to walk. I get back on the road, a familiar dance—a mile of this, a mile of that, punctuated by aches, pains, joys, cafés, music, and a landscape of people, like the GT&E utilities man who pulls his truck off the road and calls me over.

While I am on the road, I am homeless too. What makes it partly different is that my homelessness is by choice, and I am possessed by a dream.

"I know I can't give you a ride because you're working too hard, but I can give you some money to help you on your way."

Midway across the state, as I walk a stretch of what seem to be abandoned rails, I meet Modesto Herrera, a homeless man living in a clump of trees beside the tracks. Beyond the trees, just barely out of sight, a homeowner runs his mower through a yard. The sound of the motor and the aroma of the cut grass bring back memories.

Modesto sits on a plastic bucket, busily writing. Around him in neat piles are his belongings, which include suitcases, cooking utensils, clothing, a leather briefcase, and sleeping gear, beneath a clear plastic tarp. He looks up with a puzzled expression from behind his wire-rim glasses, and then a smile grows on his face that stretches out beneath his large black mustache.

By the time I leave, half an hour later, he has told me his life story, about how he lost his job as an autoworker, his home, his car, and his family. A lawsuit is under way. He brings the paper from the safety of his leather briefcase. He refuses to live in a shelter and is convinced that someday he will regain what he has lost.

I walk more and rain falls. I think of Modesto and all the other homeless people. While I am on the road, I am homeless too. What makes it partly different is that my homelessness is by choice, and I am possessed by a dream. Perhaps Modesto and I are not that different after all. A couple takes me in for the night. They recognize me from a TV show they saw years ago when they lived in another state.

Sleeping on the road again, I settle down with my portable radio to listen to the World Series. The Giants are playing back in San Francisco. Instead of baseball, I hear a report on an earthquake at the stadium. The upper deck of the Bay Bridge has collapsed and I am reminded of how fragile life is and how close homelessness and death really are.

As I progress across Indiana, I smell the leaves burning. The leaves that remain on the branches are burning rusty red and yellow autumn colors. Fewer fields are waiting to be harvested and more fields now lie empty. The hordes of grasshoppers that rise in small clouds at each footstep in the grass beside the road grow fewer. The temperature drops.

> *A cold wind blowing*
> *Through the filigree of trees*
> *Having dropped their leaves*

October 18, 1989
Fiat, Indiana

I get to the post office in Bryant, Indiana, in time to pick up my mail, which includes a suit of expedition long underwear. I walk until late that night. As I cross into Ohio, it begins to snow.

I look for a motel, but settle for a creek bridge just east of Wabash. I share the place with two geese. They move closer as the night wears on. By morning they are squawking next to my feet. I throw a pebble and they waddle off into a nearby cornfield.

It is still early morning when I squeeze from beneath my shelter and trudge through the snow and grass up to the road. The north wind stings my face and the snow collects on my beard. People look at me through the flurry in disbelief. A few wave.

When I get to Celina, nine miles later, I find a café. Feet wet, I eat and prepare to walk nine miles more to Saint Mary's. I decide that a motel is in order. Tom Hoffman, a local newspaper reporter, stops by the café for an interview. He talks above the afternoon din of customers and the Muzak oozing from hidden speakers.

I read about the California earthquake in a day-old newspaper and feel sad . . . an unusual wave of homesickness. Meanwhile the snow is letting up.

In Wapakoneta, I visit the Neil Armstrong Space Museum, the namesake being a native son. The Gemini 6 space capsule is on display along with space suits, tools, and other memorabilia of flight and space exploration. A planetarium program chronicles the first lunar landing, and the museum offers continuous live transmission from the shuttle *Atlantis* in earth orbit.

Outside, I look into the blue sky, shake my head in wonder, and continue slowly over the hills with trees in autumn blaze, past the farms and through the small towns across this new state, Ohio.

Sitting by the lake
Autumn colors reflected
Deep in a blue sky

October 29, 1989
West Lafayette, Ohio

I walk in the dark, on a narrow shoulder. A detour coupled with weekend traffic makes the walking unpleasant. Up ahead a red and orange flashing light says that the road is closed. All traffic turns left and heads north toward Route 60. I slip behind the barrier and start to walk across the dark abyss that is the bridge. Then, because I am unable to see my way, I decide to wait until morning to cross. I find a place beside the construction in the grass and stare up at the stars, happy that no traffic will pass in the night.

In Newcomerstown, I stop to visit the post office and afterward have breakfast at the local café. That is where I meet Bob and Bernie. Bob is the town's pharmacist and Bernie is a telemarketer who among other things is interested in helping troubled teens.

Bernie is the more outgoing and talkative of the two. As soon as I walk in the door, he invites me to their table for breakfast. I watch him toy with the idea of walking with me for the day. And when I mime that I am amenable to the idea, I watch his decision to accompany me appear in a sparkle in his eye.

I follow Bernie to his home and meet his wife, Judy. The plan is to leave in the morning after a good breakfast. In the morning, Judy appears with a camera and takes many pictures before we start. We stop in town to see Bob. I ask why Bob won't come with us.

"Bob, he's married to that store of his," says Bernie.

We walk 17 miles, over the hills and into Amish country; several Amish farmers' wagons roll by with horse hooves clopping on the asphalt road. Bernie chatters off and on until dark, lighting up a cigarette every now and then. With all the smoke and chatter, he reminds me of a former self.

"Do you know any tricks for going up hills?" he asks, inhaling the smoke deeply while we climb a hill.

I try to answer, but in the dark signs and gestures are futile. We stop a little farther on and knock on the door of a young couple.

Bernie asks to use the phone to arrange for a ride back to Newcomerstown.

Inside the house, the bear speaks. The bear is a novelty speakerphone. The bear's mouth moves when a voice comes through the receiver, in this instance Bob's.

"Hello?" says the bear.

Bernie looks at the bear and begins to speak.

"Hi, Bob, it's Bernie. I'm talking to a bear." For a moment, I think the bear's name is Bob.

"Jesus, Bernie, where the hell are you?" asks the bear, its mouth moving automatically without expression. It is leaning on a lamppost and wearing yellow clothing.

"I don't know, about twenty miles outside of town on 258. I'm calling to see if you'll come give me a ride home."

"It's awful late, you know, for me to be coming all that way. What about Judy?" asks the bear.

"I called but she's not home."

"She's probably worried sick. Is that Francis fellow still with you?" asks the bear. I think I see the bear's hand move as well.

"Yeah, he's right here beside me," says Bernie, looking in my direction.

"God, we thought he was going to murder you or something. We didn't believe any of his story, and you go off walking with him like an idiot. It's a wonder you're still alive. Why do you think we took all those pictures? Evidence, that's why!" Bernie's eyes grow wide, and a dumb smile forms on my face.

"Bob, I'm talking on a speakerphone, and there's this bear that says everything you say for everyone to hear."

Silence. The bear stops talking. His mouth hangs wide open.

Just then our host comes up and whispers to Bernie that he will give him a ride.

When you walk, lessons may present themselves to you in a variety of situations and disciplines, as in formal education. This is particularly true of environmental studies, which is touched by all the hard and soft sciences. But lessons presented on the path less taken are often experiential. They can even come from the mouths of bears.

"Bob . . . Bob . . . " There is no response. "Bob, I found a ride, Bob. I'm going to hang up now."

I fall asleep in the yard and leave early the next morning. Two days later, I cross the Ohio River into Wheeling, West Virginia.

At the waterfall
The highway is forgotten
In the quiet splash

November 5, 1989
Roneys Point, West Virginia

The weather turns rainy and cold. I register at a motel in town and send for my winter coat and wool pants. My shoes need repair. I find a shoemaker who can replace the worn Vibram heels with the new pair that I carry with me. I have learned over the miles that it is better to bring extra heels along, as the shoe repair shops in the smaller towns are often out of the large size that I require.

I stay in Wheeling for three days, giving interviews to the local newspaper and TV station. People stop me on the street to talk, give me their best wishes, and express their concern for the environment.

Wheeling is shoved hard against a mountain. I follow the roads that lead to a tunnel. It would cut miles off my journey. A maintenance man finishes some repairs and mimes to me that he read about me in the paper, but pedestrians are not permitted in the tunnel. He offers to drive me through and then remembers. Instead, I take the alternate route that climbs into the trees and crosses the mountain into Pennsylvania.

In the evening I stop at the Liberty Street Café in West Alexander. The sight of me taking off my pack startles a woman on her way out. She stumbles back through the doorway and whispers to the waitress, whose face changes from an expression of happiness to one of apprehension.

I walk in with a smile, which the waitress returns. Then I give them both the printed introduction. In the ensuing silence John Wayne makes his way in black-and-white through the rubble of a bombed-out building on the television in the corner. Then I hear more whispering, mixed with laughter.

"Do you enjoy your life?" the waitress asks.

I nod that I do. I have been asked this question many times, along with, "Are you happy?"

After fries and coffee, I walk back out into the night. It is raining again, with peals of thunder and flashes of lightning that illuminate the countryside. I find a field of new winter wheat and put up my bivy, a low body-length tent large enough to hold only me.

The sound of the rain wakes me once, beating down on the taut roof. I get up early in the morning, and make slow progress along the National Road. The road dates back to colonial times. On either side are occasional stone buildings and towns just as old.

In Clayville, I stop at Jerry's Shoe Repair to have a nail removed from the heel of my shoe. I neglected to check it before leaving the shoe shop in Wheeling.

In Washington, Pennsylvania, the editor of the local paper comes from behind the counter to tell me that all kinds of people walk, skateboard, or some such thing through town every few weeks. That is why he is not interested in doing a story. I wonder why he feels the needs to explain himself, though I appreciate the explanation for its entertainment value. My rule is to make myself available to reporters and the media, not to convince them to report on my journey. I am quickly out the door, and further on I find a different attitude among the editors and news reporters.

> *Rain wind and thunder*
> *The lightning flashes in streaks*
> *Road spray in my face*
>
> November 16, 1989
> York, Pennsylvania

Ten days and more than 200 miles later, the Appalachians are behind me. In Gettysburg, I do an interview for the local paper. I try to remember my elementary school visit more than 30 years earlier, the park rangers, the autumn leaves, and a split-rail fence. Did I dream it? I read a few plaques attached to the bases of statues, play music through the battlefield and for a road crew on a bridge.

There are no more mountains to cross. I send my heavy underwear and a sweater to my parents' home in Philadelphia, 100 miles east. With the increase in traffic and the city congestion, I plan to sleep the next four nights, after York, in motels. Luckily, I keep my tent. I use it for two more nights.

My route takes me through Amish country, Bird-In-Hand and Intercourse, where black carriages and horses share the highway with automobiles. I start thinking that I could get a buggy and a horse. It is something to consider. Then I remember Scott, the construction worker I met in Wisconsin, and his dream. Closer to the city I sleep out near the tracks again. The trains are no longer slow rumbling freights, but high-speed commuters that swish by with horns blaring.

My father meets me on the road two days outside Philadelphia. We find a tavern and have lunch together. He displays no judgment of me in his manner now, only concern for my safety on the road and a deep respect for the journey. It is in his voice. A violent storm of wind and rain comes up. Trees are blown down and buildings damaged.

It is rush hour when I reach the city. I walk along the Schuylkill River and then Wissahickon Creek, trying to remember that I have been here before. It all feels vaguely strange. But all the strangeness disappears as I turn onto Pike Street, the street where I was raised, and walk up the steps to the door where my parents wait. I have reached home in time for Thanksgiving.

On Christmas Day a friend from Madison, June Holte, arrives in Philadelphia by train. It is good to see her. We have made plans to walk the hundred miles to Cape May, New Jersey, together.

On January 2, 1990, seven years and one day after beginning my planetwalk at the edge of the Pacific, I touch the waters of the Atlantic at the New Jersey shore.

CHAPTER 19

Speaking from Silence: Thank You for Being Here

If your lips would keep from slips,
Five things observe with care:
Of whom you speak, to whom you speak,
And how and when and where.—Anonymous

April 22, 1990
Washington, D.C.

Keeping silent is a vow I make one year at a time. So, every year on my birthday, I ask myself if I should renew my vow not to speak. I am never sure what the criteria for speaking again should be, or if I will ever speak. When the time comes, if the time comes, I will know. So each year I ask myself, John, are you going to keep this up? Are you going to keep miming and acting out, walking and not talking?

In the early years, when my silence was new, I seemed to have a palpable need to revisit my decision. It was virgin territory, this silent landscape, a narrow path through a ragged bramble. It twisted and turned uneasily up, down, and around surprise and loneliness. I ached with old muscles unused and the growth of new ones. Words piled onto me. The later years have become more comforting, and silence more familiar, with watercolor views to everywhere. Meaning is rooted in action and lives, movement, the passing of clouds, the clarity of eyes.

Revisiting the vow is the way I keep my decision alive and fresh. It keeps the silence an act of choice. It is not like jumping off a tree-swing rope over Stony Creek. You know that once you leave that little bare patch of earth high up on the bank, there is no getting back without getting wet or dropping broken-legged on the rocky shore. If everything works right, you just get wet. Choosing silence seems like one long never-ending moment until you look down from the swing and see the water. On my 44th birthday, after 17 years maintaining a vow of silence, I look down, feel the high arc of invisible rope stretched across time and space, give up my last fear, and let go.

My stomach pushes up inside. After so many years, what will become of me? Will I vanish? Will the internal chatter, the lies, those things that drove me crazy, return? I am again venturing into the unknown.

The thin steel strings from my old S. S. Stewart banjo are exploding metallic rain at my fingers' touch. I play a tune of a thousand miles and children's smiles, seven years across America, roadside concerts and old-time festivals. The comfort of habit and the discomfort of change are beginning anew again. At the same time, I feel the excitement of a new adventure and journey. Just one more tune before I speak. When the music stops, I stretch my heart and leap from that quiet place inside.

The thin steel strings from my old S. S. Stewart banjo are exploding metallic rain at my fingers' touch.

"Thank you for being here." The words are almost inaudible, the voice unrecognizable. I turn to see where the words have come from. There is no one standing behind me. I have spoken them. I wait for the lightning to strike, but it does not. I feel the correctness with every inch of my body. No sooner have the first words escaped than I find myself still in silence, the place and the experience of silence still with me.

From the small gathering of family and friends seated in the Washington, D.C., hotel, a gasp arises, then, "Praise the Lord!" The shout goes up anonymously. Aunts and cousins murmur to each other around their tables. I speak slowly and softly. In my mind, each word presents itself to me for brief inspection. I take them into my being and will them from the silence into the existence of sound.

"I have chosen Earth Day to begin speaking," I continue, "so that I will remember that now I will be speaking for the environment."

The silence and language feel as if they belong together, as if they are part of a whole. Where they touch creation takes place and we are perhaps closest to that which is true. Believing in that truth, I propose that speech not connected to silence is without creative meaning, though it may fill the niche of a social process, as in the case of formal speech or political rhetoric.

After the words of the last sentence have come from me, I stop speaking for a moment and wait for new words. I smile, catch a glimpse of my mother's watery diamond eyes, hesitate, and start speaking again, this time about change and personal responsibility, and then about language and myth and how I have come to be on this pilgrimage. I stop again and look inside, wide-eyed at the storyteller.

There is something uncompromisingly honest in the experience of silence. It is from silence that all speech, and therefore all myth, begins. Speech is the myth of that which cannot be spoken. Without speech, there can be no theory, without theory there can be no answers. When the world of myth and theory confuses us, silence is always there, affording us the opportunity not merely to question our assumptions, but to discard them and begin again.

After so many years, I discover how difficult it is to speak. The words come slowly. I labor through the birth of each one, until I have a full litter that scamper off to live lives of their own. I stop, thinking that reading might be easier. People commonly believed that if I did not use my voice, I would lose it. Friends often paraphrased some well-known medical study, although the sources always seemed to elude them, or they thought they remembered seeing someone interviewed on one talk show or another. Many people believed that if I stayed silent long enough I would never be able to speak again, or I would go mad. Others told me that not speaking is ineffective or just plain selfish.

I reach for my master's thesis on the floor beneath my chair and open it to the introduction.

"This quote by Lynton K. Caldwell, an environmentalist, puts into words why I am on this pilgrimage. It is a quote at the beginning of *Living in the Environment* by Tyler G. Miller, the first textbook on the environment that I read.

"The environmental crisis," I begin slowly, "is an outward manifestation of a crisis of mind and spirit." I stop and breathe deeply. I discover that reading aloud is even more difficult. Sweat

begins to bead on my forehead. The thought of continuing settles within me, and I read on, consciously thinking about and forming each word that I see on the page before me. "There could be no greater misconception of its meaning than to believe it to be concerned only with endangered wildlife, human-made ugliness, and pollution. These are part of it, but more importantly, the crisis is concerned with the kind of creatures we are and what we must become if we are to survive."

After a few seconds of silence applause erupts. I go around to each table and speak to everyone individually and in small groups. In spite of the shaky start, I enjoy the rediscovery of the spoken word. Out on the street I take simple pleasure in saying hello. My first day of speaking is tiring, and I appreciate more than ever the quiet retreat of my hotel room.

The next day, I am riding my blue bike to Gallaudet, the college for the deaf. Gallaudet students had held demonstrations against the appointment of a hearing president who refused to learn sign language. As a result, I. King Jordan became the first deaf person to be nominated as the school's president. He also became one of my heroes, because through my years of silence and learning sign language I grew close to the deaf community. I had visited the school a week before and arranged to meet with him. Visiting Jordan at Gallaudet would be a highlight, albeit ironic now that I had ended my silence.

On my bike, I move with the flow of downtown traffic through timed green lights. Only a few blocks from the school, I see a sienna flash from the corner of my eye. I am struck by the car making the left-hand turn as I bike through a P Street intersection. My face presses sideways against the windshield. I can see the old woman driving on the other side of the glass, a blank expression on her face. Metal twists. My bike, then my body, crumples to the warm asphalt. As the pain and nausea rise around me, a flooding sea, I picture a baby robin crushed into the asphalt on a hot Philadelphia street. Is this how my pilgrimage is to end, dying on the street in Washington, D.C.? Maybe this is the lightning strike of retribution for beginning to speak after so long. I worry about not having done my daily painting. The pain grows more intense, and each breath requires more and more effort. Tears well up in my eyes and I begin to cry. Darkness.

"Hey man, you all right?"

The voice comes from a man bending over me. I grimace. Traffic is at a standstill and people are shouting things from far away across the street that I cannot hear. Beside me, the voice is telling me not to worry.

"I seen the whole damn thing." He keeps repeating it like a mantra, as if witnessing the event has given him control over life and death and I am saved. Slowly my eyes adjust to see a large dark face with worried brown eyes, yellowed teeth, and warm moist breath. It fills my view.

"I seen the whole damn thing," he repeats. "Don't worry, I work for a lawyer."

I have heard about people like this, I think. They are called ambulance chasers, but he is here before the ambulance has even arrived. The fact that this guy is whispering in my ear about money as I teeter on the edge of death makes me think that I am dead, or at the least hallucinating. I close my eyes and wonder if the apparition will disappear when I open them.

By the time the ambulance arrives, I have been moved to the curb, to the consternation of some of the bystanders across the street. The paramedics stabilize my left shoulder and help me into the ambulance. It is vaguely familiar, a small hospital room in off-white and green, a monitor of some sort, and a steel-plate floor with a raised design. I cannot remember having been inside an ambulance before, except maybe once on a school trip to a fire station when I was a kid. I do remember the spotted Dalmatian that rode with the hook and ladder, and then my children's book *The Poky Little Puppy.* Only when they are securing me with heavy wide straps for transport does it dawn on me what is happening.

"Say, where are we going?" I ask, trying not to sound too frantic.

The woman in front of me smiles, stops, and looks me in the eyes sympathetically.

"We're taking you to the hospital," she says, continuing to fasten me into a seat with the fabric straps. "You know, you've been in an accident."

I nod my head, and everything moves in slow motion, leaving a comet trail of sparkly light. My thoughts begin to race. I try to assess my condition. Can I walk to the hospital or will I have to take my first automobile ride in 20 years? More emergency personnel come in to see me. Howard University Hospital, they say, is about 15 blocks away.

"You know, I think I'll walk," I say nonchalantly, hoping to convince them of the wisdom of my words. There are a few laughs. I quickly follow with an explanation.

"Actually, I don't ride in motorized vehicles." There is silence, and everyone stops moving. "I haven't ridden in a car for almost twenty years." The crew looks at each other and then at me. "In fact, I . . . I . . . didn't speak for over seventeen years," I stammer, still not proficient in speaking. The words tumble out idiotically. Their eyes open as wide as pies. "Yeah, I only just started speaking again yesterday."

The moment the words slip from my mouth, I know this is going to be a hard sell. I remember all those times that people would ask hypothetical questions and make up hypothetical situations to show me how not speaking would lead to some unavoidable tragedy. If only I would speak, I could explain everything. I listened to them and smiled, often demonstrating in mime what I might do, or I explained that I tried hard to avoid those situations and felt comfortable dealing with problems as they arose. But here, now, in this bizarre scene, I am actually speaking and it looks as if I am going to be carried away in the ambulance against my will.

They mumble something to each other under their breath, then, except for one young man who stays to watch me, retreat for a private conference.

The expression on the remaining paramedic's face makes me feel that I have only convinced them that I am crazy and they will want to take me to St. Elizabeth's for psychiatric observation.

Humor is healing, so remember to laugh. While it can be offensive in certain circumstances, look for humor in your own situation and when you find it, have a good laugh at yourself. It will lighten your spirit and help you grow.

"And why don't you ride in cars?" the lone paramedic asks tentatively, as if he does not wish to set off my psychosis. The rest of the crew files in again. "Do you belong to some kind of religion? Are you afraid of cars?"

"No," I say, shaking my head slowly. My voice is feeble as I try to explain about seeing an oil spill in San Francisco Bay, but I can't bring my two hands together to form the hull of the two tankers or the collision, as I had so often done in my silence, and I have no printed introductions to hand out with my life story. Strangely enough, I increasingly feel like not speaking. I am not sure my answer is understood.

"You sure it's not some kind of religious thing?" he asks again.

I waffle an untethered hand back and forth to indicate that what he is saying is not exactly right. The spirit of charades enters the cramped ambulance, and a few guesses bounce around until one paramedic asks if it is like a principle.

"Yeah, it's something like a principle," I agree. I am a little more relaxed now that the mood is changing from "get the straitjacket" to "crazy but harmless," and "maybe we can let him go."

Behind me now, the woman paramedic is undoing a restraint around my waist.

"Principles," she mocks. "Well, honey, if you would just suspend your principles for five minutes, we can drive your butt to the hospital."

"I don't think principles work that way," I explain, as I sign the release form one of them hands me. It states that they offered assistance and a ride to the hospital and I declined, absolving them of any further responsibility.

Outside, a policewoman is waiting to take my statement, and after interviewing a number of witnesses she determines the accident is the driver's fault, "failure to yield." My attorney friend is more than disappointed that I refused the ride in the ambulance.

"No, man, what are you doing?" he shouts as I step from the ambulance. "You've blown it."

Exasperated, he explains under his breath that riding in the ambulance would have meant more money when we sued the insurance company. As for me, I am only interested in finding a safe place for my bike, and someone to help me get it there, on the way

"Principles," she mocks. "Well, honey, if you would just suspend your principles for five minutes, we can drive your butt to the hospital."

to the hospital. He assures me that the office is on the way and that his boss will let me leave my bike there. On the way, he tells me that he is not an attorney but an investigator. I fill him in on the last several years of my life, and tell him that I have just started speaking and I don't ride in cars.

"Hey man, what kind of shit is that suppose' to be?" he sneers. He is still annoyed with me for not riding off in the ambulance and securing a hefty commission for the attorney's office.

"Man, you talk crazy. You must be in some kinda bad shock or somethin'. Why you talk crazy like that? You on somethin'?" He decides he has no reason to believe me, so he does not.

With my left arm in a sling and him dragging my blue Schwinn with a crumpled front wheel, we finally reach a row house on North Capitol. Out front a shabby and faded sign announces that this is the law office of Herman Jones, Esq. The entrance is up some stairs from the street and then down a short flight of concrete steps into a basement.

"You wait here," he says, and disappears upstairs.

I wait, chatting casually with the receptionist, who looks admiringly at her long curved nails and occasionally answers the phone. In what seems like only a few seconds he is back, ushering me up a narrow staircase and into the sprawling office of a senior partner.

The large wooden desk is cluttered with paper. Around the walls are the obligatory bookshelves loaded with volumes of law books. A picture of Dr. Martin Luther King looks dreamily down on us. An air conditioner hums, drowning out the sound of the traffic. It barely cools the air.

Seated in a brown overstuffed leather chair, Herman Jones, Esq., smiles broadly and offers me his hand and then a seat.

"So, Davis here tells me you been in an accident." He nods at the man who has befriended me, standing sheepishly at the door.

"Yes," I reply, thankful for the air-conditioning. Even though it is not oppressively hot, I am still sweating from the walk. "But actually I'm here to see if you'd let me keep my bike here until I can make some other arrangements."

"No problem, no problem." He grins.

"Well, you're lucky he was there to see it, because if we have to go to trial he can be a witness," he says, rubbing his hands together. I listen politely as a large diamond ring sparkles on his right hand. "At the very least we'll be able to represent you and get you the best settlement."

"I'm thinking that since the woman was ticketed it wouldn't have to go to trial."

"That's true," he says, "but I want to hear about this walking and not talking business that Davis has been telling me about."

He folds his hands beneath his chin and listens. When I finish, he leans back in his overstuffed swivel chair and laughs so hard that he spins clear around in a tight circle, sending a pile of important-looking papers to the floor. He keeps on laughing until tears well in his eyes and stream down his cheeks. Davis looks on fearfully from the corner.

"Now that's some story. Not that I don't believe you, but you got to admit, that's some story." He puts great emphasis on the word "some" and flashes a big gold-toothed smile, and asks, "Is there anyone who could substantiate this story of yours? I mean, you have to admit it's a pretty fantastic tale." He smiles and chuckles some more to himself. Then he waves away Davis, whose expression has turned to one of sadness and loss. For sure, this guy is crazy and there will be no commission for bringing him into the office.

I think for a moment. Christine Withers from *National Geographic* magazine and Shawn Pachutnic, a reporter from the *Los Angeles Times*, covered the event of my ending my silence, and I had met the Washington bureau editor of the *Times* before I started speaking.

"There was an article in the *Los Angeles Times* yesterday. You could call the editor," I suggest. I offer a number on a scrap of paper. Mr. Jones, smiling, declines the offer and dials information. He knows all about those scams offering a phone number to some official place, only for the caller to be connected to an accomplice at some other location. It really makes no difference to me. I am as amused by Mr. Jones as he is by me. When the operator answers, he asks for the *Times*'s number and dials again.

"Yes, this is Herman A. Jones, at the law firm of Jones, Smith, and Franklin. I'm sorry to bother you, but I have a Mr. John Francis here, who was in an accident today and claims . . . Oh, you do." The smirk leaves his face.

"Yes, he's fine . . . Y-y-yes, sitting right here in my office . . . My address?" He gives his address to the person on the line, then looks over to me and asks me where I am going after I leave his office.

When I tell him I am on my way to Howard University Hospital, he repeats the information into the phone.

"No, he insists on walking . . . Oh, he has? That's very unusual, yes. Well, thank you very much." He hangs up and turns toward me; his face again fills with a toothy smile, and he folds his hands behind his head.

"Well, now," he says, "seems as though you were telling the truth. You know, it's a good thing you came to this office because we can really take care of you." He swivels his chair closer to mine. "Just think, if you had been killed in that accident, they would have just put you in the ambulance and driven you away. Same as if you were being buried, they would just put you in a hearse and drive you to the cemetery. We could help you so that won't happen." He leans closer until I can see the gold of his teeth and feel the warmth of his breath. He reminds me of his investigator, Davis. "We could write a will that would stipulate that in the event of your death you would be carried to the cemetery in a wagon drawn by mules. That would be okay, wouldn't it?" He smiles, showing all his teeth.

He leans closer until I can see the gold of his teeth and feel the warmth of his breath.

"Yeah, that's a great idea," I say. I don't bother to tell him I have heard all the "what ifs" before. I just agree and nod my head. The room seems to tilt and a brief moment of gray graininess and nausea rushes over me. I feel my shoulder throb. I am starting to feel the effects of the accident and want to get to the hospital, but before he lets me go he wants me to meet the attorney who would handle my case if I decided to go with them. Now I am tired of speaking and I retreat to the sanctuary of silence, not thoroughly convinced that starting to speak has been the right decision.

I leave my damaged bike parked in the backyard of the office and walk alone the rest of the way to the hospital. In the emergency room, I wait with the other patients. Shawn Pachutnic, the *Los Angeles Times* reporter, finds me there. He has traced my steps from the law office to the hospital to make sure I am all right and have arrived safely. After he leaves, my body finally succumbs to the trauma of the accident. I begin to shake, the room turns again to that grainy grayness, then fades to black.

The next morning a story appears in the *Los Angeles Times* about the environmentalist hit by a car, refusing the ambulance, and walking 15 blocks to the hospital.

In Washington, I move in with my cousin Ed Kirby and his wife, Dorothy. Ed is a psychiatrist, and Dorothy, a retired nurse, is an artist who paints large acrylic works of people with no faces. It is a second marriage for both of them. Ed and his first wife were both successful psychiatrists. Dorothy was Ed's nurse and her husband was an engineer. The couples were good friends socially, and when each lost their spouse to death, they got married. I guess they each had a good idea of what the other had lost and what each other needed. I know there was some talk in the family when Ed married Dorothy. It may have been because Ed's father was a Baptist minister and Dorothy is Jewish. For all I know, her father might have been a rabbi. Anyway, Ed converted and that was that.

Ed and Dorothy were at the event where I ended my silence. Their acceptance was expansive and I feel they truly understand me. They live around the corner from the hotel I am staying in and across the street from the Washington Cathedral, in a home large enough for raising their five children, two his and three hers. The kids are all grown and living on their own now. Ed's office is in the basement; he moved it there after he came home from work unexpectedly one day and found the kids rappelling from the third-floor window.

Two other cousins are also living in the house. We are all in various stages of our education in medicine, international relations, and environmental studies. I am going to stay in Washington to research and write my dissertation on assessing the costs of oil spills from tankers.

June is fast approaching as I near the end of my research and writing. I feel an added urgency to finish during the spring semester because John Steinhart, my friend, major professor, and adviser, is about to retire. I also have to figure out how I am going to defend my dissertation.

All of my class participation at Wisconsin consisted of mime and writing. That kind of participation required me to be present. After passing my preliminary exams, I left the university with some fantastic notion that I would defend my thesis via satellite teleconference. My committee accepted that I was not going to walk several hundred miles back to Madison. The fact that I am now speaking, however, has added a new wrinkle. We settle on a telephone conference call.

During most days I work at the office of the United Nations Environment Programme (UNEP) as Joan Martin-Brown's assistant. Joanie is the special adviser to Mustafa Tolba, executive director of UNEP. In the evenings I stay late and work on my dissertation. When my department decides on a telephone defense, all I need is a time and place to take the phone call. I ask Joanie and she offers her office on a day that she will be traveling.

On the day of the defense, I park myself at the end of a long conference table in the air-conditioned office. This is definitely a better place to be than Madison, I decide, as I look over my notes and the abstract of my dissertation: "Oil Spills from Ships in the U.S. and the Caribbean: Assessing the Costs and Conventions."

When the call finally comes, I am thankful that I do not have to be in the same room with my committee members. I know that room too well. I had stood out in the hallway with the family and friends of anxious dissertators, and watched sweat drip and hands tremble. But here, alone in Joanie's air-conditioned office, 500 miles or so from Room 28, all the sweat and shaking hands don't much matter. Instead, I focus on my presentation and the image of my committee gathered around the plastic speakerphone. I begin slowly.

"The study addresses two hypotheses: that changes in the oil trade, as well as its safety rules and related institutions, have resulted in a reduction in the incidence and the amount of oil spilled in the marine environment, and likewise have resulted in a decrease in damage caused by oil spills. Indications are that there are no substantial changes in incidence but a 200 percent rise in quantity from 1971 to 1985, followed by a slight decrease to 1990. Using two damage-assessment methodologies and archival data, I show that damage appears to be also increasing. These damage assessment models represent the present state of this art in the field of natural resource damage assessment, and are our only chance to glimpse the trend of natural resource damage over the last decade.

"Despite the apparent 50 percent decrease in relative damage described by the Type A procedure . . . " I speak casually into the phone as I launch into the introduction to what I hope will be a successful defense.

I explain how the different types of methodologies I have devised to assess damage to natural resources, particularly those resources that are not traditionally captured in the economics of the marketplace, such as aesthetics, clean air, and clean water, possess inherent defects, and that more sensitive models might very well show an even greater increase in damage.

In spite of the air-conditioning, sweat forms on my brow and drips down onto my face. I finish after an hour and the committee is silent. After what seems like an eon, John Steinhart, the chair, asks for questions. I answer them as best I can and hang up to wait for them to call back after their private discussion. Most of the committee has never heard me speak before. I wonder what they think.

The phone rings and John is on the other end.

"Well, how do you think you did?" he asks.

I should be able to read the happiness in his voice, or maybe it is relief, but I am emotionally drained.

"I'm not sure," I reply tentatively.

"Well, how did you feel?"

"Distant."

"Well, everyone was really pleased. Gretchen thinks it is a very important work and has offered to copyedit for you." He laughs. "I guess, though, that the general feeling is one of amazement."

"Amazement?"

"Yeah, everyone was really amazed that you could actually speak in sentences." We both laugh. And in the laughing, I realize how far I have come, across a continent. I hang up the receiver and wipe two streaks of sweat away from my eyes. My feet ache.

Months earlier Joanie had nominated me to be one of UNEP's goodwill ambassadors. She tried for several months to have her nomination reviewed at UNEP headquarters in Nairobi, Kenya, but the appointments seemed to be hopelessly tied up in a snarl of international bureaucracy and politics.

It is only after I complete my dissertation defense that I have the opportunity to meet Dr. Tolba in person. He is on a North American tour before flying to Argentina and Antarctica. A small mustached Egyptian with graying hair, he is an icon in the arena of

international environmental protection. Joanie has me positioned at the door to her office while he is visiting with her inside. When they emerge, she introduces me.

"Dr. Tolba, this is Dr. Francis, the young man I have been telling you about." I am nearly speechless when he takes my hand in greeting.

"It's good to meet you," he says. "But I am expecting a man much older after hearing about all the things that you have done."

I mumble something incoherent, and he smiles at me.

"I am appointing you a UNEP Goodwill Ambassador, because I know you will do something with the honor, and not just hang it on your wall," he says, turning to his chief of staff and asking him to have my file on his desk when he returns from Argentina.

As UNEP's walking ambassador, I join other Goodwill Ambassadors, including entertainers Raffi, Max Von Sydow, and Olivia Newton-John; British explorer Robert Swan; and Ed Nijpels, chairman of the World Wildlife Fund for Nature in the Netherlands and mayor of the city of Breda. My official title is UNEP's Goodwill Ambassador to the World's Grassroots Communities.

Ambassadors are to use their time, talents, and energy to raise awareness of central environmental issues and the work of UNEP, as well as to develop their own projects in the area of environmental education. It is a perfect match with the goals of Planetwalk and the spirit of my pilgrimage. It is also a great honor.

CHAPTER 20

OPA 90: Regulating Tankers

Trees sound like fire
Rustling leaves as hot wind blows
On summer branches

June 12, 1991
Washington, D.C.

On the day I leave Washington, the temperature climbs into the nineties and the humidity is high. I say my goodbyes, climb on my new blue touring bike, and pedal through traffic to find Route 1. The night before my cousins gave me a party and I was up late packing. Now I am tired and in no hurry to pedal through traffic on busy District streets. I ride for hours before they are behind me.

As I ride through Baltimore, gospel music mixes with Sunday morning preaching and it all pours out of the Baptist churches on North Avenue, sometimes over loudspeakers. The city's Sunday streets eventually give way to suburban sprawl and then to small towns and the rolling hills of the Maryland countryside. I stop for lunch at Conowingo Park. Located on the west side of the Conowingo Dam, on the Susquehanna River, it is a recreation area the Philadelphia Electric Company developed for employees and the public. My father has retired from the company, but my brother works at one of the coal-fired generating stations a little farther on. That makes me feel a little like being home.

My brother, Dwayne, is shorter, stockier, and nine years younger than I am. My mother miscarried once before I was born and twice between us. I left home when I was 18, so it was as if each of us got to be an only child. Dwayne grew up not in the shadow of a successful older brother, but in the hope that whatever insanity possessed me was not transferable by genetics. My father encouraged him at every opportunity not to be like me.

Lightning flashes to the north prompt the lifeguards to call everyone out of the pool as a precaution against electrocution. Until 20 minutes elapse without lightning or thunder no one is allowed back into the pool. I pedal into Philadelphia. My mother is ecstatic at the news that I have completed my doctorate. My father is his usual self.

"What are you going to do with a Ph.D. when you don't even drive a car?" He scowls.

"I don't know."

"John, will you leave Johnny alone? He is the first one in this family to get the degree, so just be proud of him."

"Java, I'm proud of him, but you tell me, what kind of job is he going to get riding around on a bicycle? Maybe he could be a bike messenger."

I know better than to get in the middle of their argument. I pack my bike and head north. Three days later, I arrive in Rahway, New Jersey, where my mother's family is having their reunion.

It is good to see that side of the family again. Little Johnny is their celebrity and they have lots of questions to ask.

"Did you really walk across the whole United States?"

"What's it like not to talk for so many years, and how did you go to school?"

I miss my uncle Carter and my dad's sister Lucy, who have died since I last saw them on the West Coast. My aunt's and uncle's acceptance of me was quieter and more gentle. My mother has convinced my father not to bring up my walking and refusal to ride in cars. I knew it would be that way, so he says nothing except to make proud fatherly noises in the face of my notoriety. But he is both curious and suspicious when he tells me about a phone call he received the previous week.

"You got a phone call from someone at the coast guard. What did you do?"

"Maybe I owe them money for some data they gave me. Who called? What did they say?"

"I don't know. It was a woman. I can't remember her name. She said she wanted to talk to John Francis and I thought it was me until she started talking about oil spills."

He finds a slip of paper in his wallet and gives it to me. I put it away and do not think about it until the next day, when I am safely across the George Washington Bridge and ensconced in New York at the home of my friends Jim and Sharon Willse. I am in the city to visit the UNEP North American regional office and meet its director, Dr. Noel Brown. Another reason for the visit is to raise funds for the overseas leg of Planetwalk and, in particular, for my participation at the Earth Summit to be held during the summer of 1992 in Brazil. I am not having much success. I decide to continue my bike ride up into New England to see the countryside and visit some friends, but first I find the slip of paper my father gave me and dial the number at Coast Guard Headquarters back in Washington, D.C.

When I arrive in Boston I have a phone conversation with Bruce Novak, the person in charge of incoming personnel.

When the call goes through, I find myself speaking with Meg Whitaker, a research assistant for the Oil Pollution Act of 1990 (OPA 90) staff. She explains that the OPA 90 staff had been formed to implement legislation passed as a result of the 1989 *Exxon Valdez* oil spill. Lawyers working on writing the actual regulations are interested in seeing my dissertation after finding it cited in a number of oil spill publications.

Meg is a graduate student in public health. She has a young, friendly, and enthusiastic voice, and before long we are talking about Planetwalk, pilgrimage, and environmental awareness.

"They could really use somebody like you here on the OPA 90 staff," Meg finally says. "Would you consider it?"

"Sure," I reply, "but what do I have to do?"

"Leave it to me," she says.

When I arrive in Boston I have a phone conversation with Bruce Novak, the person in charge of incoming personnel. Several phone conversations later I reach my friends in Brattleboro, Vermont. Bruce calls again.

"We would like you to come to Washington right away," he says. "We can send you a plane ticket overnight."

"You know," I begin cautiously, "that I don't ride in planes?"

"Oh . . . That's all right, there's the train. You can take the train and we'll reimburse you. You *can* take the train, right?" He sounds hopeful.

"Actually, I don't ride in trains either." Silence.

"You don't ride in cars either, do you?"

"No."

There is more silence on his end of the line, and I think what a pity it would be if I could not work for the Coast Guard because of my lifestyle convictions. According to my attorney friend in Washington, I have already thrown away a multimillion-dollar lawsuit because of my refusal to ride in an ambulance, and now it seems as if I am giving up the opportunity to address some of the issues my walking is all about. Not being able to work for the Coast Guard would be ironic.

"Yeah, we heard something about that," Bruce replies. I imagine him scratching his head, his mind tied up into a sailor's knot. He lets out a long "Hmmm!"

"I'll get back to you," he says, and hangs up.

The next day Bruce calls again to tell me that the director of the OPA 90 staff, Norm Lemley, wants me in spite of my, uh . . . unusual lifestyle.

"We'll work with you on this," he says. "We'd like to have you here for at least two years."

"I can only commit to one year. I'm still on an eighteen-year walking pilgrimage around the world."

"Okay, we can sort that out later. But how will you get here?"

"Oh, I can ride my bike."

"And how long do you think that will take?"

I scratch my head and make some quick calculations, savoring the moment before I answer.

"I could be there in about two months. I have to complete my visits here, and straighten out some affairs before I can return to Washington."

"Okay. We'll be waiting." His voice has a quizzical lilt, as if he never expects me to show. He hangs up.

That is it. The federal government has just recruited me to help write U.S. oil spill regulations. I can hardly believe what has just happened. I am ecstatic! To have been sitting on an oil-soaked beach 20 years earlier, wondering what I might do to help prevent such tragedies, and now to be asked by the government to help write and evaluate oil spill regulations, is overwhelming. I am filled with joy and anticipation. I need to call someone and share this news. I call my father.

On the phone, I try to contain myself, but I can feel my excitement slipping out all over the place. After the initial pleasantries, I dive into it.

"Hey, Dad, you remember last month when the coast guard called?"

"Yeah, I remember. What did they want?"

"They want me to come work for them in Washington. They want me to help write oil spill regulations. I just talked to them a few minutes ago and accepted their offer." I tell him the salary I will be paid and wait inside his pause. I know he is digesting all I have said and I wonder what his words will be after his own long silence. Then he blurts them out.

"What coast guard?"

"You know what coast guard. The U.S. Coast Guard, the same one that you talked to."

"The U.S. Coast Guard?"

"Yes, Pop, the U.S. Coast Guard."

"Well, do they know who you are?"

I smile because I know he is referring to all the times I protested against the Vietnam War and he said I would never be able to work for the government. It did not matter that protest is a citizen's right or duty. He still thinks of himself as an immigrant, even though he became a citizen long ago, and he continues to worry that one day he will be sent back.

"Yes, they know who I am."

"Who do they think you are?"

"I guess they think I'm Dr. Francis, at least that's what they call me." I am still not used to this title and my father struggles with it as well. He repeats the phrase and my professional name a few times as if it is a foreign language, alien to him, and then chases a frog from his throat. He mutters something inaudible.

"The world certainly has changed."

"Yes, the world is changing, Dad. I'll see you on my way through Philadelphia."

Two months later my father stirs from his sleep on a folding cot in the corner of my downtown Washington, D.C., apartment. It is my only furniture. Breakfast is almost ready. I can hear the traffic noise on Pennsylvania Avenue as cars pass by the National Archives. We eat at the counter without saying much. We talk a little about the 20 years it took us to get here. We travel it together. How else could we be here now? I have to leave for coast guard headquarters soon. It's only a three-mile bike ride. He wants to leave before me. We shake hands. This time the landscape of his face is without shadow. His sky is cloudless. Turning as he walks through the door my father stops, looks at me with something akin to muted pride and acceptance, and says, "You know, I don't think you are crazy anymore." He closes the door behind him. The sun is shining through the window.

Coast guard headquarters is a nondescript six-story concrete building next to Fort McNair, on the northern shore of the Anacostia River at Buzzard's Point in the southeast section of Washington. The area's name came from the buzzards that fed on the rotting carcasses of expired trolley horses, in the time before electric trolleys took their place.

I lock my bike to a fence across the street and walk to the guard station at the main entrance. Bruce Novak comes out to meet me and get me through security. He is of medium build with square features and crewcut dark hair, wearing a red-and-white-striped shirt and a dark blue tie. He extends his hand and speaks in a voice now familiar from our many phone conversations.

"Dr. Francis, it's good to meet you. Your papers have not all been signed yet, but you'll be able to start work immediately."

I follow him through two swinging doors and down a long hallway to the main office. OPA 90 staff is printed in large black letters on a square of Plexiglas. He ushers me past the secretary and into the inner office of the director.

Norm Lemley is sitting behind a large admiral's desk cluttered with papers. His intensity is palpable. Several officers and civilians stand or sit around him. They are speaking about regulations and environmental assessments. There is exasperation in the air, but when Lemley looks up and sees us at the door a grin stretches across his face and he motions for us to enter.

"Well, here is our environmentalist now." He stands and reaches across the desk to shake my hand. He is a big man in a white shirt, his striped tie loosened. Bruce tells me that he has recently been appointed a senior executive, the highest civil servant position in the federal government. I quickly glance around the office. Framed awards and citations that go with the position hang on the walls.

I am introduced to everyone in the room. Each name slips in one ear and out the other. It is a practice that I perfected during my 17 years of not speaking and not calling anyone by name. Other things are more important to me in knowing a person. The names can come later.

"We're hoping that you'll be able to help us with the environmental side of our regulations," says Lemley. "The problem is that we have to come up with the economic costs of oil spills that our regulations prevent." Everyone looks at me.

"Well, my research did include looking at how we put economic value on natural resources, so I guess I'm your man."

We chat and people ask questions about my trip to Washington and finding a place to live. Then Lemley adjourns the meeting for a more private conversation with me. I don't know what to expect, except that I can feel sweat trickling down my back. Maybe it's left over from the bike ride to the office. For a moment I am lost in my own amazement at being here, at saying words about oil spills and damage to the environment and being listened to. Then Lemley's voice brings me back from my own thoughts.

I am lost in my own amazement at being here, at saying words about oil spills and damage to the environment and being listened to.

"Your position here at OPA 90 will involve developing a way to measure natural resource damage for the various regulations. Also, after you've been here a while I want you to serve as a project manager for one of our studies, maybe the deep-water port study."

The deep-water port study, he explains, will analyze the risk of those kinds of ports relative to other modes of oil transport. The study addresses the feasibility of reducing the limits of liability from $350 million to no lower than $50 million for deep-water ports.

The only deep-water port in the United States is the Louisiana Offshore Oil Pipeline (LOOP). It is an 18-mile pipeline that allows very large oil tankers to discharge their cargo well offshore, reducing the chances of an oil spill closer to shore in more sensitive areas. Evaluating the advantages and disadvantages of the approach is complicated, with many environmental and economic ramifications to consider.

For a moment the office is quiet and then Lemley asks if I have any questions for him. I am already thinking.

"With my history of not talking and not riding in cars, you must feel that you're taking a big chance hiring me."

"I'm glad you brought that up, because it is something that I want to talk to you about."

For a moment I think that asking the question is a mistake and now I have opened up Pandora's box. He is going to tell me that I am on probation and that I better shave off my beard and ditch the earring. He leans close, as if taking me into his confidence. I feel more sweat.

"In fact, Dr. Francis, I thought the stories we heard about your silence and walking were very interesting. You have obviously been thinking and living very creatively, what we call here 'outside the box.' That's really the kind of thinking we're going to need if we're going to get these regulations written and passed. Yes, it may seem that the decisions you have made in your life have been crazy, but I want you to promise me that whenever you have any crazy ideas about how we are writing our regulations, or the economic and environmental analysis, you'll come and talk to me about them, no matter how crazy they sound. I know that's where creativity lies and we'll need that. In the end it may be just a crazy idea that we can't use, but let's look at it first. Will you promise me that?"

"Sure." I nod my head. But I am caught a little off guard, never expecting a government bureaucrat to think so progressively. I rummage through my mind for something to say. There is nothing there—no nervous chatter, no superfluous question, only silence—so I listen. Lemley looks at me for a long moment, then begins to speak.

"I don't think we're taking much of a chance hiring you. Our research staff has found your work cited in the literature. Do you know that you are the only person we could find currently doing research on the Natural Resources Damage Assessments of oil spills? That's exactly what we need for this project. Another thing is that you have a Ph.D. from the University of Wisconsin. Last time I checked they weren't giving those away, so I figure there are a lot of other people who believe you know what you're talking about." He pauses. "God, how did you do it? I mean, how did you not talk?"

I shrug my shoulders and draw a question mark in the air.

"Okay, I get it. I'm glad you're talking now. But what are we going to do about you not riding in motor vehicles? You know, sometimes you're going to have to travel, maybe across the country." He stares out the window into a parking lot across the street. "Driving is out, am I correct?"

"That's correct, but I can ride a bike."

"A bike?"

"Yes, I could ride my bicycle if it's within three hundred miles." I grab the number out of the air. Three centuries in a row is doable, but would put me at the edge of my ability.

"Yes, that would work, but we're not going to send you across the country; it would take you two years to get there and back." He laughs out loud. "Well, if you're a project manager you can send someone else. But in some instances people are going to want you to be there to speak with them. How did you defend your dissertation in Wisconsin when you were here in Washington?"

"I defended by phone, but we were going to use videoconferencing before I started talking again."

"Okay, then we can do that using a satellite communications network. There, it's all settled. Well, Dr. Francis, welcome aboard."

Lemley leads me to an office and a small desk piled with papers. When he leaves I begin my journey into learning the regulatory process. The winter passes and turns to spring. Each day I ride my bike the three miles to and from headquarters, through the cold and snowstorms that shut down the District.

One spring day, Lt. Smith from the office confides in me about what he and some others thought about me.

"Actually, we were all curious to see what kind of tree-hugger environmentalist was on his way to headquarters to work with us. We thought you were some kind of nut, but now we see that you are just one of us, a normal person who just has convictions, and we respect that." This is a high compliment. "What did surprise us, though, is that you're black."

Later in the afternoon Lemley stops by my office to tell me about a trip I am going to have to make to Philadelphia to do a tanker inspection. It is a necessary orientation for everyone charged with regulating the oil tanker industry. Lt. Commander Robert

Diaz has volunteered to accompany me on the 300-mile round-trip bike ride.

The next day Lemley asks me to have lunch with him in the cafeteria. It is not unusual, but I can sense that he has something on his mind besides just breaking bread. He walks into the cafeteria and surveys the crowd, a mix of civilians, officers, and regular sailors in uniform.

"Over here." Tray in hand, he nudges me with his elbow and I follow his circuitous path through people and tables until we find ourselves standing in front of Admiral Gene Henn. Admiral Henn is the vice commandant in charge of the OPA 90 staff. He is a very likable, approachable person, but he is still an admiral and they are notorious for not having time for idle chatter. The weeklong communication workshop that I took on how to give an admiral a two-minute briefing only served to drive home the point. After two minutes admirals lose interest, our instructor explained. I am sure Lemley is not about to engage in idle chatter.

"Good afternoon, Admiral. Mind if Dr. Francis and I join you for lunch?"

"Not at all, Norm. Have a seat."

"Thank you." We sit down and begin unloading the contents of our trays onto the table. "I think we'll be ready for the next regulatory negotiation meeting this week." The "Reg-Neg," as it is often called, is an innovative program in which the stakeholders in a specific regulation meet before a judge and negotiate all the points of interest prior to the regulation's ratification. Once the parties agree on the regulation and documents are signed, all parties give up the right to challenge the regulation in court. In this instance the stakeholders consist of the oil industry and environmental groups.

"Next week John is going up to Philadelphia for a tanker inspection." Norm slips this in between bites of a fried fish sandwich. Admiral Henn stops his own meal and looks at me.

"Oh, really. How are you going to get there, John?"

I stare back at him blankly and for the moment all words leave me and I am silent again. I mime the rotating pedals of a bicycle with my two hands.

"You're going to ride your bike?"

I nod yes.

"Commander Diaz is going with him," adds Lemley.

"That's good. Be careful."

We take a few more bites of our lunch and Lemley nudges me, then excuses us from the table. We head for the exit with our trays in hand. A smile settles on Lemley's face. "There, we've fully briefed the admiral."

Back in the office the secretary begins making all the necessary calls to plan for our trip. The oil company is concerned that I am riding a bike to the oil port in Philadelphia.

"He just doesn't ride in motorized vehicles since witnessing an oil spill in California," the secretary says. She pauses and listens to the response. "Well, yes, he has been featured on CBS TV, but I don't think that *60 Minutes* will be showing up, although they might." She turns to me and asks me to promise that *60 Minutes* won't show up. I promise. "They're worried that there might be an oil spill while you're there. They say they're sending their vice president of safety to meet you."

It takes one and a half days for Commander Diaz and me to reach Philadelphia. The tanker is docked at the Sun Oil terminal not far from the international airport. I remember stories my father told me about cleaning the storage tanks at Sun Oil. It is dangerous work. One spark could cause the most catastrophic explosion. He kept the job only a few weeks before signing on with the Philadelphia Electric Company as a lineman.

When we arrive at the terminal Richard Halluska and Tiffany Rau of OMI, the owners of the tanker, meet us at the dock. Richard is of medium build with a neat mustache, wearing a brown sport jacket and orange safety helmet. Tiffany is tall and slender, wearing khaki slacks, a windbreaker, and a safety helmet. Along with the OMI crew, a coast guard sailor is there to do the inspection. Before the inspection, however, we sit in the main cabin and sip hot coffee. After the preliminary introductions Tiffany asks about the bike ride from Washington.

As we walk upon the road we meet ourselves. And at the end, perhaps we'll find that there are no sides to take, no enemies of state, no arguments against the other. There's only death that waits. But on this tiny planet, and in this precious moment, we have the chance to live in peace together. If only we would take a walk.

"It was great! We made it in a day and a half and we had good weather." I look at Commander Diaz and he nods in agreement.

"I heard you don't ride in motorized vehicles as a protest or something. I hope you don't mind me asking, but you seem so . . . uh . . . normal." Richard looks at me, his chin resting on his folded hands.

"No, I don't mind. I'm glad you asked. It's true that I gave up riding in motorized vehicles after witnessing an oil spill in California, but I wouldn't say it's a protest. I actually believe that all of us who use oil have some responsibility for all of the pollution it causes, even the spills, and not just the oil companies or the people who transport oil."

Richard looks at Tiffany and they both look back at me, and in unison ask, "What does that mean?"

"It's just like I said, if you're using oil to get around, then you share in the responsibility for any spill that occurs, as we are all demanding more oil cheaper and faster, and in the process some of it spills."

"So what you are suggesting is a sort of shared responsibility?"

"Yes, exactly." Everyone in the cabin is listening. "Don't get me wrong, I think that oil transport companies have the greater responsibility when we're talking about oil spills from ships—just not all of it. But for the record, my research has found that most of the oil that finds its way into the marine environment comes from automobile crankcase disposal."

"Well, you're the first environmentalist that I've heard talk like this," Richard says. As he speaks the lines of tension in his face relax and a wave of relief washes over our small group.

"I think I'd like to refer to myself as an environmental practitioner instead of an environmentalist. I know it may just be a matter of semantics, but practitioner implies becoming, and doing something in order to improve. In the end I think it's about learning how to live better on Earth."

"I couldn't agree with you more. Frankly, we were a little nervous when we heard that one of the people who was going to be regulating our industry was bicycling here from Washington to do a tanker inspection because he'd seen an oil spill and didn't want to contribute to the pollution. We're relieved to find that you're someone who can see both sides and with whom we can talk."

Sitting beside me, Commander Diaz is laughing. "He's pretty much an anomaly up at headquarters as well."

The inspection of the tanker takes the rest of the day. It is my first time on such a ship—so large that people use bicycles to travel from one end to the other. How these behemoths cross the oceans and spill as relatively little oil as they do amazes me. Regulation, economics, technology, and fate all have a part. My education continues.

Back at headquarters, Lemley is happy that we have made it back from Philadelphia without incident. OMI officials have reported our visit a "unique experience." Now Lemley wants me to participate in an economic conference on the West Coast. To get me there we turn to another technology.

"Well, we're not going to send you to San Francisco on your bike," Lemley says as he shuffles through some papers on his desk.

"Instead, we're going to work with the Black College Satellite Network (BCSN) to set up a satellite link with the conference. That will solve the problem."

In an interview with the *Commandants' Bulletin* later he explains, "This is a win-win situation. The satellite link will promote UNEP's Goodwill Ambassador program and save the coast guard money, as other presenters will be able to participate without leaving Washington."

The inspection of the tanker takes the rest of the day. It is my first time on such a ship—so large that people use bicycles to travel from one end to the other.

This is not the first time that I have worked with BCSN, the coast guard, and satellite technology. Planetwalk has already produced two National Town Meetings (NTM) on environmental equity issues, and an interactive teleconference among grassroots communities on environment and development for presentation at UNCED (the Earth Summit in Brazil).

The purpose of the NTMs was to provide a voice to the historically disenfranchised and grassroots communities, allowing their thoughts to be communicated to the delegates of UNCED, and to provide a bridge for these communities to the environmental movement.

Regional grassroots organizations around the country participated, as well as the U.S. Environmental Protection Agency. One NTM focused on rural issues and the other on urban issues. We then produced a videotaped address given by me in my role as goodwill ambassador that was sent to the Brazilian television network, El Globo, to be aired during the Earth Summit. The address is a synthesis of the two NTMs.

I stay at the coast guard for a year and two months before

leaving on my bike for Martha's Vineyard, Massachusetts, to continue my pilgrimage. I have made arrangements to sail aboard the *Zorra*, a 72-foot wooden yawl. I have been working with the idea of developing a computer-based environmental education curriculum, and want to use *Zorra* as a floating classroom for students from different Caribbean islands.

Before I leave Washington I am given a civilian service award by Admiral Henn, at coast guard headquarters, for the work I have done as an enlightened environmental analyst and activist.

Somewhere between Philadelphia and New York, I stop beside the road and look back to where this journey began, and tears well up and cloud my eyes. Traffic is passing, and maybe people are staring, but I don't care. I knew that someday this would happen, that I would have to look back and see from where I've come. All I can think of is having taken that first step on an impossible journey, and now beside an interstate, I ask myself how I got here and how I have changed. I sit down in some grass and scattered litter as the rush of years and miles settles close. I bow my head, shiver, and feel a silent laugh.

If, 20 years ago, after witnessing the oil spill in San Francisco Bay, someone had told me, "John, if you want to make a difference, I want you to stop driving in cars and start walking east, and you'll make a difference," and as I turned and walked away they shouted, "and shut up, too!" I would not have believed them. But as I sit here I realize that is exactly what has happened.

"Damn, we can change the world." The words escape from between my lips and startle me, but the last five words echo in my mind. "We can change the world." And I know it's not just me, but each one of us, through our own impossible journey, has this capacity to change and make a difference in our world.

A few moments later I am back on my bike making my way north. The traffic seems more frenetic. I wonder how I have changed. Have I become a better listener? I think so, but I tell myself there will be many opportunities to practice. I leave the highway to find a quieter road.

Epilogue

June 2003, Cuba: In the tropical heat of the Cuban afternoon, sweat is pouring from my face as I strain to make the elevation of the mountain. Struggling behind me are 70 or so other souls, walkers who have joined me from the United States and Canada to Planetwalk across Cuba. Global Exchange, a human rights organization that leads reality tours around the world, has helped organize them. At the summit, I stop to rest and look out over the green forest of Pinar del Río, splashed with sugarcane, coffee, and other tropical fruit. Ever since the economic embargo imposed by the United States in 1960, travel to the island has been forbidden for most Americans. Conducting research or attending a professional conference are two of the few exceptions to the Department of Treasury's travel ban. I am here to do both, invited by the Cuban government's Ministry of Science, Technology, and Environment as a scientist and UN Environment Program Goodwill Ambassador. I am attending the Fourth International Conference on Environment and Sustainable Development in Havana, and beginning a research project to see if organic agricultural practices in Cuba can be used as a model for the Caribbean and South America.

The research project involves walking 1,000 miles across the island, visiting agriculture and sustainable development sites. My fellow planetwalkers are spending four days with me to cover the first hundred miles of Planetwalk Cuba's inauguration. We stop and listen to local experts explain about the ecology, crops, organic agriculture, and sustainable development practices. In the late afternoon buses meet the group and take them to nearby hotels to eat and spend the evening. I walk on with two Cuban scientists and camp by the side of the road. The group joins us again in the morning.

As I walk into the village of Los Tombos, a dozen children line the street with their teacher and the local government official, all waving Cuban flags. I sing "El Caminante," accompanying myself on the banjo; it is the song I wrote in Spanish about walking for the environment. The children love it.

On the last day, the red dirt road winds through a valley of verdant green fields mixed with vegetables and tobacco, on to the town of Vinales, west of Havana. The governor is waiting in the town hall for a welcoming celebration for all the walkers. Government officials make speeches about the environment and the need for peace. Then schoolchildren sing environmental songs and recite poems.

It is the first time that I have walked this far with so many. I make my final goodbyes to those who have been with me, exchanging contact information with promises to stay in touch.

"Everybody should take a piece of the earth and walk it in the spirit of peace, courageously encountering whatever they find," says one woman, echoing the sentiments of others. Many do not want to stop walking.

I had arrived by plane a week earlier. After so many years of not riding in motorized vehicles, it seemed unnatural as I stepped off the plane and into the minibus that took me to the hotel in Old Havana. During my walk across Venezuela a few years earlier I had an epiphany that changed my attitude.

Venezuela, 1994: A guard at the infamous El Dorado prison challenged me as I strolled by the main gate. "Hey you—stop! Where are you going?" In his hand, he held an M-16 that was pointed menacingly in my direction. He looked to be about 17 and frightened of this tall, dark, bearded man with sun-faded cloths and a backpack. My banjo was wrapped in a soft army-green case made of light ballistic material. I suppose it could have been a weapon of some kind. I imagine that is what he suspected: At the very least I was here to help a prisoner escape, at the worst I was the escaping prisoner. As I turned to face him something odd happened inside me. In my mind, I became a prisoner attempting a great escape.

"Come on, show me your papers," he said, gesturing to me with the barrel of his gun. "Do you have a passport?"

When I reached Brazil, I accepted my first automobile ride in over 22 years.

In my best street Spanish, I told him that I did, but I did not need to show it to him, and then I blurted out in an authoritative tone uncharacteristic for me, "I am Dr. Francis, a UN ambassador, and I am walking around the world." I waved my arms in the direction I was moving while he looked at me dumbfounded. What a great disguise for an escaping prisoner, I told myself as I continued down the road. At any moment I expected to hear the echoing report of the gunshot shatter the morning silence and feel the searing pain of a bullet rip through my flesh. Instead, the road rounded a bend and turned into the forest, leaving me alone with my thoughts to celebrate my newly won freedom.

It took several days and nearly a hundred miles of walking through the Venezuelan savannah to process what seemed to me a self-deception. I finally realized that unlike my vow of silence, which I had renewed each year after long reflection, I never questioned my decision to walk. After witnessing the oil spill in California, walking was something I just did as my way of living lightly in the environment. The annual reflection on silence made it a living decision as my life changed in and around me. I had no such process concerning walking. Though appropriate at the time, I now realized that my decision not to use motorized vehicles had become a prison, and only I could set myself free.

Also, my interaction with people in grassroots communities, their assistance and acceptance of my journey and commitment, helped me see the need for change in my life as I approached the border with Brazil. While I decided to continue my walking and sailing pilgrimage, I also decided to begin to fly and use other motorized transportation. Part of the change came from a growing sense of responsibility to my family, and my education, as well as to the communities and groups of people I was meeting on my journey, whom I might be able to help, at least as their advocate. I hoped that my decision would allow me to better address the objectives of Planetwalk and become a more effective Goodwill Ambassador. I felt strongly that walking and meeting with people especially in "disenfranchised communities" was still an excellent way to learn about their problems and their needs. It is also a way you learn about yourself. When I reached Brazil, I accepted my first automobile ride in over 22 years. A few weeks later I was on a plane headed for the United States. My parents and friends were ecstatic, especially Jean, who doubted ever seeing me again once I had left the country. She died the following year when I returned to Brazil to continue walking.

October 1996, Brazil: I arrived at the Manaus airport after a five-hour flight from Miami. It was painless compared to what I had gone through the year before when I had taken as many months to walk from La Gran Sabana, on the Venezuelan border, almost 800 miles, passing through the Brazilian rain forest to Manaus, the capital city of Amazonas, on the Rio Negro.

During my walk I had to pass through the reserve of the Waimiri-Atroari, a group of Indians that belong to the Karib language group. Since its formation, no outsiders had ever been allowed to walk across the reserve. During the 19th century, in their first contact with Brazilian society, they were known as the "Chrishanas." Initial estimates had put their numbers at as high as 6,000. Like so many indigenous peoples, they came under the pressures of economic expansionism from an invading culture, and retreated farther and farther into the forest. There they lived in relative isolation until 1968, when the Brazilian government persuaded Father Giovanni Calleri, an anthropologist, to approach the Waimiri-Atroari over a three-month period. The authorities intended to use the Indians as a labor force to build BR-174 Highway linking Boa Vista, the capital of the state of Roraima, in the north, and Manaus, the capital of the state of Amazonas, in the south. The road was to pass through several villages in the Indian territory that had not yet come in contact with modern Brazilian society.

Here the story becomes sketchy, but what is known is that the Indians, who wished no contact, especially with missionaries, killed

Father Calleri and his party on October 26, 1968. Later, indigenist Gilberto Pinto Figueiredo, who favored a humanistic approach to contact, was killed by the Waimiri-Atroari in 1974. The tribe was determined to resist encroachment and to prevent further outbreaks of epidemic diseases passed on by the highway construction workers. What ensued has been called by some genocide, and by others, an unfortunate but acceptable means to economic development. By 1977, when the fighting was over there remained only about 350 individuals, mostly women and children.

It was little wonder that when I reached Boa Vista on my way to Manaus, I was not encouraged to seek permission to walk through the Waimiri-Atroari reserve which was now transected by the BR-174 Highway. The term "highway" seemed a bit of a stretch, as in most places it was little more than a red-dirt cut through the forest and savannah that made little or no allowance for the subtleties or the topography of either.

At each side of the reserve there was a gate that was manned by the military. It was closed during the evening hours, and only the radio-equipped buses were allowed to cross after dark or, in some cases, commercial trucks that could prove they carried perishable goods.

"They are not very friendly," a Brazilian acquaintance told me. "It would be better to take the three-day boat ride from Caracarai, down the Rio Branco to Manaus."

Nevertheless I petitioned FUNAI (Fundação Nacional do Índio), for permission to cross the reserve of the Waimiri-Atroari on foot. It was an unusual request, not one they had received before. The official behind the desk was named Manuel. From behind his small and cluttered desk, he gave me the most serious expression. He just shook his head and said I was crazy. Others in the office warned against making the trip, first because of the unfriendliness of the Indians and then because of the natural dangers such as big jaguars and snakes. "There's nothing there, nothing at all. No one will be there to help you when you get into trouble," Manuel said.

My UNEP (United Nations Environmental Programme) credentials were sent to Brasília, and then to the Waimiri-Atroari program office in Manaus, to ask the Indians themselves. Two weeks later, to my surprise, the answer from Manaus was yes. The Indians would let me pass. I was at once elated and filled with dread. Manuel, my contact in Boa Vista, wrote out the conditions of my permission. I was to keep to the main road and not venture onto any other trails into the forest. I would sleep only at one of the four FUNAI posts that were spread out about 20 to 25 miles through the reserve. I was sent away with a note of introduction for Garcia at the first FUNAI post at Jundia, more than a two-week walk away.

Several weeks later I was relieved to meet him about 50 miles from the northern boarder of the reserve. He pulled up beside me in a dark blue Toyota pickup, while I sat resting in the shade of a tree by the side of the road. He was tanned and dark not only from the sun, with fine features, piercing dark eyes, and a thin broad smile.

"You must be John Francis," he said leaning from the open window. On the door a black-and-white sign read, waimiri-atroari, on top of a lethal-looking arrow. Beneath this logo, environmental protection program.

The Waimiri-Atroari program was developed in 1988 to mitigate the socio-environmental impacts anticipated from the Balbina hydroelectric dam, which was designed to provide electricity for the industrial district in Manaus. Before the reservoir flooded 30,000 hectares (almost 75,000 acres) of Waimiri-Atroari land in 1978, Indians from two villages, Taquari and Tapupuna, were relocated. The program was based on an action plan drawn up by an interdisciplinary team of technicians that involved negotiations with the Waimiri-Atroari during its conception. Areas covered by the program included health, education, environment, support for farming activities, territorial surveillance, documentation, and preservation of the community's memory. An administration was also designed to enable the Waimiri-Atroari to recover their former autonomy and to ensure them a balanced integration into Brazilian society. Sadly, in dealing with the indigenous peoples of Brazil, the Waimiri-Atroari program is the exception.

Garcia told me that he, his wife, Sonya, and their small son, Italo, lived just inside the reserve, and that I would be staying with them while things were being arranged. I was relieved to learn that I was to be accompanied through the reserve by a relay of men that would walk with me from one post to the next.

For three days I walked with them through the forest that was their home. Our common language was some Portuguese and the shared experience of moving through the environment around us. For each of the first two days two Indians accompanied me. In the evenings we arrived at a post where we would sleep and be fed. The first post consisted of a few weathered buildings where there was a health station, and the second, larger, post maintained a school where Portuguese was being taught as well as the developing written form of the Waimiri-Atroari language with its own dictionary. There were also cultivation and animal husbandry experimentation and demonstration projects that included raising fish, turtles, and tapirs.

Here I met with Robert Miller, a Brazilian land resources manager who had been working on the latest study produced by the Waimiri-Atroari program, an environmental impact analysis on the effects of the government's proposal to asphalt the BR-174 Highway, including the stretch within the demarcated lands of the Indians.

On the third day, thinking that I might not be able to keep up the pace of a 30-mile day, four Indians made up a small party that was prepared to camp out in the forest. Despite the distance, we reached the final post, about 125 miles from Manaus. Night had fallen long ago when we arrived. For the Waimiri-Atroari, walking at night was to be avoided, but we were walking in the light of a nearly full moon that made all around us magical.

When I reached the final post, I promised a machete to each Waimiri-Atroari who had accompanied me through the reserve. Now, a year later, I was back in Brazil to continue my walking pilgrimage on to Bolivia, and Argentina. But first I had this debt to repay.

This was what I had in mind as I walked into the Waimiri-Atroari Program office in Manaus. I wanted to make arrangements to visit my friends on the reserve.

Even though I had been invited back by Mario, the Waimiri-Atroari leader, I felt I needed to go through the process of getting permission. A few months earlier, I was told, a German journalist and his companion had entered the reserve by canoe without permission. Their equipment was reportedly thrown in the river and they themselves were held for a time before being expelled.

At the program office it was good to see some familiar faces. Our greeting was warm, but I learned that the Waimiri-Atroari was nearing a state of war. For several days, about a hundred warriors had blockaded the road leading to the Pitinga mining project, which boasts the world's largest tin production.

In 1981, after the company Paranapanema successfully lobbied the government to have the Waimiri-Atroari territory reduced by 526,000 hectares (more than a million acres), they installed the cassiterite mining Pitinga project on the eastern side of what had been declared the "Waimiri-Atroari Indian Land" in 1971.

To complicate matters more, to access the Pitinga mine the company built a road through the diminished Waimiri-Atroari territory, displacing two villages. In spite of the tense situation, a radio call was made to the Indians, who, with their leader Mario, were occupying the roadblock, and a few minutes later I had my permission to visit.

Two days later I was on a crowed bus to Boa Vista, though I would get off at the FUNAI post midway through the reserve. The 2 p.m. bus pulled out of the station about an hour late. Even though the road was now paved from Manaus to the beginning of the reserve, it was after eight o'clock at night and dark when we reached the post.

The driver came out with me to get my pack from the luggage compartment. A minute later the lights of a vehicle from the post could be seen approaching. The sole occupant of the four-wheel drive was a grizzled man I did not recognize. He initially questioned my being there, but after a few tense moments, the bus filled with curious passengers gazing into the darkness was on its way again, and I was bouncing up the rutted drive to the FUNAI post.

The next day, Mario, the Waimiri-Atroari leader whom I had met the year before, arrived in a Toyota pickup truck to take me to the road were the Indians had their encampment.

It was an hour away on a smooth dirt-road turn-off, which had been well maintained by the mining company. When we came up to the first checkpoint, there were about 50 men milling about. All were wearing colored shorts; some wore headdresses decorated with palm fronds and feathers. All of them had weapons, bows and arrows with lethal metal tips. (They were ready for a confrontation, but once they recognized who it was they relaxed.) Some were cooking over a smoky fire, some lounging in hammocks in the shade of trees, while others stood along the chain that stretched across the road. They lifted the barrier to let us pass.

Here there was another reunion with Waimiri-Atroari whom I knew from before. Several had walked with me. After our greeting I began handing out the machetes to them as I had promised.

"And here is Amim," said Mario, pointing to another familiar face. "You remember him?" There were big smiles as I pulled yet another machete from inside my blue pack. When I had finished we got back in the truck to complete the drive to the final security gate where the main Indian encampment was. More Indians piled into the back with their bows and and spearlike arrows. Occasionally the truck would stop and a hunting party of two or three would get out and disappear into the forest that crowded the road.

Mario explained that before the road had been built there had been two Waimiri-Atroari villages in this area, but after the road was built they had to be abandoned.

Further on we came upon a hunting party waiting in the shade beside the road. Beneath the finger fronds of a palm, lay the gutted carcass of a tapir. Clean palm fronds were laid out in the back of the truck and the animal was put aboard. This would feed the Indians for about two days. For a moment there was an air of celebration. Along the way the truck stopped again and Indians who had been fishing climbed in with their catch of tambaqui, a favorite freshwater fish that often grows to the size of a fully grown person.

When we finally reached the main encampment of about 100 Waimiri-Atroari warriors, the tension was palpable. Almost all of them ran to the gate, yelling and shaking their bows and arrows. The rest lined both sides of the road. The mood they expressed was a clear demonstration of their displeasure, and the seriousness of their concerns. I was taken aback, but Mario reassured me and I was allowed to bring out my video camera and tape what was happening.

A few moments later, in front of the band, appointed spokespersons began to tell the reason for their displeasure. They were not really interested in the money as much as they were with the future of their children and their children's children. They wanted clean water and the use of more of their usurped land as well. There was more clattering of weapons, and I was shown one of the streams the Indians said were contaminated from the mining activity.

The demonstration settled down a bit and the men went back to the various tasks of the encampment, washing, bathing, food preparation, and cooking. Women and children had been left behind in the villages. I was welcomed into the camp. "I know you," someone would say in Portuguese while touching my arm in a friendly way. It was a sign of recognition. It would be repeated many times during the day.

I was shown where to hang my hammock and passed the day with them. Later, when some reporters from Manaus showed up, I was invited to accompany them to meet with the general manager of the Pitinga mine. The Waimiri-Atroari had never gone beyond their own blockade, but Mario encouraged me to go listen to what this man would say. When we reached the administration offices, though, his plane had not yet arrived from Manaus, and the reporters were anxious to return to the encampment, where a representative from FUNAI was due to speak to them and the Waimiri-Atroari.

It was night when he finally showed up. The only light came from stars, a few candles under the security post pavilion, and the occasional flash of a reporter's camera. The atmosphere was once again tense. The Waimiri-Atroari had been at this for almost a week. FUNAI's position was to suggest that the mining operation was important to the world economy and should continue without disruption.

There was no happiness, only the clattering of bows and arrows, and steadfast determination. They said they were ready to die for what they believed. I felt sad at that possibility. I left the encampment in the morning with Marcilio, the director of the Waimiri-Atroari program office in Manaus. He was frustrated with the official position of FUNAI, and voiced his displeasure on the ride back to town.

They were still at an impasse when I left the region. Inside, I carry the spirit of the Waimiri-Atroari.

My mother died two years later. Each year until 1999, I alternated between working in the United States and walking in South America, until I had walked across Brazil, Bolivia, Argentina, and Chile, with a visit to Anarctica. Back in the United States, I married my sweetheart, Martha Smith, whom I had met almost ten years earlier when she worked at the UN offices in Washington, D.C. When I am not on the road we live together with our sons, Samuel and Luke, in Point Reyes Station.

August 2007, Russian Mission, Alaska: Four years after beginning the walk in Cuba, I found myself in the Yukon, hosted by the Yukon River Inter-Tribal Watershed Council (YRITWC), a coalition of 64 Tribes and First Nations in Alaska and Canada united in protecting the Yukon River watershed, which drains an area twice the size of California and supports the longest inland run of Pacific salmon in the world. Invited to work with the council, I am on the "Healing Journey," a canoe journey that started earlier in the summer at the headwaters of the Yukon River in Canada and is traveling approximately 1,500 miles downriver, visiting each community along the way, where traditional meals, cultural exchange, dancing, drumming, and talking circles begin to mend the past and forge a commitment to a common future. The "Healing Journey" supported by the National Geographic Society's Legacy funds and other donors will end at the 10-year anniversary Summit of the YRITWC in St. Mary's, Alaska, near the Bering Sea Coast. As the Healing Journey travels downriver, each participating community shares observations and concerns related to climate change, all of which are documented and will be brought to the Summit in St. Mary's.

Since I began using motorized vehicles to return to and from my walking pilgrimage I have been involved in several projects like the YRITWC "Healing Journey." I also speak and consult with a variety of audiences around the world, including redefining environment for the travel and tourism industry, introducing the role of ethical advisor for civilian/military humanitarian operations, and encouraging diversity and inclusiveness within traditional conservation and environmental organizations.

On Earth Day 2005, I began a walk retracing my route back across the United States, looking for differences in the landscape and the conversations. My goal is to redefine the environmental problems we face into an inclusive concept, and to form partnerships among Native and non-Native people, cultures, businesses, and organizations across America that might traditionally feel they do not share the objectives and values of environment and conservation. My thesis is that if we as human beings are an integral part of the environment, then how we treat each other and ourselves directly and indirectly effect the physical environment.

The message I carry is that each of us can make a difference in creating a better environment for us all. It is particularly poignant with today's real concerns about climate change and rising seas, which is an especially significant issue among islanders and the indigenous peoples of the north, who are already experiencing the most drastic physical changes on the planet.

As part of this mission, Planetwalk, the nonprofit education organization founded in 1982, ten years after I began walking, is developing with partners "Planetlines," an environmental, peace, and community service curriculum. Based on the concept of pilgrimage, the curriculum will serve high schools, universities, and civic groups. Through the curriculum, young people and adults of diverse cultures and economic backgrounds will gain the knowledge and tools necessary to develop their own walking pilgrimages or "planetwalks." By combining science, the humanities, and public service, participants and students will learn that they, too, can create lasting environmental and social change. My hope is that the hands-on multidisciplinary curriculum will bring education to life in schools where traditional teaching methods often struggle to engage students. With a focus on and involvement in specific pilgrimages such as future Healing Journeys and the Planetwalks, the "Planetlines" curriculum will be dynamic and inherently relevant.

Expanding awareness and collaboration among diverse groups, through the use of the Internet and other technologies, and building bridges beyond the physical boundaries of individual pilgrimages will allow us to share solutions on a scale that is necessary to solve planetary problems. This will be the quest that inspires the next generation of planetwalkers.

John Francis
August 2007